You Shall Be My People

A Continuing Heritage
Celebrating the 250th Synod of the
Reformed Church in the United States

Edited by
Robert E. Grossmann
Norman C. Hoeflinger

The Synod of the
Reformed Church in the United States
1996

ISBN 1-57579-014-9

Library of Congress Catalog Card Number: 96-68227

Published by the Synod of the Reformed Church in the U. S.

Printed in United States of America

PINE HILL PRESS, INC.
Freeman, S. Dak. 57029

TABLE OF CONTENTS

———————·•◆●◆•·———————

INTRODUCTION . . . . i - iv

CHAPTER 1   *The Reformed (Calvinistic) Character of the Early
German Reformed Church in America*
Rev. Norman Jones 1

CHAPTER 2   *The Theology of the Eastern Church and Mercersburg*
Rev. Frank Walker 29

CHAPTER 3   *The 1934 Merger*
Rev. Peter Grossmann 47

CHAPTER 4   *The History of the RCUS Since the 1934 Merger*
Rev. Robert Grossmann 87

CHAPTER 5   *The German-Russians and the Influence of
Dr. H. F. Kohlbruegge*
Rev. Norman C. Hoeflinger 125

CHAPTER 6   *The Influence of Westminster Theological Seminary
on the Reformed Church in the United States*
Rev. Howard Hart 159

CHAPTER 7   *Our Heidelberg Heritage*
Rev. Paul H. Treick 171

CHAPTER 8   *Whither the RCUS?*
Rev. Jim West 213

INDEX 223

1950 EUREKA CLASSIS SESSION—EUREKA, SOUTH DAKOTA

Front row: Pastors Walter Grossmann, Kasper Krueger, Emil Buehrer, Ulrich Zogg, D. E. Bosma, Robert Stuebbe, William E. Korn. Second row: Henry Opp, John Gramm, John Job, Oscar Griess, Jacob Stroh, Jake Feil, Henry Mayer. Third row: Fred D. Opp, Jacob Streyle, Erhardt Koerner, Reinhold Schortzmann, Calvin Ackermann, Ervin Annan. Fourth row: Fred Odenbach, Christ Opp, Rudolph Hilgemann, Ruben Bittner, Jacob Koerner, Henry Hieb, Jacob Mehlhaff.

1958 EUREKA CLASSIS SESSION—EUREKA, SOUTH DAKOTA

Front row: Jake Mehlhaff, Gust Schnabel, D. E. Bosma, Bruce Cole, John Mehlhaff, Robert Stuebbe, M. Nonhof, A. Walma, Calvin Ochsner, M. Wortman, W. Smedes, E. Heckenlaible. Second row: Fred Opp, B. J. Haan, A. Bender, C. Stuebbe, K. J. Stuebbe, C. Van Til, H. Heeren, Gottlieb Dockter, M. De Vries, Jacob F. Mettler, Henry Opp. Third row: Henry Hieb, Wm. Mettler, Herbert Koerner, H. Hueneman, Emanuel Ochsner, Gideon Keorner, R. Spangenberger. Fourth row: E. Buehrer, Wm. Mehlhaff, R. Klaudt, Oscar Griess, N. Hoeflinger, J. Cooper, E. Dockter, Jacob Feil.

1960—50TH ANNIVERSARY SESSION OF EUREKA CLASSIS—HERREID, SOUTH DAKOTA

Front row: Wm. Mettler, Harold Opp, K. J. Stuebbe, Thomas Beech, Wm. Korn, Wm. Stoller, E. Buehrer. Second row: Jacob Feil, Fred Klinge, Wm. Mehlhaff, Reinhold Spangenberger, Fred Opp, D. E. Bosma, Oscar Griess, Edwin Wagner. Third row: Peter Grossmann, R. Johnston, L. Gross, H. Stevens, Calvin Ochsner, A. Kirschenmann, Karl Wiegand, Rudolf Opp, Leonard Neifer, Geo. Gerretsen. Fourth row: Harvie Conn, J. Galbraith, Calvin Stuebbe, N. C. Hoeflinger, R. D. Stuebbe, C. Ploeger.

INTRODUCTION

The volume you hold in your hands celebrates the anniversary of a very special work of God's grace and providence. We celebrate in the year of our Lord 1996 the 250th annual meeting of a national assembly of ministers and elders of the Reformed Church in the United States. While the remnant of the Reformed Church in the United States which continues today could only be considered extremely small in the way that human society measures size, it does constitute a real continuation of the biblical, Christian, Protestant and Reformed teaching and life of God's people on earth that has characterized them since the time of the Protestant Reformation. Indeed, because God's dealings with His people are one throughout history, it is our conviction that we are looking here at the same grace of God that saved the patriarch Abraham and his believing ancestors right back to the first humans needing salvation, Adam and Eve. While it is with fear and trembling that we place ourselves in the line of God's true people, for we are truly fallible and earthen vessels, we do not hesitate to recognize and confess the unity of God's true people in all of history, for that is one of the cardinal teachings of Scripture and of the Reformed faith.

The occasion of this volume is indeed important to the life of our denomination. A history of 250 years of annual assemblies itself goes back before the Revolutionary War and the founding of our Nation. Actually, the history of our Church is longer than 250 years for our first continuing congregations were founded 271 years ago in 1725, and German Reformed worship services were held before 1710. A good part of this fascinating history is unfolded on the pages that follow. Nevertheless, we must be careful to observe that in terms of world history, and even in terms of Protestantism, our Church is quite young. The Heidelberg Catechism, the central confession of our members, was written in 1563, over 150 years before the founding of our first congregations here in North America. This European Protestant background of our Church will also find reference on the pages of this book. Finally, the history of our Church is but a tiny portion of the history of God's covenant dealings with His people, and even less than tiny in the face of His own eternal existence. "For with the Lord, one day is as a thousand years, and a thousand years as one day" (2 Pet. 3:8).

On these pages we will have reference to the work and faithfulness of many men and women, and of their endurance and triumphs as well. But let it be said here and now, right at the beginning, that man deserves no credit for what we find in the way of labor or even in faithfulness to God, **for all of this is what God Himself works in His people**. Therefore this book is dedicated to the glory of Almighty God, the only Creator and Savior of all things visible and invisible, and is published by the Synod of the Reformed Church in the U.S. in humble thanksgiving for what He has given and worked in us. Furthermore, we have no pretensions that the Reformed Church in the United States is unique in any of this, for both our blessings and our temptations have been such as are common to mankind. We recognize and confess with joy and satisfaction that we have brothers and sisters in Christ all over this great nation, and literally to the ends of the earth. It is indeed a great encouragement to us that we have biblical ecumenical relationships with a number of church denominations of like precious faith, both in the United States, and in Europe and Africa. And it is even more encouraging to know that God is calling forth His people out of every nation, and tongue and tribe, and that these folks too are our brothers and sisters in the Lord.

The makeup of the Reformed Church in the U.S. today is that of melting pot America. We began and continued for many years as a mostly German background Reformed Church. Nevertheless, this Church did participate fully in American life, beginning with participation in the American Revolution, a participation which included personal contact with George Washington and hiding the Liberty Bell under the floor of one of our churches while the British occupied Philadelphia. Today our membership still includes congregations of mostly German extraction, but we also have congregations containing only a small minority of such people. Indeed, we seek to attract people of every race and background into our churches to participate with us in what we believe is the authentic life and worship of Christian people.

On the pages of this celebration book, or *Festschrift*, as such works have come to be called, even when they are written in English, you will find sections on the history, theology and various influences that have affected our Church over the past 250 years. The past history of our Church, and the influences of our brothers and sisters in other Reformed and Presbyterian Churches has given us a goodly and godly heritage of sound theology and biblical practice. We are far from perfect, indeed, we are often beset by personal and community sin. Nevertheless, we seek to live up to this heritage and carry it with us in full confidence that our faithful Covenant God, who has helped us hitherto, will also enable us to pass it on to succeeding generations.

To live in the United States of America in 1996 is an unsettling thing for Bible-believing Reformed Christians. We see all around us the decay of the moral fiber and Christian faith upon which our society was founded and through which it has prospered. We cannot help but compare our days and our task to those of the young Prophet Jeremiah, who was sent by God to call Judah back to submission to Him and His word. Jeremiah prophesied, but Judah did not listen and God's judgment followed. Certainly that possibility is something we must consider today. Our fathers and mothers were immigrants, many for the sake of religious oppression. Shall our children be the same? But we have no time to speculate, "he who has put his hand to the plow and turns back" is not worthy of Christ's kingdom. Let us labor on, pray and work for the conversion of our nation, and be ready to serve the Lord no matter what He sends. It is He who sends, and it is He who saves, whether we are faithful or not. Therefore let us be faithful, lest God saves and we are a part of the problem rather than a tool in His hand for good.

The writers of our chapters are all ministers in the Reformed Church in the U.S. They come from diverse backgrounds to serve in one Church with one heart and one mouth. Some of us are sons of the Reformed Church, others have come to us from elsewhere, but all are committed to the one true God who sent His Son to die for our sins. Rev. Norman Jones, pastor of Hope Reformed Church at Pierre, South Dakota, has written our opening chapter on the strictly Reformed character of the Reformed Church in the U.S. during it founding generations. The Rev. Frank Walker, of Bakersfield, California, provided the chapter on the Mecersburg Theology, a development at the Seminary of the RCUS which held great implications for our later history. Rev. Robert Grossmann, of Garner, Iowa, has written on our most recent history, that since the continuing Reformed Church in the U.S. remained free of modern ecumenical entanglements by separating from the Merger of 1934. His brother, the late Rev. Peter Grossmann, provided the chapter on the Evangelical and Reformed Merger of 1934, the historical dividing line between those who have left the old Reformed Church and those who have continued its existence. The Rev. Paul Treick, pastor at Modesto, California, has written the chapter on our beloved Heidelberg Catechism, the creed which is to this day memorized by each covenant youth preparing for communicant membership. The Rev. Howard Hart of Lincoln, Nebraska, contributed a chapter about the influence of Westminster Theological Seminary in Philadelphia, Pennsylvania, on the Reformed Church, a major influence indeed. Our oldest active pastor, the Rev. Norman Hoeflinger, pastor at Lincoln Valley, North Dakota, has written the chapter on the influence on our denomination of the German theologian Herman Kohlbruegge, an influence that also needs to be known and measured in order to understand our history. Finally, the Rev. Jim West, pastor of Sacramento (California) Covenant Reformed Church has contributed a chapter discussing the future of our Church. A special thanks is due to Rev. Paul Treick, who handled the computer typesetting for this book.

We, the editors of this volume, place it in your hands knowing full well that it is lacking in many respects. As busy pastors we have not been able to edit every jot and tittle. Yet we believe our brothers have provided a valuable historical resource, not only for retrospect, but also for considering the future of our little Church. We pray that God will use this book for these purposes, and even more fervently that it will please Him to use the Reformed Church in the United States to glorify His name and spread His Gospel in the years ahead.

Rev. Robert Grossmann, Rev. Norman Hoeflinger

March 1996

C H A P T E R   O N E

The Reformed (Calvinistic) Character of the Early German Reformed Church in America

Rev. Norman L. Jones

✠ Introduction

✠ The Evidence of the Reformed Character of the Church in Germany

✠ The Evidence of the Reformed Character of the Pennsylvania Coetus: Boehm, Schlatter, Congregational Organization and the Coetus, Creeds, Ministerial Oaths, Worship & Liturgy, Education

✠ The Conflict with Anti-Reformed Heresies

✠ Conclusion

INTRODUCTION

What were the religious beliefs of those early German emigrants who left their homeland and braved the dangers of ocean travel to settle in the new land called America? This question is an important one for us as the German Reformed Church in the United States (RCUS) was begun by many of those early settlers. The theology and worship of the Reformed Church in the United States has undergone several twists and turns in the past two-hundred and fifty years, and at times it could be questioned whether the RCUS was really "classically Reformed" and true to the orthodox Calvinist tradition. There have been theological developments in the RCUS that were decidedly not in keeping with Reformed orthodoxy. This volume tells about such matters.

Coming closer to our own day, we must be honest with ourselves at this point in history. Serious problems have indeed plagued our churches at various points in its history. It does no good to try to excuse these things.

So we come back to our original question, Was the original theology of the German Reformed churches of America flawed? Were our doctrine and practice weak from the beginning, from an orthodox point of view, so that the serious, religious problems which developed over the years were a natural result of that weakness? It is our contention that the theology and practice of the early RCUS was truly orthodox Calvinism, and that later aberrations can not be laid to the theology of the founding fathers. What then was the theology of these founding fathers?

To answer this question we must get back to the original documentation and the historical circumstances that led to the founding of the RCUS in the first half of the eighteenth century in the colonies, particularly the colony of Pennsylvania. There is extant, but not readily available, a large amount of historical material that covers the religious history of the Reformed Germans in the colonies. Dr. Joseph Henry Dubbs, a historian of the German Reformed Church, lists 71 volumes and articles in a bibliography dealing with the German Reformed Church in Europe and America.[1] Most of this material is in the German language. By far the greatest researcher and writer on the history and theology of the German Reformed Church in America is the late Prof. J. I. Good who wrote numerous volumes of minute detail giving the history of our church, as to its main leaders, work and theological developments. It is the work of these two scholars that we shall rely upon primarily in the argumentation of this chapter. Much of what we shall say will be more or less a paraphrase of what these men have written. Also, we should give credit to our own Rev. Robert Grossmann who has carefully analyzed the overall history of the RCUS from its beginning to the present day and written a history in outline form that is very valuable to all who are interested in our church.[2]

The theology of the early German Reformed Church in America can easily be determined by examining a number of different evidences. We shall consider two main lines of evidence which demonstrate the orthodox, Calvinistic character of the early RCUS: The evidence from the Reformed character of the Church in Germany, and the evidence of the orthodox character of the German Reformed

---

1 Joseph H. Dubbs, *The American Church History Series, Vol. 8* (New York: The Christian Literature Co., 1895), pp. 214-220.

2 Robert Grossmann, *Outline History of the Reformed Church in the United States*, 1725 - 1995 (Garner, IA: Elector Publications, 1995).

Coetus (pronounced *see-tus*)[3] (i.e., synod/classis) in Pennsylvania.

THE EVIDENCE OF THE REFORMED CHARACTER OF THE CHURCH IN GERMANY

To understand and appreciate the nature of the Reformed convictions of the pastors and people who emigrated to America and established the first German Reformed churches, which led in turn to the formation of the first coetus and then to the RCUS as a denomination, we need to examine the Reformed church in Germany, particularly the Palatinate area from which most of the German Reformed Christians came.

THE HOME OF THE HEIDELBERG CATECHISM

The Protestant Reformation was born by God's Spirit in Germany and Switzerland. In Germany it was Martin Luther who ignited the spark which eventually set Europe and England ablaze. The Reformation in Germany was originally Lutheran in nature, but soon experienced the more purified Reformed doctrines and practices which emanated from John Calvin's ministry in Geneva, Switzerland, 1536 to 1564, and from his predecessor, Ulrich Zwingli (1484-1531) in Zurich, Switzerland. The historian Charles Miller notes that "Although Calvin's primary personal influence was in Geneva, in Switzerland, and in France, Calvinism was to have considerable influence in the area now known as Germany. Then, among the more than two-hundred states and cities which constituted the Holy Roman Empire, it (Calvinism) was generally a continuation of Zwinglianism and more generally in conflict with Lutheranism than with Catholicism."[4]

Miller summarized the religious situation in Germany in the mid-1500s as follows:

The most important German Reformed movement was in the Palatinate, a major principality in southwestern Germany. Here from about 1545 to 1620 Calvinism was to flourish. Because the elector was friendly with the German emperor, the area did not

---

3 J. I. Good explains that "the word *coetus* is taken from the organization of John à Lasco, who first organized the ministers at Emden in northwestern Germany into a coetus in 1544. It was a synod with limited powers, and still exists as the oldest Reformed organization in Europe, except one, the Venerable Company of Geneva, founded by Calvin. Or its name may also have been taken directly from the deputies of the North and South Holland synods, whose united organization, when it met at the Hague to transact business for Pennsylvania, etc., was called a coetus. So South Holland synod had two coeti — one at the Hague, composed of its deputies, and the other in Pennsylvania." J. I. Good, *History of the Reformed Church in the United States, 1725 - 1792* (Reading, PA: Daniel Miller, Publisher, 1899), pp. 331, 332.

4 Charles Miller, *The Rise and Development of Calvinism,* chap. 2 (Grand Rapids, MI: Calvin College, syllabus, no date), p. 11.

become Protestant until late in the Reformation, in 1545.

Legally the Peace of Augsburg in 1555, which caused the French Reformed Church Calvin had served in Strassburg to be closed and ended Calvinist influence in Hesse, denied individual religious freedom in Germany and permitted the princes the right to choose only between Lutheranism and Catholicism in their territories. However, Elector Frederick III of the Palatinate, one of the seven electors of the Holy Roman Empire, was so disgusted by the controversy within Lutheranism that he welcomed Calvinist ideas.

High Lutheranism at the time was moving back toward Catholic practices, reintroducing Latin in the services and the veneration of the Virgin. Moderate Lutheranism led by Melanchthon was in retreat. In the face of this conflict, Elector Frederick invited Zwinglian and Calvinist teachers to come to the Palatinate. Under the influence of these men Elector Frederick moved the church of the Palatinate toward Calvinistic doctrine and practices without abandoning the Augsburg Confession. There were no feasts to the Virgin; altars, baptismal fonts, religious pictures and even organs were removed; Latin was abandoned in all liturgy; and public and private morality was enforced.[5]

With the arrival of these Calvinistic scholars in Heidelberg to preach and teach in his new university, Elector Frederick III ("The Pious") soon asked them to draw up a confession of faith in the form of a catechism to define the Protestant religion of his realm, the Palatinate. The result of the work of Caspar Olevianus and Zacharias Ursinus was the Heidelberg Catechism, published in German in 1563. Three years later Frederick was called on by the Diet (the parliament of the Holy Roman Empire) to defend his catechism in view of the fact that according to the Peace of Augsburg (1555), the only two legal religions to be permitted in the Germanic Augsburg Empire were Catholicism and Lutheranism. Frederick gave such a magnificent defense of his catechism before the Diet that his realm, the Palatinate, was permitted to be the exception to the rule.

That the Heidelberg Catechism is a standard of Calvinistic theology there can be no question. The two authors were Calvinists, Olevianus himself having

5 *Ibid.*, p. 12.

studied under John Calvin. The catechisms of Calvin and à Lasco[6] were closely followed, and one can easily see a similarity of phraseology between the Heidelberg Catechism and the Calvinistic Belgic Confession which was published two years earlier.

The charge sometimes made that the Heidelberg Catechism is more "Melanchthonian" (from the "low" or moderate Lutheran theologian, Philip Melanchthon), than Calvinistic is without foundation. The Catechism teaches total depravity (Questions 5, 8), sovereign election (Questions 26, 31, 52), the forbidding of pictures for worship (Questions 96 - 98), the perseverance of the saints (Questions 1, 31, 51, 54); Calvin's view of the article of the creed, "He descended into hell; Calvin's view of the division of the Ten Commandments and the petitions of the Lord's Prayer; and his view of the sacraments. Each of these points is contrary to Lutheran-Melanchthonian theology. Indeed, the Melanchthonian theologians and princes opposed the Heidelberg Catechism very strongly.

Other evidence could be adduced to prove that the Palatinate was a center of Calvinism in spite of the fact that three times the official religion of that state was changed in the course of the turbulent sixteenth and seventeenth centuries. The Palatinate became a refuge for thousands of Huguenots (Reformed) who fled from France after the St. Bartholomew's Day massacre (1572). The Palatinate Liturgy (1563) which provided for exclusive psalmody (a Calvinist distinction) was in effect for 100 years in the Reformed Churches, until 1657. The closeness of the Dutch Reformed church, which was staunchly Reformed, to the German Reformed Church is an obvious fact. The Hollanders "borrowed" the Heidelberg Catechism from the Palatinate as their own precious expression of the Reformed Faith.

We should also consider that the great Synod of Dort, held in Holland (1618-19), at which Arminianism was officially condemned by the Dutch Reformed Churches, and by many Reformed theologians from other countries, **including** theologians from Germany. The Elector of the Palatinate delegated three theologians to the synod who signed their names to the completed document, The Canons of Dort. Likewise, did the four theologians from the German Landgrave of Hesse, the four from the churches of Bremen, and the two from Emden.

---

6 John à Lasco (1499-1560) was a polish scholar and theologian. He came in touch with the German and Swiss Reformers and broke with the Roman church, becoming an influential Reformer. He is credited with founding the Reformed Church in Friesland (North Holland), and organizing the ministers into a coetus. He spent many years in London ministering to the foreign Protestant refugees. He returned to Poland to establish the Reformation there. He published an influential book on church discipline, a confession of faith and a catechism.

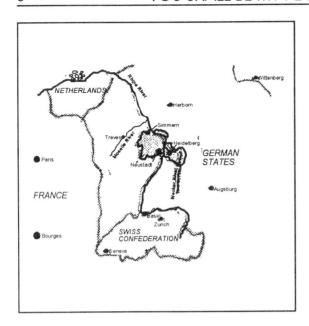

The Palatinate. The name of two little countries of the old German Empire. The two Palatinates were one political unit until 1620. One was called the Upper Palatinate. The other, the Lower or western or Rhenish Palatinate. The Lower Palatinate comprised territory west of the Rhone River and south of the Mosel River. In the Reformation period it was the greatest of the German states, and its ruler was one of the seven electors who chose the Emperor of the Holy Roman Empire. The Rhineland-Palatinate state today is an area of 7,660 sq. miles and the population in 1990 was nearly four million.

Not only were the German Reformed churches anti-Arminian, they took the lead in what became known as Federal or Covenant Theology.[7] The German theologian Johannes Coccerus (John Kock) advanced the theological idea of the covenant, the seeds of which are to be found in Calvin, Olevianus and Ursinus. Covenant theology was developed further in the writings of Herman Witsius and the English Puritans, and incorporated into the Westminster Confession and Catechisms.

This then is some of the theological background, the spiritual legacy, which the early German Reformed emigrants brought with them when they came to these shores. They were Calvinists!

---

7 Clouse summarizes the development of covenant theology as follows: "Covenant Theology. Sometimes called 'Federal Theology,' this system describes the relationship between God and man in the form of covenants. One of the features in the development of Calvinism, it was especially popular with the Puritans and the Reformed theologians of Germany and Holland in the latter sixteenth and during the seventeenth century. . . .Covenant theology in a strict sense began in Germany when a number of Calvinists such as Olevianus and Ursinus emphasized the idea of the covenant of God with man and the believer's mystic union with Christ. Parallel with this German movement was the British development of covenant theology which was sometimes related to political thought. . . .William Ames became the leading British exponent of federal theology, which in a moderate form appears in both the Westminster Confession and the Savoy Declaration. Debtor to both British and German schools, John Coccerus published a book *Summa Doctrinae de Foedere et Testamento Dei* (1648), which has the most elaborate explanation of the covenant principle produced to that time." Robert G. Clouse, *The New International Dictionary of the Christian Church*, article on "Covenant Theology" (Grand Rapids, MI: Zondervan Pub. House, 1974), p. 267.

THE GREAT EXODUS FROM GERMANY

Something should be said here about why so many Germans left their homeland and migrated to America. This is a rather involved story, but our people should be made aware of its fascinating and pathetic character. The primary reason for the mass migrations from Germany in the late 1600s and the following decades can be said in one word: war!

The poor land of Germany had been a battleground for many decades as the armies of various nations fought for control of this area. These battles were both politically and religiously motivated.

The following is a historical digression, but it should be useful to explain the motivation of thousands of Germans who made the life-changing decision to brave the perils of the sea and face an unknown environment, never to see their homeland again.

Church historian William Toth describes the devastation of Germany resulting from the Thirty Years War (1618-1648):

> (The Thirty Years War was a period) of unceasing warfare, involving plunder, rapine, intrigues, and constant death. All Germany lay prostrate. Business had succumbed completely; schools and churches were left without leaders; cities and villages smoldered in ashes; and once-fertile farms sank into unbelievable neglect. The extent of physical destruction staggers the imagination, and the toll of human lives remains forever unknown.... Historians agree that the after effects of this war thwarted German life for a hundred years.[8]

After the Thirty Years War came the French aggression led by Louis XIV. Louis' armies invaded the Palatinate with some 50,000 men and many German towns were reduced to ashes. In 1689 French cavalry surrounded the country around Heidelberg and set fire to a dozen more towns. In all, more than 1200 communities, Catholic and Protestant alike, fell victim to wanton devastation. Four hundred thousand inhabitants of Baden and the Palatinate were made destitute. The men who attempted to defend their wives and daughters were murdered. Others were driven from their towns and villages into the snow and ice of winter to look for shelter.[9]

By the Treaty of Ryswick (1697) the French occupied the

---

8 Dunn, David, *et al.*, *History of the Evangelical and Reformed Church*, Part 2 (New York, NY: Pilgrim's Press, [1961], 1990) pp. 7, 8.

9 *Cf.* Dunn, David, *et al.*, *op. cit.*, pp. 8-10.

Palatinate, Breisach, Freiburg, Phillipsburg and Strassburg. . . . Philip the Catholic puppet ruler of the Palatinate, enforced his right to impose his religion throughout his new possessions, especially since over 1,922 places in the Palatinate had already been re-Catholicized during the course of the war.[10]

Next, after a brief interval, came the War of Spanish Succession (1701-14), during which western Germany once more experienced the devastations of armed conflict.

In the commotion of those times bands of German people quietly left their homeland for England and then to other lands. Pennsylvania became the destination of many of these homeless Germans. Toth gives the following statistics: By 1727 the immigrants numbered about 20,000 in Penn's colony. By 1742 another 18,000 were added. Six thousand more arrived by 1748, and between 1749 and 1754 nearly 32,000 more came through the Port of Philadelphia alone. In 1776 Benjamin Franklin told the British House of Commons that of the 160,000 white people in Pennsylvania about one third were Germans.

How many of these immigrants were Reformed? We will never know. In 1730 it was reported, according to Toth, that the Reformed holding to the old confession constituted more than one half of the whole number of German immigrants, about 15,000. The principal source of these people was the Palatinate and the nickname "Palatine" was commonly used for all German immigrants.[11]

By this historical digression into the miseries of the Palatines we can better understand the mentality and motivation of those brave souls who struggled to reach a land of religious and political freedom.

We shall now turn to the Reformed character and principles of these, our spiritual forefathers, who laid the foundation for the RCUS.

THE EVIDENCE OF THE REFORMED CHARACTER OF THE EARLY GERMAN COETUS (CLASSIS)

John Philip Boehm (1683-1749)

All historians of our church recognize John Philip Boehm as the earthly father of the German Reformed Church in America. It was he who laid the foundations for what was to become the RCUS. Boehm came to "Penn's Woods" in 1720 as a school teacher from Worms, Germany. Being a very able and devout Reformed Christian he was prevailed upon to conduct worship services for the

---

10 *Ibid.*, p. 10.

11 *Ibid.*, pp. 4, 5.

Reformed people who did not have the services of an ordained pastor. For five years he ministered the Word to the farmers in his area without any compensation. He was even prevailed on to baptize children and administer the Lord's Supper. Reluctantly he heeded the requests of the people, knowing that it was contrary to Reformed Church order for an unordained man to administer the sacraments. Altogether he helped organize thirteen congregations in a territory now comprising eight counties in Pennsylvania.

When an ordained minister came on the scene from Germany in 1727, the Rev. George Michael Weiss, and saw what was happening, he vigorously protested that Boehm's ministry was not in accordance with Reformed church polity. Upon Weiss' insistence that Mr. Boehm seek ordination, the consistories involved sought the help of the Dutch Reformed consistory in the colony of New York. The New York consistory, in turn, contacted their Classis in Holland. This lengthy process was finally concluded when Classis Amsterdam permitted the New York consistory to ordain Mr. Boehm (1729). His previous acts of ministry were also declared valid. As a result, both Boehm, and Weiss promised to submit their work to the authority of the Classis Amsterdam in Holland and this established the German Reformed-Holland Reformed connection which lasted until 1793. This ecclesiastical connection between the Pennsylvania and Holland Reformed churches became a most blessed relationship, as the Holland church working together with the Heidelberg Consistory in the Palatinate[12] provided the Pennsylvania Reformed Church with ecclesiastical oversight and financial help for over half a century -- without which the German Reformed Church in America would probably not have remained intact.

This binding ecclesiastical connection between the churches of Pennsylvania and the strong orthodox Reformed church in Holland demonstrates the truly orthodox character of the German Reformed Church. The Dutch, if nothing else, were insistent upon orthodoxy!

Michael Schlatter (1716-1790)

If John Philip Boehm should be called the Father of the German Reformed Church in America, Michael Schlatter should be called its Founder. It was Schlatter (born July 14, 1716 in St. Gall, Switzerland) who became the instrument in God's hands to organize the independent Reformed congregations into an organized body called a *coetus* (which can be translated *synod*, or, as we have preferred, *classis*).

The Rev. Schlatter was a highly energetic young man who loved a challenge. He came from a prominent Reformed family in St. Gall and was raised

---

12 It should be noted that as early as 1728 the Consistory of Heidelberg, fully aware of its inability to help the immigrant Germans to establish churches in the new world, appealed to the synods of South Holland to help these impoverished brethren. The Dutch did so with great compassion.

in a strict Calvinist church of that city. He studied briefly at Leyden, Holland, and was eventually ordained to the ministry. He returned to Switzerland for a few months and served as an assistant pastor. Through a providential series of events he found himself visiting the Heidelberg Consistory just after that body had received a request from the Amsterdam Classis for a German minister to be an organizer of the independent Reformed congregations in Pennsylvania. At this time, Rev. Boehm was an old man and not able to further the development of the churches into an organized denomination.

Schlatter (a single man) accepted the challenge by the Heidelberg Consistory and the synods of Holland, and made arrangements to come to Pennsylvania in 1746.

To understand and appreciate this development in the story of our church and our great indebtedness to our concerned Dutch brethren, we are reprinting as an appendix at the end of this chapter Professor Good's account of the arrangements and instructions the Holland "deputies" made with Rev. Schlatter to organize a coetus.

Arriving in Philadelphia September 1746 after a harrowing sea voyage, Schlatter plunged into the work set before him. He immediately took trips to visit the aged Rev. Boehm and the other ordained pastors J. Reiff, Dorsius and Weiss. He also visited the churches to help solve any problems they might have, such as niggardly pastoral support. On October 12, 1746, Schlatter called Boehm, Weiss and Rev. Rieger to meet in Philadelphia to make preliminary plans for the formation of a coetus as per his instructions from Holland. Unordained preachers in the area were not invited. The first meeting of an organizing coetus was held the following year in Philadelphia, on September 29, 1747, and was attended by 32 ministers and elders. Schlatter was also installed as the pastor of the Germantown and Philadelphia congregations in January of that year. Yet he still managed to take extensive trips to visit the churches, sometimes preaching daily. As Dubbs notes:

> From northern New Jersey to the Valley of Virginia there was hardly a Reformed congregation which he did not visit, except some of those which were supplied by independent ministers.. He succeeded in establishing 16 charges, each consisting of several congregations.[13]

Schlatter estimated that there were 30,000 German Reformed people in Pennsylvania with 53 small churches and four settled pastors!

In 1751 Schlatter went back to Holland to report on the ecclesiastical conditions in Pennsylvania and to try to raise more funds. His published appeal

---

13 Dubbs, *Ibid.*, 282.

resulted in the collection of £12,000. On his return to America he brought with him six young ministers and 700 Bibles for distribution to churches and families. The condition that the Dutch synods always laid down when they provided money for the German churches in Pennsylvania was that they continue to be subject to the authority of the Holland church.

In the four years between 1747 and 1751, Schlatter traveled over 8000 miles (mostly on horseback) and preached 635 times. In 1755 he was induced to resign his pastorate in Philadelphia and become involved in other charitable activities (charity schools) and still later he became a chaplain in the Royal American Regiment. During the War for Independence he was imprisoned as an American patriot because he refused to continue as a chaplain in the British army.[14]

The RCUS can be thankful to God for the Rev. Michael Schlatter, and for the Holland church for their great contributions to the formation of the German Reformed Church in America.

CONGREGATIONAL ORGANIZATION AND THE COETUS

J. H. Dubbs states that the earliest German Reformed congregations in this country were organized in strict accordance with the polity of the churches of the Palatinate. As early as 1563, Elector Frederick ordered that the churches in the Palatinate should elect elders and deacons following the pattern of the other Calvinist churches.[15] Dubbs goes on to say:

> The pastor, elders, and deacons in each congregation constituted a body which was officially termed *Consistorium* (Consistory) or *Presbyterium* (Presbytery), but was popularly called *Kirchenrath* (church council). Ordinarily one half of the Consistory was annually retired from active service; but the eldership was nevertheless regarded as a permanent vocation, and the men who had once been ordained to this office retained its functions, though they might be temporarily relieved from labor.

According to this pattern, which was familiar to the Reformed everywhere, the earliest American congregations were constituted; and there is no evidence that any other form of government was even suggested.[16]

The constitution prepared by Pastor Boehm in 1725 was used by the 13 congregations which he organized. Dubbs says that a few copies survive, and a few

---

14 Article on M. Schlatter in *The New Schaff-Herzog Encyclopedia* (Grand Rapids, MI: Baker Book House, 1950). Vol. 10, pp. 239, 240.

15 Dubbs, *op. cit.*, p. 264,

16 *Ibid.*, pp. 264, 265.

extracts taken from the *Mercersburg Review* (October 1876) are reprinted in his book.[17] Boehm's Constitution follows the general principles of congregational government found in Europe, many of which operated under the Church Order of Dort. It does contain some unique provisions as one can readily see.

Professor Grossmann summarizes the Reformed features of Boehm's Constitution as follows:

1. It reveals a thoroughly Reformed position.

2. It sets forth a well-organized consistorial government with strict discipline.

3. It accepted the Three Forms of Unity, as they are known today. (Note: This point will be discussed later.)

4. It was adopted (with necessary modifications) as the Constitution of the Coetus (Classis) which was organized in 1747.

5. It clearly recognized the authority of the Classis by submitting the congregations to classical authority in those functions which belong to a Reformed Classis.

6. It was accepted by Classis Amsterdam which had oversight over the church polity in the American German Church. This meant that the Constitution was in agreement with the Dutch Confessional standards and the Church Order of Dort.[18]

September 29, 1747 was the date of the organization of the German Reformed Coetus. It took place in the Philadelphia church with four ministers and 28 elders present. In the following year (Sept. 28, 1848), the second coetus met and adopted Boehm's constitution. Prof. Grossmann summarizes the significance of this historic event:

a. At the request of Holland, the ministers and elders present signed the Heidelberg and Canons of Dort as their creeds, although Rieger refused because of scruples on the doctrine of reprobation "in the sense of Calvin." Later Rieger agreed and signed. . . .

b. Boehm signed the minutes as president, and Schlatter sent a report to the Holland deputies.

c. With some additions for coetal use, Boehm's 1725 Constitution was adopted as the church order for the coetus including the

---

17 We have reproduced it as an appendix.

18 Grossmann, *Ibid.*, pp. 15-16.

following statement: "(This church order) shall be kept inviolate according to our best ability, in order that we may hold steadfastly to the Heidelberg Catechism, all the formulas of unity and the Synod of Dort, and neither we nor our descendants shall be permitted to add anything thereto, to take anything therefrom or to acknowledge anyone as their regular minister before such a one, as well as everything else, be submitted by the consistory of the congregations to the Very Reverend Classis of Amsterdam or to their delegates and approved by the same, and at all times the answer received shall be final." (No Congregationalists these!)

d. This constitution provided that aggrieved parties could appeal to the coetus and that no minister should officiate in the charge of another without permission.

e. This constitution of the coetus is exactly the same as that adopted by Boehm's three churches in 1728. It was originally written in 1725 by Boehm. He then submitted it to the Dutch pastors in New York, who revised it and sent it to Holland. The Dutch synods approved it and it was sent back to America where Boehm's congregations approved it in 1728. (See Minutes and Letters of the Coetus, p. 41, in the Records of 1748.) The constitution itself begins on page 47 in the Minutes and Letters.[19]

A further proof that the Coetus operated under a constitution patterned after the Church Order of Dort (1619) is to be seen in the practice of the *censura moram* (examination of conduct) at the annual meetings of the coetus. It went like this:

The letters from Holland were read, and the state of the churches minutely considered. Then the elders were for a time dismissed, and the *censura moram* was held, at which the character of individual members was investigated and advice given with regard to future conduct.[20]

This procedure is taken directly from the Church Order of Dort, Article 81 (cf. the older Christian Reformed edition).

THE CREEDS

As we've seen, the coetus in 1748 adopted the Calvinistic Heidelberg Catechism and the Canons of Dort. These were reaffirmed at the Coetus of 1752; and the Coetus of 1765 again refers to them. J. I. Good mentions an incident in

---

19 *Ibid.*, pp. 24, 25.

20 Dunn, David, *et al.*, *op. cit.*, p. 38.

1787 in which a certain Mr. Hautz was ordained by the Coetus without awaiting the consent of the Holland Classis. He had signed "an oath of agreement with the doctrines, usages and regulations of the Biblical Reformed Church." The Holland Classis rebuked the Coetus for this action because this oath did not specifically mention the Holland creeds. This, of course, would have meant The Three Forms of Unity: The Heidelberg Catechism, The Belgic Confession and the Canons of Dort.[21] The Coetus in 1790 defended its action by declaring that the "doctrine, customs and ordinances of the Reformed Church" implicitly included "the Netherlands Confession of faith and Church Formulas. . . ."[22]

OATHS OF THE MINISTERS

Professor Good says that all the ministers who were sent over from Holland, and there were quite a number over the course of time, were required to give adherence to the Dutch creeds,[23] and this was true of those received by the coetus in America, who, before they would be approved by the Amsterdam Classis, must pledge agreement with the Dutch creeds. Indeed, they were said to have signed the Formula of Unity which meant the three creeds. The oath of the early ministers who were sent over from Holland to the German Reformed church reads as follows:

> We, the undersigned, acknowledge by this subscription that we hold ourselves, with heart and mouth, to all those formulas whose maintenance the preachers of the coetus of Pennsylvania under the Netherlands synods shall help to secure.[24]

This oath, says Good, is on record from extant copies of calls from 1752 to 1784, hence it was the requirement of all the ministers serving in the Coetus.[25]

WORSHIP AND LITURGY

The Calvinistic character of the German Reformed worship is instructive. Professor Good summarizes the original worship as follows: "The early [German Reformed] church was non-liturgical. It used a free service in the regular Sabbath worship, although it used forms for special occasions, such as the sacraments,

---

21 Good, *op. cit.*, p. 675.

22 Hinke, William, ed., *Minutes and Letters of the Coetus of Pennsylvania 1747-1792* (Philadelphia: Reformed Church Publication Board, 1903).

23 The term "Dutch Creeds" should not be misinterpreted. They refer to the Heidelberg Catechism (German), the Belgic Confession (French) and the Canons of Dort (the work of an **international** synod held in Dordrecht, Holland). The Dutch Church early recognized the biblical truth of these creeds and adopted them as their Three Forms of Unity. The unity of the Reformed Churches around the world is not based on ethnic background but on the truth of the Word of God.

24 Good, *op. cit.*, p. 675.

25 *Ibid.*, pp. 675-676.

marriage and ordination."[26] He proves this assertion by showing that there was never any mention of a liturgy in connection with the coetus meetings. Prayer is always mentioned in the Minutes as "fervent prayer," "an earnest prayer," etc. In the Holland correspondence, the only time liturgy is mentioned is in connection with the forms for the sacraments, marriage, and ordinations, and not with the ordinary Sunday services. Good says that there was no liturgy published during the entire period of the Coetus (1748-1792), the reason being that the Reformed used only the simple Palatinate Liturgy. The Palatinate Liturgy had no responses, and the prayers were not mandatory.[27]

Good says that the Reformed followed the Palatinate Liturgy in the observance of the Church Year. The five special days of worship were: Christmas, Good Friday, Easter, Ascension and Whitsunday (Pentecost).

There was no altar in the Reformed churches, only the communion table. In those cases where the Reformed and the Lutherans shared the same church building, the Reformed never used an altar, only a table. Good remarks, "It was not until the controversy began in the church about 1860 that altars — high altars — began to be spoken of and introduced. They would have been a novelty to our fathers of the Coetus."[28]

CHRISTIAN EDUCATION

The Protestant Reformation with its renewed interest in Bible reading by the laity, immediately stressed the importance of Christian schools for the children. This was true for both the Lutheran and Reformed churches. Professor Dubbs comments that "Every German regarded it as a religious duty to teach his children to read the Bible and the catechism, so that they might be properly prepared for confirmation and holy communion."[29]

The Reformed churches in Germany required catechetical instruction and the maintaining of Christian schools (see Heidelberg Catechism, Question 103). Toth describes the emphasis on education for the covenant children in Protestant Europe:

> Schools also were entering a period of renewed strength and vigor so that they were steadily whittling down the rate of illiteracy among Germans. A study of the lists of German immigrants in the first half of the eighteenth century shows that 74 percent of the

---

26 *Ibid.*, pp. 678.

27 *Ibid.*, pp. 678-680.

28 *Ibid.* pp. 680-682.

29 Dubbs, *op. cit.,* pp. 241, 242.

male immigrants were able to write. This high rate of literacy, unusual among Europeans at that time, was neither accidental nor incidental. It was rather the result of a long tradition of commitment to the idea of education embodied in the support of higher schools of learning as well as parochial schools. Protestant princes took the initiative in fostering education. As early as 1559 a state-church school system had been organized in Wurttemberg, followed by Brunswick in 1569, Weimar in 1619, and Gotha in 1642. By the middle of the seventeenth century most of the German states had adopted some state-church plan of education. As a rule, both Lutheran and Reformed churches were accustomed to engage a minister as well as a schoolmaster — providing them with a stated salary and a home — and to set up high educational standards. The effectiveness of these schools, of course, fluctuated with the vicissitudes of the times, but never waned completely. Whenever the state failed to provide the necessary schools, the churches rallied to the challenge involved in maintaining the standard of literacy among their numbers. Educational leadership came from the universities, which generally were a special responsibility of the rulers. At the beginning of the eighteenth century universities, like those at Heidelberg, Herborn, and Marburg, came to new life, and others, like the one at Halle in 1691, were founded. The German-Swiss universities of Zurich, Basel, and St. Gall stood high among European institutions devoted to the cultivation of learning. The foundations for an aggressive educational leadership in later periods were thus substantially laid.[30]

Following the tradition of the old country, the schoolmaster in those early colonial days, was a very important person. Dubbs comments on his activity in the Reformed community:

> (The schoolmaster) was ordinarily the most educated man in the community (next to the pastor.) In a fully organized congregation he was regarded as the pastor's chief assistant. He not only taught the children to read and write, and to sing the chorales which the fathers loved so well, but he also instructed them in the Bible and in the catechism. If no pastor was present, the school teacher would often read sermons at the Sunday services and take charge

---

30 Dunn, David, *et al.*, *op. cit.*, pp. 21,22.

of funeral services.[31]

The following observation by Dubbs showing the close connection between the Reformed congregation and the Reformed Christian school for mutual support is of great importance:

> (We must) recognize the great value of the system of parochial schools as it prevailed in this early period. Indeed, it is difficult to see how without them the Reformed Church could have been established in this country. Pastors, though earnestly longed for, were slow in coming; and if it had not been for the imperfect ministrations of a better class of parochial teachers — most of whose names are now forgotten — the great number of the earlier churches could hardly have been founded.[32]

School teacher John Phillip Boehm was just such a person, and mightily used by God to perform a service that resulted in the founding of the RCUS!

The above comments illustrate the fact that the Christians — almost all Christians — in that era never conceived of education and religion as two separate compartments of life: secular and sacred. Such a dichotomy would have been unthinkable to them. Education was a religious function, or in Reformed terms it was a *covenantal obligation* required by the baptismal vow to raise up the child in the fear and admonition of the Lord. So the church building and the church school building were two important buildings to be erected when the Reformed settled a community. The two men to be supported were the pastor and the school teacher. The two institutions worked together in the minds of the early Reformed.

---

31 Dubbs quotes a typical contract made by a school teacher between himself and a local church: "On this 4th day of May, 1747, I, the undersigned, John Hoffman, parochial teacher at Lancaster, have promised, in the presence of the congregation, to serve as chorister, and, as long as we have no pastor, to read sermons on Sunday. In summer I promise to hold catechetical instruction with the young, as becomes a faithful teacher, and to lead them in singing; and also to attend to the clock. On the other hand, the congregation promises me an annual salary, consisting of voluntary offerings from all the members of the church, to be written in a special register and arranged according to the amount contributed, so that the teacher may be adequately compensated for his labor.

"Furthermore, I have firmly and irrevocably agreed with the congregation on the aforesaid date that I will keep school on every working-day during the entire year, as is the usual custom, and in such manner as becomes a faithful teacher. In consideration whereof they promise me a free dwelling and four cords of wood, and have granted me the privilege of charging for each child that may come to school the sum of five shillings for three months and for the whole year one pound. I promise to enter upon my duties, if alive and well, on the 24th of November, 1747.

"In testimony whereof I have written the above document and signed the same with my own signature, to remain unchanged for one year from date. Sealed with my usual signet.   — John Hoffman, Teacher."

32 Dubbs, *Ibid.*, pp. 243-244.

In the area of covenant education, it must be admitted, our German Reformed forefathers were far ahead of many of us in the RCUS today. They sacrificed to give their children an education that was in keeping with the doctrines of the Reformed faith. How much are we willing to sacrifice to do the same for our covenant children? Their commitment to Reformed education did much to preserve their churches from extinction, as Dubbs noted. Likewise, unless our Reformed parents today catch the vision and begin to understand the covenantal requirements for Reformed education, whether in an organized day school or in a home school (which is increasingly becoming the preferred option today), our churches will not survive! The covenantal education of our baptized and confirmed youth is not a mere luxury, it is the   requirement of God's Word, and   understood by our Reformed forefathers as the requirement of the holy baptismal vow. May we learn from those early Reformed Christians before we see more and more of our youth succumb to secular humanism and become spiritual dropouts.

THE CONFLICT WITH ANTI-REFORMED HERESIES

To be Reformed means to be opposed to all doctrines and practices which are not biblical and not in keeping with the Reformed creeds.

Accordingly, the early German Reformed Church had its share of trouble with anti-Reformed sects and doctrines that found Pennsylvania to be a fertile ground for their cancerous growth. Penn's colony was a haven of freedom, not only for the orthodox Christians, but also for many cultic groups. Professor Good lists, along with the Lutherans and Reformed, such groups as Dunkards, Mennonites, Schwenkfelders, Quakers, Inspirationists, The New Born, Labadists, Ronscorfers, etc.[33] It was a "wilderness of sects."

It is not necessary to go into detail about the various heresies that confronted the Reformed churches in those early days, but we'll mention a major one that has received a lot of attention.

"THE CONGREGATION OF GOD IN THE SPIRIT"

This was a movement organized by the Moravian Brethren, an Anabaptist group, led by one Count von Zinzendorf of Moravia.[34] Zinzendorf arrived in Pennsylvania and was greeted by a leading Reformed elder in the Germantown

---

33 Good, *op. cit.*, p. 200.

34 Zinzendorf, the son of a high Saxon official, was in government service before becoming an influential religious leader. He had connections with Lutheranism, Pietism, the Reformed, Roman Catholicism and non-churchly groups. He invited Bohemian Protestant refugees (United Brethren) to settle on his estate at Bertheldorf (1722) which became known as *Herrnhut*. It became the center for a world-wide missionary outreach by their missionaries known as The Moravian United Brethren. Zinzendorf became their superintendent and traveled widely to evangelize for the movement.

church, Henry Antes. Plans were made to organize a spiritual communion of Christians from whatever denomination or sect. This communion was to be called "The Congregation of God in the Spirit." Zinzendorf claimed to have authority to ordain both Lutheran and Reformed ministers (!). He said he held to the Augsburg Confession (Lutheran). Again, he could represent the Reformed, for he had been ordained by the head of the Reformed Church of the Electorate of Brandenburg, Jablonsky, who was also a Moravian Bishop.[35]

This man must have had an impressive, charismatic personality. He had a powerful influence on many Christians in the various denominations, especially the Lutherans and Reformed. Elder Henry Antes, who had been a close associate of Pastor Boehm in earlier days, could now say under Zinzendorf's influence, "I am Reformed; I am Lutheran; I am a Mennonite — a Christian is everything!"[36]

A sympathetic writer (professing to be Reformed) many years later had this to say about the aims of the Moravian movement:

> The avowed purpose of the Congregation of God in the Spirit was not to supersede the existing denominations, but to form a superior organization of sincere followers of Jesus, who should cultivate the higher graces of the Christian life, guide by their pious influence the bodies they represented, and maintain a godly fellowship, leaving the congregations to attend to minor and temporal affairs as before.[37]

Professor Grossmann has summarized the conflict between the staunch Reformed and Zinzendorf and his followers in the Philadelphia area:

a. This began in 1740 when Henry Antes, a "pious (Reformed) elder of Falkner Swamp," had (George) Whitefield preach there in the morning and Bishop Bohler, the Moravian in the afternoon.

b. The Moravians soon began ecumenical work among all the Germans in Pennsylvania which eventually led to "the Congregation of God in the Spirit," a Moravian union movement. Zinzendorf planned to establish the "tropes" (circles of believers) system which they used among the state churches in Europe, among the Germans in America.

c. Zinzendorf himself came to Pennsylvania in December, 1741,

---

35 Good, *Ibid.*, p. 203.

36 Dubbs, *op. cit.*, p. 272.

37 Henry S. Dotterer, *Boehm's Reformed Church* (Norristown, PA: Herald Printing and Binding Rooms, 1891), p. 36.

and met with Elder Antes on the way to Bethlehem, Pennsylvania, where the Moravians were laying out a colony.

d. Zinzendorf was able, with the full cooperation of the Reformed pastor in Germantown, Rev. John Bechtel, to gather a number of meetings among the many parties of German Christianity in Pennsylvania. However, it was not long before the Seventh Day Baptists pulled out and only parties of Lutheran and Reformed continued to attend.

e. Into this situation old Rev. Samuel Guldin stepped as a great adversary of the Moravians. He published a pamphlet against them at his own expense, sold half and gave the other half away, thus raising considerable opposition (to Zinzendorf's movement).

f. The union movement eventually went wholly into the Moravian church, and with the strong opposition of (John Philip) Boehm for the Reformed and Muhlenberg for the Lutherans the union movement itself died.

g. This was the greatest theological controversy among the Reformed in this period and though some families were lost to the Reformed churches, no congregations were lost. The Germantown church came back fully to the Reformed Coetus and the pastor, Lischy, also came back after rejecting his earlier conversion to Moravian principles.[38]

It was especially Pastor Boehm who took a stand against Zinzendorf's proselytizing efforts which, as Grossmann has indicated, included the defection of the (unordained) John Bechtel. Bechtel became the main assistant for Zinzendorf among the German Reformed. He was ordained by the Count into the Reformed Church! He then proceeded to publish his own catechism, *Bechtel's Catechism* (1742) that was decidedly antagonistic to the Heidelberg Catechism. Bechtel's Catechism was introduced into all the congregations which joined The Congregation in the Spirit.[39]

Pastor Boehm was not taken in by the Zinzendorf Moravians. He had been forewarned by the Holland Classis of this heretical influence. In fact, a book had been written by an Amsterdam pastor, G. Kulenkamp, exposing the Moravian theology as one of "enthusiasm, fanaticism, and corrupt mysticism"[40] which was sent to Boehm. Boehm subsequently had several personal unfriendly encounters with

---

38 Grossmann, *op. cit.*, pp. 39,40.

39 Good, *op. cit.*, p. 213.

40 *Ibid.*, p. 225.

Zinzendorf, by mail primarily. The basic disagreement between the two sides was over the issue of predestination and reprobation. Boehm heartily affirmed the Canons of Dort and Zinzendorf rejected them. On one occasion, Zinzendorf wrote to Boehm, "I am not inclined to the doctrine of an absolute reprobation, as a doctrine which in my religion is confessedly held as fundamentally and wholly erroneous."[41] In August of 1742 Boehm published his first attack on the Moravians called *True Letter of Warning, Addressed to the Reformed Congregations of Pennsylvania.* In it he not only condemns the heretical doctrines of The Congregation of God in the Spirit, he expresses his deep sorrow for those who had been his close friends in the Reformed faith, such as Elder Henry Antes, who had defected. It was Henry Antes who had persuaded Pastor Boehm to seek ordination many years earlier.

The Moravian Congregation of God in the Spirit represented at least three heresies that the conservative Reformed pastors rejected: Arminianism, Pietism, and a false ecumenism based on spiritual feelings (mysticism) rather than truth..

Professor Good speaks of the strong influence of pietism among the Germans, including the Reformed Germans. He speaks of a good and a bad pietism! He writes, "The Reformed Church from the beginning was pietistic. What was the Reformation but a great revival? And our church, which grew out of the Reformation, partook of this spirit."[42] Perhaps we're caught up in semantics here, but the usual understanding of pietism is that it is an overemphasis on subjective religious experience, often involving mysticism, and a preference for "spiritual experiences with the Holy Spirit" over against the objective truth of the Bible (i.e., doctrine). Men like Rev. Boehm were strongly opposed to the "fanatics," the "enthusiasts," as these pietists were called. The Calvinists were *pious*, but they should not be called "pietists."

The tendency of pietists is to ignore doctrinal differences among Christians and focus on their "spiritual oneness." This in turn promotes ecumenicity at the expense of truth and confessional boundaries. The conservative Reformed Germans resisted this temptation to have fellowship at the expense of truth. Even merger with the Presbyterians was not to be, because of some (minor) differences between them. Boehm, for example, did not like it that the Presbyterian form of worship did not use liturgical forms for the sacramental and extraordinary occasions.[43]

Later in her history different "spirits" would enter the RCUS, which were unconfessional and which caused grievous damage to the Reformed character of the

41 Dubbs, *op. cit.,* 274

42 Good, *op. cit.*, p. 592.

43 *Ibid.*, p. 679.

faith and worship of our denomination. About these matters other chapters in this book will explain.

In our day there are always men of an ecumenical frame of mind who put "love" and "unity" ahead of truth and theology. They are dangerous people, even though they talk loudly of their spiritual experiences. As Reformed people we must ever be sensitive to the relationship between truth and love, between doctrinal differences and unity with other professing Christians. We must indeed seek to cultivate unity with other Christians (John 17:21), but only on the basis of shared doctrinal convictions.

CONCLUSION

The purpose of this chapter has been to demonstrate that, quite apart from what happened to the Reformed Church in the United States in the nineteenth and twentieth centuries, the early German Reformed Church was based squarely on orthodox Calvinism, in both theology and worship.

That theology is articulated in the Three Forms of Unity which teach the absolute sovereignty of God in creation, providence and redemption. The Five Points of Calvinism, as taught in the Canons of Dort, were basic to our theological foundation. The other doctrines elucidated in the Belgic Confession were our theological property and heritage.

We trust that the evidence presented in this chapter will convince all our RCUS people, and others who have been skeptical about us, that we began as an orthodox, Calvinistic, Reformed denomination. True, we have lost much of our heritage from time to time and trifled with it; but by God's amazing grace to us sinners we have begun to see a genuine return to the Faith of our Fathers in recent years. Indeed, already we are beginning to hear murmurs from some quarters that "the RCUS is a small, hyper-conservative denomination" that is far too intolerant toward other denominations in the ecumenical scheme of things! So be it, if our witness is based entirely on God's Word!

These words from Professor Good are a fitting conclusion to the early history of the American German Reformed Church:

> The Church during the period of the coetus was evidently strongly Calvinistic and predestinarian. The matrix in which our Church was born was Calvinism. Melanchthonianism was not thought of under the Dutch control. For sixty-four years (long enough to mold a Church for its future) the Church was distinctly Calvinistic.[44]

And to this we add, Amen! Thank God!   🍎

---

44 *Ibid.*, p. 674.

APPENDIX A

The Commission and Instructions Given to Rev. Michael Schlatter by the Amsterdam Classis Prior to His Leaving for the Colony of Pennsylvania in 1746[1]

The Classis deputies gave Rev. Schlatter the following:

1. An introduction to the German Reformed Church of Pennsylvania, giving his reasons for being sent thither.

a. Because originally the settlers in Pennsylvania were from the Palatinate and Switzerland, to which two countries Holland was under the greatest obligations of gratitude, because from them the light of the Gospel first streamed to Holland.

b. Because the Pennsylvania congregations are attached so loyally to their time honored Reformed faith, and

c. because Pennsylvania would become thus a safe asylum for the oppressed brethren of their faith of Europe when driven out by persecution.

Then they gave two reasons for not being able to do something for Pennsylvania before.

1. They could not get a clear idea about the Church in Pennsylvania.

2. Because they had hitherto lacked a suitable German minister, although they had sought for one for fifteen years since 1731. They then say that they believe they have found a proper person in Rev. Michael Schlatter, one of the 26 ministers of St. Gall. He was of good family, well educated, understanding Hebrew, Greek, German, Dutch and French. After being admitted as a candidate to the ministry in 1739 he had visited the five great universities of Holland and the principal Protestant universities of Germany. He was willing, because of the great need of Pennsylvania, to go there, and they recommend them to give him a cordial reception.

2. They also gave Schlatter the following instructions about his work in Pennsylvania:

1. He was to organize the ministers and congregations into a coetus, which should meet annually.

a. It should subscribe to the Heidelberg Catechism and the Canons of Dort with heart and voice.

b. It should consider the concerns of the Church, the members being appointed president and secretary in rotation, beginning with the oldest.

---

1 Quoted from J. I. Good, *op. cit.*, pp. 305-308.

c. It should correspond with the deputies of the synods of Holland, and render reports of their work as a coetus. The deputies allow Schlatter half a year as a sufficient time in which to do this. After that he was to take charge of a congregation.

2. He was to fulfill the duties of a church officer known in Holland as the visitor extraordinary. He was to visit the congregations and find out their condition, how many members each congregation had, whether they were steadfast in the faith, whether they paid a fixed salary to their minister and how. (The deputies say they were willing to aid the congregations in Pennsylvania, but they were not willing to divert the money which was already used to aid more than a hundred Reformed congregations in various parts of the world.)

3. Where there was no congregation as yet, he was to gather the most intelligent and zealous Reformed together, and learn how much money they would be willing to raise for the salary of a minister, and also how much they would pay toward building a church. He was then to install elders and deacons in those churches.

4. He was to ascertain how the 130 Bibles sent over to Pennsylvania in 1742 had been distributed. He was also to bring the money accounts of Reiff to a desirable settlement.

5. At the end of the first half year he was to hold a coetus, act as president and send a faithful account of its proceedings to Holland. That having been done, he was to take charge of a congregation and become pastor. They gave him money only for his traveling expenses and for half a year's work, but hoped that the Dutch and the Swiss churches would contribute toward this worthy cause. This instruction was dated May 23, 1746, and was signed by all the deputies. They placed in his hand a passport of both the Dutch and English governments, and committed him into the hands of Him who rules the wind and the waves. He sailed from Amsterdam, June 1, 1746, on his mission to, complete the organization of the Pennsylvania Reformed Church, by organizing the coetus.

APPENDIX B

Articles from Rev. John P. Boehm's Church Constitution of 1725[1]

(It is agreed) that all the members of Consistory now in service in all the three villages shall be recognized and remain in their offices for their appointed term. Then all the members of the congregation shall, with the Minister and the rest of the consistory, choose new members of consistory. But at the same time all the members of the congregation shall transfer, each to his own consistory, all power and right henceforth to choose the consistory from year to year by a majority vote; since, through the increase and spreading abroad of the congregations, it is not practicable for all the members to meet just for this purpose.

The persons chosen shall be propounded for three Sundays each in his congregation, to see if any one makes any lawful objection; and, if not, they shall be ordained at the third announcement.

If it should happen (as we hope it will not) that one or more of the consistorial persons should walk disorderly, or create strife and division in the congregations, he or they shall be timely warned by the rest to give over such courses; and if they will not comply, they shall be put out of their offices; and others shall be chosen in their place out of such as have last been in service, and be regularly ordained, and then serve. And so in case any one dies in office.

When any Elder or Deacon goes out of office he shall be exempt for two years and then may again be chosen; or even earlier, if it is deemed necessary by the consistory for the time being.

The Minister, Elders, and Deacons, and the whole congregation shall determine the time when, on the Lord's Day and other days, and the places where, divine service shall be held.

The rite of Baptism shall always be administered, without a fee, at the close of worship. Besides the Elders, there shall be witnesses at the baptism; and this edifying custom shall not be lightly altered. The witnesses must be sound in doctrine and blameless in life.[2]

---

1 Quoted from J. H. Dubbs. *op. cit.*, pp. 267-270.

2 The custom of having witnesses (sponsors) at baptism was common until a comparatively recent date, but has now become unusual. At present. even when sponsors are admitted, parents are required personally to assume the baptismal vows in behalf of their children. In early days there were sometimes as many as five sponsors at a single baptism, and their names were duly entered on the records of the
(continued...)

The Holy Supper shall be administered twice a year in each place where public worship is maintained. No one shall be admitted unless upon confession before the consistory and evidence of an upright life, or upon proper testimonials from other Reformed congregations, according to the Church Order of the Synod of Dort, anno 1618 and 1619. All the members shall constantly, as they are able, attend worship and appear at the preparatory sermon; and those who neglect this shall be spoken to by the consistory as they shall judge necessary. The old shall diligently instruct the young in the Reformed religion, and thereunto shall carefully provide for their hearing God's Word in preaching and in catechizing; so that the young may also come to the Lord's table. All the members of the three congregations shall have the right to commune in any one of them, no lawful hindrance existing, so long as they have the same minister.

The bread and wine for the Lord's Supper shall always be provided by the Deacons, who shall also collect and disburse the alms, and make faithful account of the same. The members of the consistory, whether Elders or Deacons, to whom the church chest and property are intrusted, shall annually make account of their administration before the congregation, and for this purpose shall keep a true record of receipts and expenditures. And the account, when approved, shall be signed by the minister in the name of all as satisfactory.

In order to meet the necessities of the church, the Deacons shall always collect the alms at the end of service.

If any member, male or female, fall into lewdness, such shall be under censure of the consistory until they promise and give evidence of amendment.

The office and duty of the Minister shall be to preach the pure doctrine of the Reformed Church according to God's Word, and to administer the Seals of the Covenant at the proper time and place, to adhere strictly to the Confession of Faith of the Reformed Church, to explain in order the Heidelberg Catechism, and to catechize, and with the Elders to exercise discipline. He shall not, without necessity, omit to hold service at the prescribed time and place at Falckner's Swamp, Skippack, and White Marsh.

A consistory shall be held at least every half-year, and the Minister shall record all ecclesiastical proceedings in a book.

And if he should be inclined to go away, whether because called elsewhere or for other lawful reasons, he shall as soon as practicable give the congregations

---

(...continued)

church. At a later date the number was limited by custom to a single pair. Conscientious sponsors were careful to see to it that those for whom they had become sureties were faithfully instructed and prepared for confirmation and the holy communion; and instances were not rare when children, on the death of their parents, were adopted by their godparents.

notice, so that they may not be left in distress, but may seasonably provide another suitable man. The Minister, also, shall in all other things bear himself as becomes a true servant of Christ, under Him the Great Shepherd of the sheep.

The Minister, Elders, and Deacons shall maintain a careful oversight of the congregation, and shall appear at the appointed time and place to hold consistory, nor omit the same without ample cause. They shall, to the best of their ability, faithfully execute the foregoing orders, each according to his office. Whoever knows of any offense committed by one of the consistory, or by any other member, shall feel bound in conscience to make it known, not through malice or hatred, but to remove scandal. The accused person shall not demand the name of his accuser, nor obstinately deny his proved faults, nor wickedly continue therein; such as do so shall be disowned as members of the congregation till they promise and show amendment of life.

And if any one allege anything against the doctrine or life of the minister, or of any member of consistory, or of any other member, they shall abstain from everything injurious or slanderous, and not avenge themselves, but refer the matter to the consistory, who shall be bound to use all diligence to remove such scandal.[3]

---

3 Editor's note: Dubbs leaves out the section on Adherence to this Constitution — the section which dates it to 1728 and 1729 *and* which includes adherence to "the Heidelberg Catechism, all the Formulas of Unity and the Synod of Dort. . . ." See *Minutes and Letters of the Coetus of Pennsylvania*, p. 52. *Cf.* also a footnote on page 49 which reports a vertabim copy made by Boehm himself and dated March 18, 1744 — some two years *before* Schlatter was sent over.

Bibliography

Berkhof, Louis. *Systematic Theology* (Grand Rapids, MI: Wm.B.Eerdmans Pub.Co.,1939, 1960).

DeJong, Peter Y. *Crisis in the Reformed Churches: Essays in Commemoration of the Great Synod of Dort, 1618-1619* (Grand Rapids, MI: Reformed Fellowship, Inc., 1968).

Detwiler, Jones. *Proceedings of the 150th Anniversary of Boehm's Reformed Church.* (Norristown, PA: Herald Printing and Binding Rooms, 1891).

Douglas, J. D., Gen. Ed. *The New International Dictionary of the Christian Church* (Grand Rapids: Zondervan Pub. House, 1974).

Dubbs, J. H.. *The American Church History Series.* Vol. 8, "The Reformed Church, German" (New York, NY: The Christian Literature Co., 1895).

Dunn, David, *et al. History of the Evangelical and Reformed Church:* Part I, chaps. 1, 2 (New York: Pilgrim's Press, 1961, 1990).

Grossmann, Robert. *Outline History of the Reformed Church in the United States, 1725-1995* (Garner, IA: Elector Publications, 1995).

Good, J. I. *History of the Reformed Church of Germany, 1620-1890* (Reading, PA: Daniel Miller, Publisher, 1894.

_____ *History of the Reformed Church in the U. S, 1725-1792* (Reading, PA.: Daniel Miller, Publisher, 1899).

Miller, Charles D. *The Rise and Development of Calvinism.* Chap. 2: "The Historical Development of Calvinism in Switzerland, France and the Germanic Empire" (Grand Rapids, MI: Calvin College, no date).

Psalter Hymnal. (Grand Rapids, MI: Publications Committee of the CRC, 1934).

*The New Schaff-Herzog Encyclopia of Religious Knowledge (*Grand Rapids, MI: Baker Book House, 1950).

C H A P T E R   T W O

The Theology of the Eastern Church and Mercersburg

Rev. Frank H. Walker

When a seminary goes bad, the denomination it serves usually follows right behind. This observation, sadly enough, summarizes the history of the Reformed Church in the United States in the mid-nineteenth century.

Three professors — Friedrich Rauch, John Williamson Nevin and Philip Schaff — wielded their influence at the RCUS seminary in Mercersburg, Pennsylvania, between 1837 and 1863, promoting a dialectical approach to church history, a view of the sacraments and the church that was more Lutheran than Reformed, and a Hegelian idealism. Because few RCUS pastors were acquainted with the German philosophy and theology from which these ideas arose, the new thought marched successfully forward. There appears to have been no one in the RCUS at the time with the competence to thwart the sheer brilliance of the Mercersburg men. A few pastors tried but the results were less than successful.

This chapter tells the lamentable story of the negative influence of worldly thought on the church of Jesus Christ.

THE RCUS NEEDS A SEMINARY

During its formative years, the RCUS benefited greatly from the guidance and assistance of Classis Amsterdam of the Reformed Church in Holland. The Dutch church, for example, sent the Rev. Michael Schlatter with a commission to organize the German Reformed churches of the colonies into a coetus (similar to a Classis but without self-determination) within six months. After he did so, Classis

Amsterdam continued to advise the coetus and review its minutes. Lacking authority to ordain ministers, the coetus was completely dependent on Holland to approve all ordinations of ministers.

This arrangement had one obvious drawback: due to the distance between the Netherlands and the American colonies, the Dutch brethren found it impossible to provide an adequate supply of pastors for the struggling immigrant church. Thus, in 1793 (the year the German Reformed Church reorganized as an independent Synod) congregations outnumbered pastors by almost four to one. Preachers were so hard to come by that many churches had become accustomed to hearing a trained preacher as infrequently as once a month (and often less).

Following its separation from the church in Holland, the RCUS began educating its own ministers under the tutelage of especially skilled pastors. While this method of 'parsonage training' seemed to offer adequate instruction, it fell far short of increasing the number of qualified ministers. Solving the problem of the four to one ratio proved harder than was first imagined.

The Synod of 1820, meeting at Hagerstown, Maryland, sought again to remedy this undesirable situation by taking the first steps toward establishing a theological seminary. It chose Dr. Philip Milledoler of New York to be its first Professor of Theology, offering him a starting salary of two thousand dollars per year. Milledoler, however, held this call for nearly two years before he finally declined it, accepting instead the presidency of Rutgers College in New Brunswick, New Jersey. In an effort to encourage support for a seminary, the 1820 Synod also adopted the following resolution prohibiting the parsonage training of students for the ministry:

> Resolved, That no minister shall hereafter have the privilege of receiving a young man in order to instruct him in theology, but may only direct him in his preliminary studies.

Apparently, this resolution was directed specifically against Dr. F. L. Herman, who was the only minister at the time training several young men for the pastorate. This action of Synod outraged Herman, who immediately set himself against the proposed seminary. The ensuing controversy, the failure of Synod to raise adequate funds to establish a theological institution, the unfounded suspicions of the laity and Milledoler's decline of the call doomed the project almost before it began. Another effort to establish a theological school in Harrisburg, Pennsylvania, proved equally as disastrous.

Though its first attempts to establish a seminary never bore fruit, the Synod of 1824 received an invitation from Dickinson College — then a Presbyterian institution — to establish a seminary on its campus in Carlisle, Pennsylvania. This offer was almost too good to be true. The college agreed to provide classrooms and permitted theological students to attend certain other lectures without charge. Its only stipulation was that the Professor of Theology appointed by the RCUS must also assume the chair of History and German Literature in the college proper. In the minds of most, the benefits of such an arrangement far outweighed any inconvenience the professor might have to endure; therefore, the RCUS accepted the offer without delay. With Dr. Lewis Mayer as its only professor, the theological school began operation on March 11, 1825, with an enrollment of five students.

Four years later, the seminary moved to York, Pennsylvania, and in 1832 it acquired the services of Dr. Friedrich Augustus Rauch, who taught mostly in the classical school. Only thirty-five students completed the seminary's course of instruction before it relocated again in 1837; this time it moved to Mercersburg, Pennsylvania. Not willing to leave York, Mayer resigned his position. However, at the request of Synod he reconsidered his decision but resigned permanently in 1839. With Rauch's health declining, the Synod of 1840 extended a call to Dr. John Williamson Nevin, a Presbyterian who was then a professor at the seminary in Allegheny, Pennsylvania, to fill the position of Professor of Systematic Theology. Nevin's knowledge of the German language and contemporary German theology made him uniquely qualified for the job in the eyes of those who elected him. When Rauch died in 1841, Nevin, assisted only by a teacher of Hebrew, assumed complete control of the seminary.

The Synod was by no means satisfied that this arrangement should continue indefinitely. Hoping to attract a German professor to continue Rauch's work, the Synod of 1843 elected Dr. F. W. Krummacher of Elberfeld, Prussia, as his successor and dispatched Drs. T.L. Hoffeditz and B.S. Schneck to present the call to him in person. To their dismay and under pressure from the Prussian government, the German pastor declined the call. J. I. Good surmises that "the later controversy [i.e., the controversy surrounding the Mercersburg professors, specifically the liturgical question] would probably never have occurred" had Krummacher (a strict Calvinist) accepted,[1] but this seems rather unlikely for two reasons: (1) it underestimates Nevin's ability, and (2) Krummacher lived only two years after rejecting the offer of the Synod. In any case, Hoffeditz and Schneck, not willing to return without a German professor to nominate to the vacancy at Mercersburg, consulted with the leading theologians of Germany (including John Augustus William Neander and the conservative E.W. Hengstenberg), who referred them to Dr. Philip Schaff. Though a rather young man, Schaff had already distinguished himself as an extraordinary lecturer at the University of Berlin. He accepted the invitation to come to America, was ordained to the ministry (April 12, 1844), and, after a six-week trip to England,

1 J. I. Good, *History of the Reformed Church in the U.S. in the Nineteenth Century* (New York: Board of the Reformed Church in America, 1911), p. 205.

was installed as Professor of Church History and Biblical Literature on October 25 of the same year.

As one can easily see, the establishment of a theological seminary occupied the attention of Synod for more than two decades. However, the controversy that emanated from Rauch, Nevin and Schaff, its chief professors, would affect the church well into the next century. Their doctrine became known as Mercersburg Theology.

FRIEDRICH AUGUSTUS RAUCH

The first of the renowned Mercersburg theologians, Friedrich Rauch, was born in Hesse Darmstadt in 1806. Following his education at the University of Marburg, he began teaching at Giessen before migrating to the United States in 1831 for political reasons. Here he first taught German at Lafayette College, and later took up his work at the classical school and seminary of the RCUS, conveying Hegelian idealism (though apparently without its inherent pantheism) to his students, who received it with enthusiasm. This state of affairs left Mayer extremely distressed.

In 1840, Rauch published his *Psychology, or a View of the Human Soul, Including Anthropology*, which was intended to introduce the German type of philosophy to his American students. It was also to be the first in a series on conservative Hegelian thought. However, his untimely death at the age of thirty-four left a far more extensive work on ethics unfinished.

Rauch's short life might seem to betray a lack of influence, but this is far from the case. Nevin, his successor, utilized "psychological theories learned from Rauch in relation to the Eucharistic presence, the nature of the risen Christ, and the conception of the final resurrection state," using a vocabulary and set of categories unfamiliar to American theology.[2] Professor T. Appel carried Rauch's influence to Lancaster in 1853. There he used Rauch's courses in psychology and ethics, adding material gleaned from Daub, Rosenkranz, Steffens and Schubert. Horace Bushnell also claimed to have learned much by reading Rauch's *Psychology*.

JOHN WILLIAMSON NEVIN

Born in Franklin County, Pennsylvania, on February 20, 1803, John Williamson Nevin grew up within twenty miles of Mercersburg, the town whose name would become synonymous with his own theology. His education at Union College, from which he graduated in 1821, was financed by his uncle, Captain John

---

2 James Hastings Nichols, *Romanticism in American Theology* (Chicago: University of Chicago Press, 1961), p. 104.

Williamson. Several men whose careers later became somewhat noteworthy attended Union at the same time, including George Doane and Alonzo Potter, who became Episcopal bishops; Robert J. Breckinridge, President of Jefferson College, superintendent of public education in Kentucky, and theology professor at Danville; William H. Seward, Governor of New York and Lincoln's Secretary of State; William Kent, law professor at Harvard; and Laurens P. Hickok, theology professor at Auburn and President of Union. Nevin's conversion seems to have occurred during the 1819–20 school year when Asahel Nettleton toured the area during the Second Great Awakening.

Two years after his graduation from Union, Nevin entered a course of study at Princeton Theological Seminary, where Charles Hodge had just been promoted to the professorate. Nevin had distinguished himself so well as a student (especially in Hebrew) that, when Hodge went abroad in 1826 for two years of advanced instruction, he invited Nevin, whose studies were nearing completion, to teach his classes in his absence. Not sure of a call to the ministry and lacking an appointment elsewhere, Nevin accepted Hodge's offer, viewing it as an opportunity to test his gifts.

When Hodge returned in 1828, Nevin left New Jersey to assume a teaching position at Western Theological Seminary, a newly opened Presbyterian school west of the mountains. Since Western Seminary did not need him immediately, Nevin lived at home, preached occasionally in a few local churches, and lent loyal and fierce support to the growing temperance movement. His uncle, Dr. Hugh Williamson, advised him earlier: "Take care, my boy, that you do not learn to smoke, for smoking will lead to drinking and that is the end of all good."[3] When he finally arrived at the site of the new school in December 1829, to his disappointment he found neither building nor library. Instead, all classes were conducted in the session room of the First Presbyterian Church of Pittsburgh, where they had begun just two years earlier.

At Western Seminary, Nevin occupied himself, in characteristically "puritan"[4] manner, with the social issues of the day. He continued to preach against alcohol, citing the cholera epidemic of 1832 as an example of "the Scourge of God" for the manufacture, sale and use of demon spirits. His devoted opposition to fancy fairs, theaters, horse-racing and slavery made him well known within the Pittsburgh Synod.

The decade of the 1830s introduced several changes in Nevin's thinking.

---

3 Good, *op. cit.*, p. 109.

4 Early in his career, Nevin held the Puritans in very high regard, but later he looked on them with scorn and contempt. Both his earlier and later views were extreme.

He turned more and more from an objective and intellectual comprehension of Christianity to a subjective and experimental apprehension, relying on the wisdom of Puritan mystics of the seventeenth century. Creation, he wrote in *The Friend* (Jan. 15, 1835), is pervaded by the presence of spiritual realities, "the idea of which must be stirred up in the soul itself before either they or their shadows can be apprehended as they are." His poems, many of which also appeared in *The Friend*, reflect a heavy preoccupation with the contrast between this present transitoriness and the eternal verities of the world of truth. Interestingly, Nevin successfully evaded conflating faith with feeling, as the rising Transcendental Movement did.

But perhaps the greatest influence on Nevin at this time, at least according to his own admission, was the German historian Neander, from whom he learned to regard religion as a communion with spiritual realities, something to be experienced and not learned. He was particularly captivated by Neander's historical perspective, which, as he came to understand more of its implications, began to affect his outlook on every other subject. Through this historical perspective, he began to appreciate the value of opinions other than those of orthodox Christianity, viewing even heresy as necessary for the development of Christian doctrine. Nevin later declared that his soul had been awakened to a new historical consciousness by reading Neander.

When the RCUS called Nevin to teach at Mercersburg in 1840, how much his views had already changed or how much he was aware of whatever changes may have occurred is hard to say. At any rate, the 1840s brought an even more drastic change to his theology than the previous decade; he gradually turned more away from the old Reformed position on predestination, the sacraments and the apostasy of Rome, and more toward a broad eclecticism. Though it would be too much to credit Schaff with this change, there can be no doubt that Schaff confirmed his catholic tendencies. Doubtless, he regarded the call as providential in light of his recent interest in the German language and contemporary German theology. It also offered him a chance to return to his native Cumberland Valley, to live among the Pennsylvania Germans with whom he was already so well acquainted. Neither did he regard transferring from Scottish Presbyterian to German Reformed, from the Westminster standards to the Heidelberg Catechism, as a problem. He believed, instead, that both the Presbyterian and Reformed communions sprang forth from the same mold. He even wrote at the time that the German catechism had, in fact, laid the groundwork for the Westminster Confession. Further, he saw an affiliation with the RCUS seminary as an opportunity to test the depth of learning of his German-educated colleague, Dr. Rauch. With these considerations in mind, Nevin readily accepted the call and moved to Mercersburg.

Although Rauch's early death prevented him from developing the theological aspects of his psychology, Nevin carried on from Rauch's beginning. He had already taken an interest in the doctrine of the Lord's Supper while at the seminary in Pittsburgh, concluding that American churches in general, even those of Reformed persuasion, had exchanged Calvin's high view of the sacrament for the low view of the Puritans, a position which he maintained at Mercersburg in opposition to the prevailing (as he saw it) Zwinglian or "rationalistic" doctrine of the RCUS. Rauch's work provided him with the necessary psychological categories for a defense of his position. The believer's union with Christ, he taught, must not be conceived of as a merely moral union but as a transfusion of the soul and body of one into the other. Accordingly, Nevin located the atonement not in the propitiatory death of Christ (as the catechism teaches), but in the incarnation itself; that is, by "an organic union of the Incarnate Word with humanity, **as a whole**, and this in order to form a basis for the regeneration of the **race**."[5] Therefore, believers are not saved by the sufferings and death of Christ but by Christ conveying to them the very substance of his incarnate life. This impartation of Christ's theanthropic life (Nevin's definition of justification) finds its consummate expression in the Lord's Supper.

In his most profound work, *The Mystical Presence: A Vindication of the Reformed or Calvinistic Doctrine of the Holy Eucharist*, Nevin developed his doctrine of the Supper as follows:

> According to the old Reformed doctrine, the invisible grace of the sacrament includes a real participation in his person. That which is made present to the believer, is the very life of Christ himself in its true power and substance. The doctrine proceeds on the assumption that the Christian salvation stands in an actual union between Christ and his people, mystical but in the highest sense real, in virtue of which they are as closely joined to him, as the limbs are to the head in the natural body. They are in Him, and He is in them, not figuratively but truly; in the way of a growing process that will become complete finally in the resurrection. The power of this fact is mysteriously concentrated in the Holy Supper. Here Christ communicates himself to his Church, not simply a right to the grace that resides in his person, or an interest by outward grant in the benefits of his life and death, but his person itself, as the ground and fountain, from which all these other blessings may be expected to flow . . . .Christ first, and then his benefits. Calvin will hear of no other order but this. The same view runs through all the Calvinistic symbols. Not a title to Christ in his benefits, the efficacy of his atonement, the work of his spirit; but

---

5   B.S. Schneck, *Mercersburg Theology Inconsistent with Protestant and Reformed Doctrine* (Philadelphia: J. B. Lippincott & Co., 1874), p. 14.

a true property of life itself, out of which only that other title can legitimately spring.[6]

To be sure, Nevin did not teach a corporeal presence of Christ in the sacrament, a position which he emphatically denies in the same book, but he nonetheless exalts the sacraments above other acts of worship, even assigning to them an intrinsic efficacy. Concerning baptism, for example, he says,

> If the sacraments are regarded as in themselves outward rites only, that can have no value or force except as the grace they represent is made to be present by the subjective exercises of the worshiper, it is hard to see on what ground infants, who are still without knowledge or faith, should be admitted to any privilege of the sort.[7]

Anything less than this mystical view of the sacraments, he argues, "becomes necessarily an unmeaning contradiction" and is a sure sign of the sectarian spirit of the modern church with its diminished view of the church and its sacraments. The intrinsic value of the Supper, to return to the subject at hand, lies precisely in the believer's participation in the true humanity of Christ, especially in the life of his glorified state.

For Nevin, the Lord's Supper was "the very heart of the whole Christian worship," in which "the entire question of the Church" finds its center and core. He says, "Our view of the Lord's Supper must ever condition and rule in the end our view of Christ's person and the conception we form of the Church. It must influence at the same time, very materially, our whole system of theology, as well as all our ideas of ecclesiastical history."[8] This is about as good a summary of Nevin's contribution to Mercersburg Theology as one can find.

In this debate, Nevin accused Hodge of holding to a merely memorial view of the Holy Supper. Hodge responded by calling Calvin a "crypto-Lutheran" and charging him with making serious concessions to Lutherans to gain their favor. While it is rather unfortunate that Hodge took this extreme and ill-founded position, the fact that Nevin was able to elicit it from the greatest theological giant of the day shows how truly clever he was.

The Mystical Presence was followed the next year by *The History and Genius of the Heidelberg Catechism*, which began as a series of essays published

---

6 John Williamson Nevin, *The Mystical Presence: A Vindication of the Reformed or Calvinistic Doctrine of the Holy Eucharist* (Philadelphia: J. B. Lippincott & Co., 1846), p. 122.

7 Nevin, *Mystical Presence*, p. 149.

8 Nevin, *Mystical Presence*, p. 3.

by the author between 1841 and 1842. In the latter book, Nevin portrayed the catechism as the glory of the sixteenth century Reformation. If he had meant by this that the catechism reflects a pure Calvinism coupled with a heartfelt love of the truth, true heirs of the Reformation might readily agree. But for Nevin the catechism is the result of both Lutheran and Reformed influences: its view of the sacraments is Calvinistic, but nearly everything else comes from Philip Melanchthon.[9] Nevin's explanation of the rite of confirmation is clearly Lutheran:

> Confirmation is no sacrament of course; but it is a beautifully significant ordinance, in which the sacrament of baptism may be said to come finally to its natural and necessary completion. Baptism becomes complete only in the personal assumption of its vows on the part of its subject. This calls for **some** rite; and it is certainly hard to conceive of any more appropriate in itself, or less open to the charge of superstition, than the scriptural ceremony which the Church has in fact employed from the earliest time for this purpose.[10] Accordingly, the "genius" of the catechism, at least in part, is its ability to mediate between the two branches of the Reformation.

PHILIP SCHAFF

When Philip Schaff arrived in the United States in the summer of 1844, it would not be long before he would meet one with whom his own views so thoroughly agreed that together they seemed to share one mind. About this time, he wrote in his diary: "I think I could not have a better colleague than Dr. Nevin. I feared I might not find any sympathy in him for my views of the church; but I discover that he occupies essentially the same ground that I do and confirms me in my position. He is filled with the ideas of German theology."[11]

Born in the Grisons, a canton in east Switzerland, on January 1, 1819, Schaff would eventually become one of the most influential theologians of the

---

9 Philip Melanchthon's views underwent some change between the early years of the Reformation and his death. His early views suggest a strong disposition to predestination and supralapsarianism, while his later writings lean more toward synergism. This was due in part to a perceived overemphasis by the Swiss Reformers on the sovereignty of God. Apparently, in making the claim that the catechism reflects Melanchthon's influence, Nevin, who had also abandoned a strict Calvinistic understanding of predestination, refers to Melanchthon's later views. In any case, we must regard Nevin's contention as spurious, unfounded, and contrary to the historical purpose of the catechism.

10 John Williamson Nevin, *The History and Genius of the Heidelberg Catechism* (Chambersburg, PA: Publication Office of the German Reformed Church, 1847), p. 160.

11 D.S. Schaff, *The Life of Philip Schaff* (New York: Charles Scribner's Sons, 1897), 103, quoted in Nichols, p. 64.

nineteenth century. Unlike Nevin, whose theological journey seems to have lacked an occasion, Schaff's ideas (except his high-church views, which he garnered from the Saturday evening gatherings of Ludwig von Gerlach) thoroughly reflect his experiences and German education. When he was fifteen, the preacher at Chur recognized his unusual talents and arranged for him to study at the Kornthal academy in Württemberg. Kornthal was, at the time, a pietist colony. During his first year there, Schaff experienced a conversion after the pietistic manner and was confirmed by a local Lutheran pastor. This would forever leave its imprint upon his character and learning. As a result he abandoned the hope of becoming a poet (though he would later prove himself more than adequately gifted in his command of languages) and turned his attention instead to the study of theology.

Shortly thereafter, Schaff entered the gymnasium at Stuttgart. There he mastered Latin, Greek and Hebrew in preparation for a university education. After two years of preliminary study, he applied to the University of Tübingen, the foremost leader in higher criticism and Hegelian philosophy. There he met Ferdinand Christian Baur, who applied the critical methods to the documents of the New Testament to reconstruct the "actual" history of their time, and Isaac Dorner, who helped students learn Hegel and Schleiermacher (as his reputation has it) without losing their Christian faith.

From Tübingen, Schaff went to Halle and studied under F.A.G. Tholuck. Tholuck identified the controlling factor of current theological thought as *Entwicklung* (evolution or development). Tholuck seems to have had a particular interest in American students, attracting men of the caliber of Charles Hodge and Henry B. Smith.

Within a few months, Professor E.W. Hengstenberg invited Schaff to Berlin to assume a position tutoring the children of Prussian nobility. He began with the son of Baroness von Kroecher, who allowed him sufficient time to attend the university lectures of Hengstenberg, Neander and Leopold von Ranke.[12] Though he had learned the principle of historical development from Baur at Tübingen, Neander, whose views were also far from orthodox, seems to have been more influential in the development of his religious thought. In fact, the faculty of the University of Berlin later sent him a testimonial, praising his eight volume *History of the Christian Church* as "the most notable monument of universal historical learning

---

12 For a fascinating survey of the leading schools and professors of nineteenth century Germany by one who had firsthand knowledge, see Philip Schaff, *Germany; its Universities, Theology, and Religion; with Sketches of Neander, Tholuck, Olshausen, Hengstenberg, Twesten, Nitzsch, Muller, Ullmann, Rothe, Dorner, Lange, Ebrard, Wichern, and Other Distinguished German Divines of the Age* (Philadelphia: Lindsay and Blakiston, 1857).

produced by the school of Neander."[13] As with Schleiermacher, Neander believed that the heart of true religion consists of the experiences of the church out of which religious thought grows.

After two years of tutoring (the second of which he spent traveling in southern Europe), Schaff, at the age of twenty-three, returned to Berlin and began offering courses as a *Privatdocent* in the New Testament and the theology of Schleiermacher. Even at this early age, Schaff had earned the heartiest recommendation of the leading thinkers of mid-nineteenth century Germany, both conservative and otherwise: F. W. Krummacher, Tholuck, Hengstenberg, Neander and Dorner. These were the men who directed the representatives of the RCUS to Schaff in 1843 and counseled him to accept the post at Mercersburg.

Schaff's arrival in the United States was greeted with both approbation and disappointment. Some lauded his exceptional learning and abilities, especially for one so young (only twenty-five at the time); others heard about his ordination sermon, in which he criticized German Americans as being in danger of succumbing to various sectarian interests, and deplored his coming.

If Nevin laid down the first principle of Mercersburg Theology (viz., the centrality of the person of Christ in the life of the church), Schaff provided the second (viz., the principle of historical development); and he wasted no time doing so. At the opening of the Synod in 1844, Dr. Joseph Berg, pastor of the First Reformed Church of Philadelphia and the retiring President of Synod, preached on the historical background of the Reformation, making the rather preposterous claim that the apostolic church had been preserved unchanged throughout the entire Middle Ages by the Waldenses. Schaff's inaugural address, *Das Prinzip des Protestantismus* (translated into English the following year and published with a lengthy forward by Nevin) was aimed directly at Berg, just as Berg's sermon seems to have been aimed at him. In this address, Schaff countered Berg with another absurdity: that the Reformation was simply the natural development of the best in the medieval Catholic tradition. The printed version of this address contained an appendix of 112 theses; according to Thesis 31, " . . . the Reformation is the greatest act of the Catholic Church itself, the full ripe fruit of all its better tendencies, particularly of the deep spiritual law conflicts of the Middle Period, which were as a schoolmaster toward the Protestant doctrine of justification." Schaff's friend Gerlach, who openly described his own position as *evangelische Katholizität*, used to speak of the Reformation as the finest flower of the Middle Ages and longed for an eventual reunion of the two parties. With somewhat less enthusiasm for Catholicism, Schaff adopted his friend's view.

---

13 D.S. Schaff, 467, quoted in Nichols, p. 69.

Almost as soon as *The Principle of Protestantism* appeared in print, the Mercersburg professors found themselves on trial for heresy. However, this had little effect on their productivity. Schaff began his first full year of teaching with a lecture to his church history class on historical method. Again, this lecture was translated by Nevin and published the following June (1846) as *What is Church History? A Vindication of the Idea of Historical Development.* Later, Schaff reproduced this and expanded it in the first volume of his church history series. Its purpose, of course, was to clarify, explain and defend his position.

Relying on Hegel's dialectic, Schaff compared church history to the growth of a plant, which, in the course of its life, goes through various stages of development, each negating and yet fulfilling that which came before it. Likewise, the epochs of church history build on those that preceded them, adding their own contributions and offering solutions to previously unanswered problems. Church history, he argued, shows the unmistakable imprint of divine wisdom in that God uses each period of the church's development to bring to light some hitherto undiscovered truth. It is the great or distinctive ideas of each age that make it different from all others. The doctrines of justification by faith alone (the material principle) and *sola Scriptura* ("Scripture alone": the formal principle) he regarded as the great ideas of the Protestant Reformation. Actually, Schaff reductively considered these doctrines as one, since the Word cannot be correctly understood apart from faith. The Word he saw as the form, and faith its content; Scripture is spirit, and the believer's appropriation of it is life. He maintained that, although Christianity is theoretically complete in Christ, its inner life was only gradually appropriated and implemented by the church. The Reformation was only one step in the process. Schaff's "Protestant Principle" was the principle of the development of the church, not of this or that doctrine (or even the collection of doctrines) taught by the Reformers.

On the other hand, Schaff also found certain "diseases" dominating the history of Protestant churches. Lutherans tended toward theological rationalism, which made its first appearance more than a century after the Reformation began. It began, ironically, as an anti-intellectual reaction of pietism to scholastic orthodoxy; then moving into Biblical criticism and Hegelian pantheism; and ending with Feuerbach redefining religion as the deification of human experience. The disease of the Reformed tradition is sectarianism (or "sectarism," according to Nevin's translation), by which Schaff meant the practical and organizational fragmentation of the church. The chief culprit here was seventeenth century Puritanism. None of the Reformers, he argued, advocated unbridled liberty for individuals, but rather a liberty that subscribed to the authority of divine truth. Puritanism, however, prostituted the Reformation principle by emphasizing the conversion experience of individuals; it was, therefore, spiritualistic (rejecting forms of worship), unhistorical (disdaining the elements of Catholicism preserved in the Reformation tradition) and unchurchly (neglecting the broader picture of the church as the Body of Christ). Furthermore Puritanism, because of its influence on American religious thought, had communicated these traits to American religion in general. Now, it might seem that rationalism and sectarianism have little in common, but Schaff saw them as the two sides of a single coin: rationalism being nothing more than theoretical sectarianism, and sectarianism being practical rationalism. His third disease of Protestantism was political revolution. Schaff regarded the Reformation's contribution to culture in a primarily negative sense. By this, he meant that the Reformers, instead of advocating social change, merely stood by as the forces already present worked for improvement. Their heirs, however, used revolution to advance the authority of Christ in the political realm.

Schaff further contended that even the diseases of Protestantism had some limited justification. Rationalism, for example, purged the church of many of its erroneous and exaggerated opinions. Sectarianism also, by protesting against real faults of the orthodox church, contributed to its proper development. Even Puritanism offered a heightened sense of a Biblical moral responsibility and self-discipline — characteristics too often lacking among Protestants in general.

To the dismay of many, Schaff's heresy trial ended with his exoneration. The reason, according to Sydney E. Ahlstrom, was that "none of his assailants knew what the German Reformed standards were."[14] Not too long afterward, Dr. Berg, author of the charges against Schaff, resigned his Philadelphia charge and transferred to the Dutch Reformed Church. However, the trial so shook the denomination that Nevin eventually resigned from the seminary and concentrated more on the college. Schaff also resigned in 1863, taking a position at Union Seminary in New York. As early as 1847, the Dutch Reformed Church voted to end its relationship with the RCUS; the theology of the Mercersburg professors was, no doubt, a factor in its decision.

THE LITURGICAL CONTROVERSY

If worship articulates the theology of a church, the most practical articulation of Mercersburg Theology came with the liturgical controversy that began in 1847 when the East Pennsylvania Classis sought to have either the Palatinate liturgy reprinted or another based on the catechism approved. The resulting controversy shook the RCUS all the way down to its foundation, almost tearing it apart.

However, the problem was far more general than this suggests. Two factors

---

14 Sydney E. Ahlstrom, *A Religious History of the American People*, vol. 2 (Garden City, NY: Image Books, 1975), p. 58.

forced the RCUS to consider the liturgical question *before* Nevin and Schaff came along. We see this in the fact that the Synod of 1820 appointed a committee of five leading ministers to consider the possibility of translating and printing the old German liturgy. In 1821 this committee reported that nothing had been done. Its report the next year recommended only the printing of the Palatinate order with some slight modifications, but little was actually done at the time. The matter surfaced again in 1834. Seven years later, the Mayer liturgy was approved but only by four Classes. If anything, this history shows (contrary to the claims of Mercersburg adherents) that there was very little enthusiasm for ritual in the church.

The first factor that drew the attention of the RCUS to a consideration of liturgy was the anglicization of the church; that is, with English replacing German as the language of the people (especially in the east), even the Palatinate model had become unserviceable. Of course, the Palatinate liturgy, which was never used in the RCUS in any substantial way, was also becoming harder and harder to obtain.

Second, the influence of Puritanism had cast disdain on set forms of worship, contrary to the semi-liturgical worship in the early Reformed churches. Pre-composed prayers, it was said, hampered the work of the Spirit in converting the unconverted. Free prayer (with its omissions, disorderliness and solecisms) was becoming the American standard. However, this had the lamentable effect also of limiting congregational participation to the singing of an occasional hymn. By contrast, the Palatinate liturgy included set prayers for the regular Lord's Day service and special prayers for Christmas, New Year's Day, Good Friday, Easter, Ascension and Pentecost. It also included a schedule of Bible readings for the entire year. Following the pattern established by John à Lasco, the communion was celebrated monthly with appropriate preparation observed beforehand. Its order of service for the Lord's Day (which focused on the sermon) was more rigid than one might suppose. The usual service began with a blessing and psalm, followed by a confession of sin, a prayer for the saving apprehension of the Word and the Lord's Prayer (in unison here and throughout). A Scripture reading and the sermon came next, and the service concluded with another confession of sin (in unison), a declaration of forgiveness to the penitent and of condemnation to the impenitent. Then followed the Lord's Prayer (the second time), a series of prayers with various themes, the Lord's prayer (or a rather lengthy paraphrase of the same), a psalm and the Aaronic blessing.[15] Though services were formal, there was not the slightest hint of a Mercersburg style altar worship; the German order was decidedly a pulpit-liturgy (i.e., designed for use by the pastor, not the people). It is also highly doubtful that many early fathers of the RCUS even knew what was in the Palatinate model

---

15 Jack Martin Maxwell, *Worship and Reformed Theology: The Liturgical Lessons of Mercersburg* (Pittsburgh: The Pickwick Papers, 1976), pp. 90 - 91.

although Boehm encouraged its use as early as 1748.[16] Though the RCUS looked to the Palatinate liturgy as a "model," none of its early liturgies (the Germantown liturgy of 1798, the Weisz liturgy of 1828, and the "Mayer liturgy" of 1841) contained special forms for the Lord's Day service. Though the RCUS had never been strictly liturgical, the Palatinate liturgy precipitated many of the questions that reappeared in connection with the Mercersburg movement. This forced the RCUS to decide what kind of worship it would endorse. How to decide was not so easy.

The Synod of 1848 erected a committee, chaired by Dr. J.H.A. Bomberger, to study the issue and offer recommendations, but this committee failed to act. When Synod met the following year, various opinions were expressed; some wanted set forms only for the sacraments and other special services, while others preferred forms for the regular services as well. Bomberger successfully argued for the latter, asserting that a regular liturgy offers the best opportunity for corporate worship. The Synod then formed a second committee, larger than the first, giving it the responsibility to begin developing such a liturgy. Nevin, who had already begun referring to the table as an "altar" and had expressed his preference for vestments and other liturgical devices, was chosen to head this committee.

However, Nevin knew that his views on worship were vastly different from those of most RCUS ministers at the time. He argued, for example, that a central pulpit must give way to a pronounced altar; but few others looked for anything more than forms for special occasions, allowing considerable room for extemporaneous prayer. Nevin even despaired of affecting the church in any significant way. His own committee recommended nothing more than a translation of the Palatinate liturgy. The battle raged both in print and in personal correspondence.

Nevin resigned from the chairmanship of this committee in 1851 (the same year he tendered his resignation from the seminary) and was replaced by Schaff. Like his predecessor, Schaff had also voiced his preference for an altar worship, complete with gowns and candles, but was far more optimistic about success. Chaired by Schaff, the committee proposed four forms for the regular Sunday service, two for baptism and a form for the solemnization of marriage. Not surprisingly, the committee made it clear that it had adapted the forms of the Greek and Latin churches of the third and fourth centuries. The Reformation's contribution was, more or less, limited to its hymnology, since (as Schaff saw it) the liturgical developments of the sixteenth century embraced little more than translations and purifications of those that preceded them. To promote congregational participation, the committee further proposed the publication of a book, similar to the Anglican

---

16 By the mid-nineteenth century, the Palatinate liturgy had become so rare that Nevin admitted in a footnote in his book on the catechism that he had only once seen a copy of it. See Nevin, *Heidelberg Catechism*, p. 153.

Book of Common Prayer, to be used by the people. Abandoning the old Reformed practice of preaching consecutively through various books of the Bible, this proposed prayer book would include a pericope system of Scripture readings and thematic collects based on the ecclesiastical calendar.

Schaff's plan received the approbation of the 1852 Synod. It seems likely, however, that most RCUS ministers did not fully grasp the intent of the committee's proposals. Even Dr. Henry Harbaugh, the committee's secretary and himself a proponent of Mercersburg altar worship, labored under the assumption that the committee would produce a liturgy basically of the Reformed model.

The Synod of 1857 finally approved the completed liturgy for provisional use. Some churches received it almost without noticing a change. In others it caused considerable strife and division. Though it sold three printings in its first year, James Hastings Nichols asserts that it was probably not used regularly by more than a dozen congregations.[17]

It soon became evident that this provisional liturgy had not provided the church with a functional tool. In 1863, the General Synod gave permission to the Synod of Ohio to prepare another liturgy and encouraged the Eastern Synod to continue revising the 1857 provisional liturgy. Three years later, the revised *Order of Worship* was completed. A Western Liturgy appeared the next year.

Opponents of the revised *Order*, at a meeting held September 24, 1867, protested its use in the church, and founded Ursinus College in an attempt to preserve the old Reformed theology and worship. This new college received the formal recognition of the Synod in 1872.

The battle over a liturgy continued for several years until the General Synod of 1878 appointed a Peace Commission to find an amicable solution. This committee was reappointed in 1881 and submitted a revised (and compromised) *Directory of Worship* in 1884, which it then referred to the Classes for their adoption. With the consent of the Classes, the General Synod of 1887 ratified the new *Directory*.

LESSONS OF HISTORY

There can be no doubt that the RCUS lost more than it gained as a result of establishing a seminary at Mercersburg. Yes, some members, and even entire congregations, sought fellowship from other sources. A few of its more orthodox ministers, including Berg (who transferred to the Dutch Reformed Church) went elsewhere. But members, congregations and even ministers can be replaced. We see

---

17 Nichols, *Mercersburg Theology*, p. 305.

that this is so when we consider that the number of RCUS ministers increased fifty times in the nineteenth century, while the number of members grew by fifteen times. Yet, at the same time the RCUS gave up something of far greater historical importance — much of its Reformed heritage.

Instead of allowing the doctrines of the Reformation to control policy, a practical matter (the need for more ministers) became the dominant consideration. Then came the misguided notion that German professors, or at least professors who were well acquainted with German thought and life, would serve the church best. However, these German professors had adopted the new German philosophy, which they soon introduced to their students at Mercersburg. By redefining the nature of Reformed theology and church history, Mercersburg Theology gradually replaced the theology of the Reformation. And since worship is the articulation of theology, the Mercersburg movement required a new liturgy. This, in turn, started the liturgical controversies of the mid-1800s.

Did the RCUS get what it wanted? If we define its wants in terms of its priorities as they were actually settled upon, it would be impossible to come to any other conclusion. But priorities are not always so neatly arranged; therefore, it seems best not to malign the motives of our forefathers, but to learn from their mistakes. The compromised theology and liturgy that came because of their decisions paved the way for the infamous and disastrous 1934 merger of our church with the Evangelical Synod of North America.

To avoid leaving such a legacy to our children, we must retain sound doctrine as our highest priority. Jesus said, If you have my doctrine, you have life. The Bible, which we accept as the Word of God, must be set before our people first. All other considerations must be secondary to it.

1968 EUREKA CLASSIS SESSION—HOPE, SUTTON, NEBRASKA

First row: Rev. R. Grossmann, Rev. R. Stuebbe, Rev. V. Pollena, Rev. Sam Allison, Rev. N. Jones, Rev. D. W. Treick, Rev. Wm. Warren. Second row: Rev. J. Zinkand, Rev. R. Gibbons, Rev. L. Gross, Rev. C. J. Stuebbe, missing, missing. Third row: Rev. N. C. Hoeflinger, Rev. P. Grossmann, Rev. C. Ploeger, Rev. C. W. Powell, missing. Fourth row: Albert Stegmeier, Art Mettler, Harry Hieb, Calvin Streyle, Elmer Hieb, Albert Stoller, missing, Ray Mettler. Standing: Rev. H. Stevens, Don Monteath, Robert Horn, Ernest Gibbons, Harley Bittner, missing, Bushman, Ben Mettler, Ted Koerner, Don Greimann, Herbert Koerner, Rev. E. Buehrer.

CHAPTER THREE

The 1934 Merger

Rev. Peter Grossmann

I was born, grew up, and was educated in the environment with which much of this project is concerned. My Father and Grandfather before me were ministers in the Reformed Church in the U.S., the former for just 22 years, the latter for some twenty years. The subject here dealt with, then, is one that is close to my heart and interests, indeed, a vital part of my life. Because of my close associations with the work, the problems and the people of the Eureka Classis of the Reformed Church in the U.S., I have, particularly since the beginnings of my studies at Westminster Theological Seminary, become more aware of the implications of the position that this part of the Church has held during the past quarter century. I believe that it is important that a study be made of the background of, and stand against, the Evangelical and Reformed merger of 1934.

Specifically, my purpose in the writing of this paper[1] has been first to gain information and present it in unified form (which to my knowledge has not yet been done), and, secondly, since the state of the Reformed Church has been for many years the intimate concern of my family, to examine my personal involvement in the Eureka Classis.

INTRODUCTION

As it stands today, the Eureka Classis of the Reformed Church in the U.S. occupies a unique position in the history of that ecclesiastical body. It carries on the

---

1 This is from a student paper for Professor Paul Wooley. It was written in 1960 while Rev. Grossmann was a student at Westminster Theological Seminary in Philadelphia.

traditions and theological heritage of the old German Reformed Church, having re-mained basically biblical and Reformed through the years. The Classis at the time of this writing has weathered a quarter century of criticism, attack on organization and personalities, and has in fact successfully staved off the engulfing octopus of modern ecumenicity! In all fairness it must be said that the history of the Eureka Classis over the last twenty-five years has been proof positive of the wonders of the grace of God in His preservation of the truth. And yet, they are few who recognize the Classis as a church. Very seldom does one see any reference to this body in the literature of the Church of the age. Those who even know of its existence as a Reformed Church are small in number indeed. Those who do know it, however, know that it is truly a part of the body of Christ on earth, and they also marvel at the tenacity and solidity of its people and teaching. Today (1960 ed.) the Classis is stronger than ever. It is growing yearly and with the growing membership there comes an increasing awareness of the far-reaching power of the Word of God. Ecclesiastical and theological position are not the only unique characteristics of the Classis. It is almost in its entirety made up of people of Russian-German origin. The national spirit is strong among the rural peoples of the Midwest, and though we might criticize this evident exclusiveness, it has also served to bind the organization together and protect it from within against the onslaughts directed against it by individual persons and the Evangelical & Reformed Church (E & R). Thus the spirit of nationalism which is so strong among people of Germanic origin has served to good effect in most cases.

There are several things I would like to discuss and evaluate in this paper. As a background I shall go back to the early history of the Reformed Church in this country, and also review as much as materials available allow, the origins of the Eureka Classis. I will be in the main concerned with the Evangelical and Reformed merger of 1934 and what came of that union and what its effects have been on the Eureka Classis. There is, unfortunately, only a small amount of information available to me concerning the Evangelical Synod of North America and I will therefore not be able to give as complete a history of that body as of the Reformed Church in the U.S.. However, it is not my purpose to investigate all the ins and outs of the mergers but instead, the forces in the Reformed Church which led to it. Thus I feel that the lack in this part of my investigation will not materially affect the direction which I intend to pursue. As this paper is read, it will be noted that I have referred to a large number of individual congregations and people. It is these that make up the Church of Christ, and their activities and influences are essential to this work. It will also be seen that there is not available a large amount of written material for consultation. Many of the events are too recent to be included in written history and furthermore, my own personal experiences in the life of the Classis are the basis of much of what I write. It is hoped that this will not detract greatly from the value or accuracy of this discussions but will indeed contribute to the interest of the subject matter. My principle written sources have been the histories by James I. Good on the Reformed Church in the U.S. up to 1910, the *New Schaff-Herzog Encyclopedia of Religious Knowledge*, two publications of the Eureka Classis, *The Witness* and *Reformiertes Gemeindeblatt* and numerous letters and essays from my father's personal files. He kept carbon copies of all the letters he wrote during his ministry and I have found them invaluable in gathering specific information about disputes within the Classis and about doctrinal differences with the E & R in particular. I have used also a great many pamphlets and the like published by the E & R, especially from the 10 years immediately following the merger of 1934. These will be specifically mentioned throughout this paper as I have made use of them.

In my research and in the writing of this paper I have been greatly indebted to the following: my mother, for the interest she has shown in this work and the advice and guidance she has given me in the gathering of materials; the Rev. K.J. Stuebbe of Manitowoc, Wisconsin, for the direction obtained in his maturity of years; and to the Pastors D.E. Bosma of Eureka, South Dakota, and William E. Korn of Menno, South Dakota, for the contribution of various written materials.

Philadelphia, Pennsylvania, April 1960

THE CHURCH AND THE MERGER OF 1934

EARLY HISTORY OF THE EUREKA CLASSIS

In the years prior to 1910 it became clear to certain German Reformed leaders in the Dakotas that they were a conservative group living inside of a less than conservative denomination, the Reformed Church in the United States. They therefore overtured the Northwest Synod of the RCUS to constituted them as a German-speaking classis in the Dakotas. With permission granted, the first session of the Eureka Classis was held at Scotland, South Dakota, beginning on June 7, 1911. The Eureka Classis was constituted in the same geographical area as the North and South Dakota classes of the same Synod, but was a separate classis actually formed to maintain the theological position of its pastors and congregations. Members of the Eureka Classis differed from the majority of the members of the Dakota Classes and in order to avoid further dissension and conflict the separate Classis was organized. Besides elders representing various charges, the founding ministers of this new Classis were Henry Treick of Scotland, SD, Edward Scheidt of Kulm, ND, Gustave Zenk of Eureka, SD, Henry Sill of Herrick, SD, William Wittenberg of Garner, Iowa, William J. Krieger of Tripp, SD, and William Feige, chaplain at the Veterans Hospital in Hot Springs, SD. Scheidt was elected president of Classis and Zenk was Stated Clerk. The position of the Eureka Classis was based on biblical, Reformed doctrine, and it has maintained that position to the present day. These men took as the motto of their Classis, 1 John 9, "Whosoever transgresseth, and abideth not in the doctrine of Christ hath not God. He that abideth in the doctrine of Christ, he hath both the Father and Son." At that same first meeting in 1911, it was determined that a school be established and the Scotland Academy was founded as a result. Scotland Academy continued for some years and provided high school education for many people in rural Dakota who would never have had this benefit except for its provision by the Eureka Classis.[2]

This was the beginning of the Classis which for the past fifty years has been active in the affairs of the western segment of the Reformed Church in the United States, and has actually continued this denomination long after the rest of it dissolved into a modern ecumenical merger. The Eureka Classis and its conservative nature was the result of an immigration of German-Russian people to the Dakotas and Nebraska during the last decades of the nineteenth century. These folks were descendants of the Germans who had moved to Russia one hundred years earlier and had maintained their religion and language as a separate component of the Russian society. With changes in the Russian Czar's attitude toward these Germans, and with the increased agitation toward an overthrow of the Russian Czar's government, these

2 "The Eureka Classis Merger History," *The Witness* (Green Bay, WI: Reformed Publication Society, Jan. 1945), p. 5.

people began to leave Russia by the thousands, even though they had established prosperous farms in the southern Odessa region of Russia.

During the early years of settlement in the Dakotas, Christian instruction and preaching were hard to come by. Most of the ministers in the last decade of the nineteenth century had come from Germany and were responsible for people spread over broad areas. At first, worship services were held in farm homes, and out of doors in good weather. Soon, however, churches began to spring up on the land and in the towns and villages that had themselves followed the railroad as it crossed the plains. Often the country churches were built before those in the towns and the rural people hung on to their country churches for many years, some of them not closing until the 1950s. Names associated with the early days of work among the German Reformed Dakota pioneers included Rev. Reu, the first German Reformed pastor in the Eureka, South Dakota, area, Rev. Nuss, and Rev. C. Bonekamper,[3] as well as several of the men involved in establishing the Eureka Classis.

It is worthwhile to note here that all of these men based their teaching first on the word of God, and were Reformed in their interpretation of it. Very close to their hearts were the teachings of the Heidelberg Catechism. This little book had journeyed to Russia, and then to the United States with this new wave of immigrants. It is not surprising that they joined the Reformed Church in the U.S., which also held the Heidelberg as its creed, though less tenaciously and less specifically than did these new immigrants. Among the German Russians, the Catechism was used right alongside the Bible, and these two books were often the only source of instruction in both Christian principles and in reading for the younger generation. There had been a drift away from strict subscription to the Heidelberg on the part of officers and from its careful teaching to the upcoming generations in some parts of the RCUS, but among these new immigrants there was still a living adherence and understanding of this precious creed. As soon as was possible, all families had their children instructed and confirmed in the principles of the Catechism. Often a talented young man in the neighborhood would teach the younger children until such time as an itinerant minister could be obtained to administer the rite of confirmation. Though the situation among these country folks was often poor, their religion was very important to their lives.

This is the historical background of the Eureka Classis, a body which came to play an important role in the Church in the west. Just what that role was we shall see after looking at events leading up to the Evangelical and Reformed merger of 1934.

---

4 James I. Good, *History of the Reformed Church in the United States in the 19th Century* (New York: Board of Publications of the Reformed Church in America, 1911), p. 631.

THE CHURCHES BEFORE THE MERGER

THE EVANGELICAL SYNOD OF NORTH AMERICA

This ecclesiastical organization with which the Reformed Church in the U.S. merged in 1934 has its roots in the Evangelical Church of Germany. The Evangelical Synod of North America was the American version of the State Church of Prussia, formed by the uniting of the Reformed and Lutheran Churches of northern Germany in 1817. This particular union was brought about as a political expediency, but its spirit had its origins in the German reaction to eighteenth century pietism. This reaction made for the de-emphasis of doctrine and consistent Biblical teaching, and opened the way for the formation of the Evangelische Kirche Deutschland (EKD) out of which came a large portion of evangelical thought in the United States in the mid-nineteenth century. There were several evangelical bodies in the United States, some dating back to colonial times which also grew out of the EKD, however, the one with which we are here concerned, the Synod of North America, developed later than this.

The German Evangelical Synod of North America was founded on October 15, 1840 at the Gravois Settlement near St. Louis, Missouri, by six German ministers. It had at its inception twelve congregations and 353 members. Its official name was "Der Deutsche Evangelische Kirchenverein des Westens". Its membership was made up of recent German immigrants to this country who had settled on the banks of the Mississippi River. Early expansion of the Synod caused its name to be changed to the Synod of the West in 1866, and in 1877 to German Evangelical Synod of North America.

This Church took as its standards the Augsburg Confession, Luther's Catechism and the Heidelberg Catechism. With this disparity, even inconsistency, in confessions it was necessary to adopt a mediating resolution: these confessions were to be accepted by members of the Synod "… in so far as these agree; but in their points of difference the German Evangelical Synod adheres strictly to the passages of Holy Scripture pertaining thereunto and avails itself of that liberty of conscience prevailing in the Evangelical Church."[4] As will be shown later in this paper, the above resolution became the basis for the Evangelical and Reformed merger of 1934 and is one of the elements of that union which has led to a very significant weakening of Christian teaching and practice.

"The object and purpose of the German Evangelical Synod in general is the advancement and extension of the Kingdom of God, but especially the establishment and expansion of the Evangelical Church among the German population of the

---

3 *The New Schaff-Herzog Encyclopedia of Religious Knowledge*, (Grand Rapids, MI: Baker Book House, 1953), vol IV, p. 468.

United States of America."[5] This statement of purpose at the organization of the Evangelical Synod was one which the Church carried out to its fullest expression. Missions among the German-Russian settlers of the northwest soon became an important work for the Church. All the plains-states saw the growth of the Evangelical Synod during the last three decades of the nineteenth century.

The Evangelical Synod was divided into eighteen districts, which later grew in number to twenty-one, and these held annual conferences. There was a General Conference every four years. The delegates were chosen by ballot in the district meetings, one representative for every twelve minister-members, and one layman for every twelve congregations. Authority was centralized in a Board of Directors elected by each General Conference.[6]

Characteristic of the Evangelical Synod, as of all churches of foreign origin in this country, was the process of "Americanization." In 1925 the word "German" was dropped from the name of the Synod. There was also a continuing revision and expansion of interests and activities. By 1907 there were 102 home mission congregations. External expansion took place mainly in the areas to the north and west of St. Louis, on the plains among the German-Russian immigrants. Provisions were made early for the use of English in worship along with German. The language of the old country, however, persisted until the 1950s in rural areas, as it did among Reformed and Lutheran Churches. In 1927 a new constitution was adopted following the lines of modern ecumenical thought. This document embodied a blend of Presbyterian, Congregational and Episcopalian forms of worship and church government.[7]

From the beginning, the Evangelical Synod had been interested in church union movements. Through the years ecumenical conversations were held with the Moravians, the United Brethren, the Evangelical Church and with the Reformed Church in the U.S. The conversations with the latter lasted for some years and resulted in the merger of 1934. The ecumenical spirit had long been part and parcel of the thinking of the leaders of the Evangelical Synod of North America.

From a publication of the merged church in 1940 this line of thought is evident.

> With the turn of the new century it became apparent that the rising
> generation would not be restricted by the narrowing conceptions of
> the past. . . . Stirred by the zeal more effectively to meet the

---

5 *The New Schaff Herzog Encyclopedia*, p. 468.

6 *Ibid.*

7 *Twentieth Century Encyclopedia of Religious Knowledge*, edited by Lefferts A. Loetscher, (Grand Rapids, MI: Baker Book House, 1955), Vol I, pp. 404-405.

religious needs of the time, the spiritual glow of the first generation was in many ways recaptured. . . Now as a new day is breaking, we pause for a moment to reassert the faith of our fathers in the spiritual cause of the Kingdom. True to the union spirit in which it was conceived and the union tradition which characterized its development, the Evangelical Synod unites with the Reformed Church for the perpetuation of the spiritual heritage which is common to both and for the consummation of which each has laid down its life. As in final retrospect we look back upon the way in which we have journeyed it would be presumptuous to measure the grace of God in terms of human accomplishments. But rather, as we stand on the threshold of a new era, we look forward to the revelations of God's grace which are yet in store for those who spend their lives in selfless devotion for the cause of His Kingdom.[8]

As to comment on this quote, let it suffice to say that the two Churches certainly did lay down their lives for the cause of union! Both bodies exist now as one in a great amorphous mass, and both committed ecclesiastical and doctrinal suicide for the purpose of "furthering the Kingdom of Christ on earth!"

At the time of the union in 1934 the Evangelical Synod of North America was composed of 1254 congregations, with 1227 pastors and 281,598 members in 21 districts.

THE REFORMED CHURCH IN THE UNITED STATES[9]

Our discussion of the Reformed Church in the U.S. will be more complete than that about the Evangelical Synod of North America. As stated in the Introduction, the reason for this will be to better trace the growth of the ecumenical spirit in the German Reformed Church in this country and to show how these developments led up to and allowed for the merger of 1934.

HISTORY — PERIOD OF THE COETUS

The Reformed Church in the U.S. traces its origins back to the Reformed Church in Germany and Switzerland. The reformation tradition of the RCUS goes back to Ulrich Zwingli, and today there are those congregations among the German Reformed which trace their heritage to Zwinglian teachings even more than to Calvin's. The simplicity of the order of worship, especially, is based on Zwinglian

---

8 *Two Eras: One Past-One to Come*, (issued by the Anniversary Committee of the Evangelical and Reformed Church, 1940), pp. 32-34.

9 *Schaff-Herzog Encyclopedia*, vol ix, pp. 436-437.

forms. However, Zwingli alone was not the spiritual ancestor of the German Reformed bodies, but the majority of the Reformers are to be included in their doctrinal history. Bullinger, Calvin and Elector Frederick III of the Palatinate are in particular looked upon as the fathers of German reformation thought. The Heidelberg Catechism, which was published first in January 1563, has ever since been the doctrinal standard and book of teaching of the German Reformed people.

The first of the German Reformed in the North America came from the Palatinate, Switzerland and western Germany. The first minister among these pioneers was probably Samuel Guldin, from Bern, who came to this country in 1710. The first German congregation was founded in 1714 at Germania Ford, Virginia, but it later dissolved. In 1725 John Philip Boehm headed the first complete congregational organization at the villages of Falkner Swamp, Skippack and Whitemarsh, Pennsylvania. Boehm was a school-master from the Palatinate and had lived for some five years on a farm near Montgomery, Pennsylvania. He had served these three congregations as "reader" for those five years. Under his leadership the congregations were organized along traditional Reformed lines, with elders and deacons administering the churches. Boehm subsequently organized at least thirteen congregations covering an area which now comprises eight counties. All these churches accepted Boehm's Church Order based on the principles of Calvin, the Heidelberg Catechism and the Canons of Dort. In the years that immediately followed, German Reformed congregations were formed in the basins of the Delaware-Schuylkill and the Schuylkill-Susquehanna Rivers. A congregation was organized in Philadelphia by George M. Weiss in 1727.

In 1729 Boehm was ordained by the Dutch Reformed Church in New York under the auspices of the Classis of Amsterdam, which at that time controlled the Dutch Church in the New World. This brought the German Reformed congregations into contact with the Reformed Church in Holland. This relationship lasted until 1792. In 1742 Count Zinzendorf tried to organize all the Pennsylvania Reformed churches with the Moravians as the leading body. As he conceived it, all the churches in the Commonwealth would eventually come under Moravian administration. This plan was opposed by Boehm and Guldin and they were successful in keeping the Reformed Churches out of this union.

In September of 1747, the Coetus of Pennsylvania was organized at Philadelphia under the leadership of Michael Schlatter who had been sent to America for this purpose by the Dutch Reformed Church. This move continued the work that Boehm had begun. At that time there were four ministers and representatives from twelve charges in the Reformed body. The second Coetus was held in 1748, at which meeting the Heidelberg Catechism and the Canons of Dort were officially accepted by the Church. From 1741 to 1751 several suggestions were made by the Dutch to unite the German Reformed with the Presbyterians. These met strong opposition and failed. In 1792, after a long period of peaceful cooperation with the Holland Church assemblies, the coetus declared itself independent, and the relationship with them was ended.

PERIOD OF THE SYNOD

The first Synod met at Lancaster, Pennsylvania, on April 27, 1793. There were twenty two ministers present, representing 178 congregations and some 15,000 people. Among the first problems to be faced was that of educating ministers to serve the rapidly growing Church. As was the custom in early America before the time of organized theological seminaries, a number of ministers undertook the education of prospective pastors. Prominent among them were Helffenstein, Hermann and Becker. Another question which came up was the use of English in the worship services. From the time of this first Synod, English began to be gradually introduced into the churches, a process which took over 150 years to accomplish!

The year of 1820 saw the formation of classes within the Church and at the Synod meeting it was decided to open a theological seminary, which finally took place five years later. The seminary was located first at Carlisle, Pennsylvania, with Dr. Lewis Mayer chosen to be the single professor. (He was to be given $1000 a year as salary.) A few years later the seminary was moved to York, Pennsylvania, then in 1836 to Mercersburg. Dr. John W. Nevin came to teach in 1840, and 1844 saw the coming of Dr. Philip Schaff to the seminary. These last two men were soon to make their presence widely felt in what came to be known as the "Mercersburg Theology" and the liturgical movement in the Reformed Church in the U.S.

From 1829 to 1844 there was a revival movement in the Church, as in others of the time. This affected the churches of America by introducing a less doctrinal and more emotional Christianity which also distrusted the historic denominational structures and educated ministers. In 1845 Schaff's speech, "The Principle of Protestantism," gave rise to a period of controversy which lasted until 1878 when a Peace Commission was organized to quiet the storm in the Church. The Mercersburg Theology was further advanced by speeches by Nevin and Schaff. A significant one by Nevin was entitled "The Mystical Presence," and Schaff delivered another called "What is History?" At the meeting of the Synod of 1847 a liturgical movement began which after ten years finally obtained the provisional acceptance of a new and complex church liturgy. Though the credit for this cannot all be given to Nevin and Schaff, their activities and ideas found a large following in the Church. When we discuss the Mercersburg Theology later on, we shall see just what the liturgical movement and the new theology meant to the traditional Christian and Reformed position.

There was of course opposition to the ritualistic movement in the Church, and in 1867 this resistance resulted in the Myerstown Convention of the old Reformed side and the founding of Ursinus College. In 1869 the Western or low-church liturgy was published to counter-act the high church movement. Active liturgic controversy in the RCUS was ended in 1878 by the Peace Commission which attempted to mediate between low and high church adherents, especially by introducing a mediating directory of worship. Though this formally ended the struggle, its developments and results were to be felt for years to come, indeed, up to the merger of 1934. It is significant to note that the various publications of the Evangelical and Reformed (the merged) Church tend lightly to pass over this controversy which almost broke the Church in two. The opinion of this writer is that this policy of not mentioning or discussing in detail the Mercersburg Theology and liturgical controversy is entirely in keeping with the strong ecumenical spirit prevalent in both the Evangelical Synod and the Reformed Church of that time.

DOCTRINE - WORSHIP - GOVERNMENT

We have seen that the Reformed Church in the U.S. was Reformed, Calvinistic and Presbyterian. Its standards were the Heidelberg Catechism and the Canons of Dort. As time went on, the Calvinism in the Church diminished and some Arminianism crept in. When Nevin came to Mercersburg from the Presbyterian Church, he was looked upon by many as cementing ties with that Calvinistic body.

It will be well for us to examine more fully the details of the Mercersburg Theology. The proponents of this line of thought claimed that it was neither Calvinistic nor Arminian, but "Christocentric." The "spiritual real presence" of Christ was emphasized in the Lord's Supper, as was the objective efficacy of the sacraments in themselves. Salvation was seen as coming through outward membership in the visible church. These emphases led to an involved liturgical form of worship in which the communion table was replaced with an altar and outward participation was the important thing. William Rupp of Lancaster, Pennsylvania, led the broad-church opposition to these teachings. The Western and German-speaking parts of the Church retained the "free" liturgy, that is, they used set forms only for the sacraments, weddings and ordination. In contrast, the Mercersburg Theology gave rise to a complicated set form of Sabbath worship as well as for special occasions. The new movement stressed the authority of the higher church courts, while the old Reformed part stressed importance of the local assemblies of the Church. In fact, as time went on, the General Synod centralized power and gained more and more authority.

These were the essential differences between the liturgy and theology of Mercersburg and those of the old Reformed position. The thought of Nevin and Schaff, which in large part gave rise to the Mercersburg Theology, was based not upon consistent Biblical belief or exegesis, but upon the philosophies of Schelling and Hegel. Nevin was known to be very spiritualistic, even a mystic, among the thinkers of the day. Schaff held, according to historian James I. Good, not to Reformed, but to a mediating position between that of Schleiermacher and the Old Reformed. Schaff had grown up in the Lutheran Church of Germany, studied in a pietistic school and at Tübingen, where he was strongly influenced by the Hegelian professor F.C. Baur. He later studied at Halle and Berlin where he came under the influence of the more conservative Neander and Tholuck. "His theological views were from the Lutheran university at Tübingen, his historical ideas from Neander of the Evangelical Church of Germany, composed of Lutheran and Reformed. It was not until he came to this country that he promised adherence to the Heidelberg Catechism and our Reformed doctrines. . . .But he came representing a new and different theology, the Mediating theology of Schleiermacher, but of the right wing, inclining toward orthodoxy. . . . Prof. Jacobs, of the Lutheran Theological Seminary of Philadelphia, says, Dr. Schaff's ideal on coming to Mercersburg was the foundation of a German-American Church, uniting the Reformed and the Lutheran, that is, he was unionistic, rather than Reformed."[10]

As we move into the next chapter on the Evangelical and Reformed Merger of 1934, it will become evident that the united Church was built upon many of the aberrations and deviations from Reformed thought which characterized the Mercersburg Theology and the high church liturgy of the nineteenth century. We shall notice particularly these developments in the E & R Church, which came out of the trend away from orthodoxy in the Reformed Church in the U.S.; the centralization of power and authority in the higher church courts (characteristic also of the Presbyterian Church in the USA); the fast-dwindling importance of the Bible and its teachings; the move away from being a confessional church as the Heidelberg Catechism was shunted to one side; and concomitant with this, the growth of the teaching that the Word of God is not powerful to save, thus degrading the power of the Holy Spirit in the preaching of the Gospel; the use of altars and the growth of an altar-liturgy; and finally, but by no means least important, the incipient idea that Christ was not divine but mere a great teacher who best embodied in history the ideals of the commandments and laws of God. This last has grown out of the refusal to accept the Bible as the authentic, authoritative, and infallible Word of God, it being only a book about the history of a peculiar people and the development of the unusual religious consciousness of Israel. When the Bible reaches such triviality in the minds of the people, and especially, the ministers of a church, Jesus Christ is no longer for them the second Person of the Trinity in such cases, it is inevitable that the practice of religion takes on elaborate liturgical and social forms to compensate for this loss. Indeed, the most seriously diabolical result

10 Good, *History of the Reformed Church*, pp. 209-210.

is that a man-centered religion goes under the name of Christianity. In reality it is blasphemy to apply the Biblical concept of the Christian religion to such a prostitution of the central doctrines and practices of the faith!

As we turn now to look at that historical year of 1934, let us keep in mind the previous discussion of change in the Reformed Church, and we shall see that the merger of 1934 was indeed the culmination of century-long trends in the Church.

THE EVANGELICAL AND REFORMED MERGER OF 1934

PRINCIPLES AND DETAILS OF THE MERGER

TEACHINGS OF THE E & R

The first definite approach to union was made as early as 1922 when Commissions on Closer Relations were appointed by both the Evangelical Synod of North America and the Reformed Church in the U.S.[11] After several years of negotiation, a Plan of Union was submitted to the two bodies and approved by a large majority of both. On June 26, 1934, the "supreme judicatories" of both Churches met simultaneously at Cleveland, Ohio, "and on the evening of that historic day, members of the General Synod of the Reformed Church and of the General Conference of the Evangelical Synod marched side by side into the Zion Evangelical Church, partook together of the Lord's Supper and signalized the consummation of the union in the handclasp of Presidents Dr. Paul Press and Dr. Henry J. Christman."[12] What a happy and historic day in the lives of the members of those two Churches!

But was it a great day for all? Let the words of an old pastor in the Reformed Church answer that question, words which this staunch defender of the faith spoke to the author only a few weeks ago. I quote him as closely as I can remember:

> When we marched down the street to the Evangelical Church and everyone turned to go inside, I had a terrible feeling in my heart. After the two presidents shook hands, everyone stood up and sang "Our God Our Help," but I remained seated. The man standing next to me grasped my arm and tried to pull me to my feet, saying, "Man, get up and sing, doesn't the spirit move you?" I walked out of the building and wept bitter tears. . . .

There were many that day who felt as did this man, and many were to

11 *My Church: Whence, What, Whither* (Department of United Promotion, Evangelical and Reformed Church, Philadelphia, 1943), p. 15.

12 *My Church,*, p 15.

grieve not just that night, but for years to come, over the great travesty perpetrated upon the members of two large and significant Churches.

But what was it that affected these men so, men who had given their lives to the work of the Kingdom, men whom one would think should be happy that unity among the children of God was being forwarded? A quote from the 1936 constitution of the E & R will show us one thing which affected the Reformed people in this way.

> The doctrinal standards of the Evangelical and Reformed Church are the Heidelberg Catechism, Luther's Catechism and the Augsburg Confession. They are accepted as authoritative interpretation of the essential truth taught in the Holy Scriptures. Wherever these doctrinal standards differ, ministers, members and congregations, in accordance with the liberty of conscience inherent in the Gospel, are allowed to adhere to the interpretation of one of these confessions. However, in each case the final norm is the Word of God.[13]

From the historic Reformed point of view the problems inherent in this statement are self-evident; since the Heidelberg Catechism and the Lutheran confessions contradict each other at a number of points, there is here no confessional integrity. This statement on doctrinal standards is essentially the same proposition set forth by the Evangelische Kirchenverein des Westens in 1840. The Reformed half of the merger accepted this unworthy statement, expanded it somewhat, and thus gave up much of what it had stood for through so many years of trial. To this day the modern ecumenical movement proclaims the advantages of such "doctrinal liberty." The problem with this is that historically and biblically, the Christian church has been built upon doctrinal unity, not doctrinal freedom. It is not surprising that those who so highly prize doctrinal freedom find it easy to suggest reassembling the Protestantism with the Roman Catholic Church.

From the same page of the E & R publication (footnoted above), *My Church, Whence - What - Whither*, we find additional information about this confessional laxity.

> As was written before the consummation of the merger: "Both the Reformed Church and the Evangelical Synod are confessional churches, yet they are not heavily burdened with confessions of faith," so now it may be said that the united Church uses "the basic confessions of evangelical Protestantism in Germany in the sixteenth century," not to compel its members to think in sixteenth

---

13 *Constitution and By-laws of the Evangelical and Reformed Church*, Part I, Section 3, pp. 5-6.

century molds, but rather to preserve the historic continuity with the great liberating principles and ideals of the Reformation's return to original Christianity. . . . Characteristic of both churches, Reformed and Evangelical, was an irenic spirit and zeal for the cause of cooperative Christianity. Both were original members of the Federal Council of the Churches of Christ in America. It is not too much to expect that our united Church will continue to take a leading part in the ecumenical movements of the future. . . Dr. Philip Schaff's motto has well been quoted as expressive of the ruling spirit of our Church: "In essentials unity, in things doubtful liberty, in all things love."[14]

What we see here is a new and to us unacceptable view of the confessions. We see here the idea that the church is in some sense "confessional," but not too much! It is as if they meant to say, "We'll not be bothered overly much by the fact that we say we adhere to confessions." When one body claims to hold equally to three conflicting confessions, we can be sure that there will either be disunity if doctrine is taken seriously, or even worse there will be the conclusion that doctrine is unimportant. It is this latter idea which clearly controls what is written in the above-mentioned booklet. With this approach to doctrine, we should not be surprised to find what we do in the United Church of Christ (UCC), inconsistency in teaching and emphasis is the order of the day as one travels from congregation to congregation.

In explanation for the name "Evangelical and Reformed," this statement is offered, "It is not a placing of two denominations side by side with each other. There is now only one denomination, an organic union, not a juxtaposition of two, not even a federal union." (from a pamphlet, *My Church and I*). From another pamphlet comes this assertion, "We are a Church establishing union on the basis of a mutually recognized unity of the spirit rather than on the basis of mutually agreed articles of faith."[15] If this is true for all of Christianity, as many would have us believe, then there is nothing to prevent the organic union of all organizations which have some remote claim on the name "Christian."

One more look at the E & R constitution reveals the following peculiarity. We turn to page 28 where we read the following about "Applicants for Temporary License." "In special cases a temporary license for one year periods or less may be granted by the president of the Synod with the approval of the President of the Church authorizing the applicant to preach the Gospel, **and** to administer the sacraments and rites of the Church." According to Reformed principles and

---

14 *Constitution and Bylaws of the Evangelical and Reformed Church*, Part I, Section 3, pp 5-6.

15 *The Evangelical and Reformed Church: What We Are and What We Do.*

according to the teaching of the Scriptures, this provision hardly needs comment. If ordination is not required before one administers the sacraments, ordination either becomes a high-church priestly office that goes far beyond the sacraments to the power of forgiving sins, or it sinks to the level of any unofficial act of worship or service.

Moving on now to the issue of salvation, the following quote of a prayer from a suggested worship service for Young Peoples' Day, January 19, 1936 is instructive: "Almighty God, ceaseless creator of the ever changing worlds, clothed in mystery, yet manifest in the cosmic urge moving in all nature to more perfect forms; we thank Thee for Thy continued presence in the mind and heart of man, making him ever discontent with things as they are, urging him forever onward and upward on his way — We thank Thee, O God, for exalted visions of the eternal destiny of man, and for all the dreams of a divine society on earth, foretold by Jesus in the glad tidings of the Kingdom of God."

Such high-flown language is difficult enough for the average young person in the Church to fully understand, but more important, there is here again manifest the man-centered humanism that passes for Christianity in so many Churches of today. The effect that this has had on the young people of the Church is sad to behold, for once introduced to a man-centered Gospel, they are even more resistant than before to the biblical Gospel of salvation through grace alone.

As we observe the pervasive social Gospel and do-goodism that permeated the writings of the merged Church after 1934, we see the tremendous attraction this must have had for the young people of that generation, especially those who felt the Church was opposing them by requiring them to worship in the now foreign language of their fathers. That the Eureka Classis was able to successfully oppose this liberal spirit and continue the existence of the RCUS must be credited to God's sovereign grace and power.

THE MISSION HOUSE

This institution, at Plymouth, Wisconsin, was founded in 1862 to supply the western portions of the Reformed Church in the U.S. with German speaking pastors and teachers. As far as its influence in the merger of 1934 is concerned, there is not much written material available. However, it is significant that the Mission House has been, since at least the late twenties, known to be mediating in its theology. Even as far back as 1906 the Eureka, South Dakota, congregation objected to the teachings of a professor there, H.A. Meier. Since the seminary in particular (there are also an Academy and College on the same campus) dealt with church people in Germany, the influence of continental rationalism and neo-orthodoxy had early effects on the type of thought found among faculty and students. Karl Barth made a great impression on the Mission House with his commentary on Romans, and at least as early as 1935 his works were being translated into English by Mission House professors. Although some of the men on the faculty of the Seminary were defenders of the Reformed faith, the philosophical rationalism of the "old country" and that of American liberalism was popular among the students and younger professors. In time much of this influence was incorporated into the material being taught. But in spite of this evolution in theology, during the middle fifties, for example, the Wellhausen documentary hypothesis on the Pentateuch was still being propounded. There is today (1960 ed.), an odd admixture of a few Reformed concepts with the latest in theological development.

When the fateful year of 1934 dawned, the Mission House was all too ready to move along with the large majority of the Reformed Church into the merger with the Evangelical Synod. There have been those who since that time have recognized the mistake that was made, but few, if any, have had the fortitude to come out of an organization once they have joined its ranks.

ECUMENICITY

This is the magic word in the E & R today (1960 ed.). All is to be put aside if it does not coincide with the purposes of organic unity. The important thing in the Church above all else is the work to unite all of Christendom under one flag. The attitude is that the Reformation of the sixteenth century was a shame and a travesty, but the ecumenical movement, the union of the Reformed Church in the U.S. with the Evangelical Synod of North America, and more recently the union of the E & R with the Congregational Churches of America, have been the most important and inspiring events in the history of the twentieth century Church!

Conversations with the Congregationalists got underway before the E & R was five years old, and in 1943 a Primer of Union was issued. This work resulted in the formation of the United Church of Christ in June, 1957. Ecumenicity is now being pushed in the new organization with the same vigor as was the social Gospel in the thirties and early forties. The glories of the visible church are made so much a part of the emphases of the Church that once again the Good Tidings of salvation in Christ Jesus take a back seat in the preaching and work of the Church. Once again we see the culmination of the trends of a generation in the United Church, just as the liturgical movement and Mercersburg Theology of the nineteenth century had so much to do with the Evangelical and Reformed merger of 1934.

We have looked now at the merged church in some detail. This is what the men of the Eureka Classis had to fight. And fight they did, for in many ways there was little that was gentle or even brotherly about the struggle which grew out of the union in 1934. It was a life or death struggle for the Reformed faith, one that today is still occasionally renewed.

We now turn to the position and work of the Eureka Classis, the continuing Reformed Church in the U.S., against the Evangelical and Reformed Church.

THE REFORMED CHURCH IN THE U.S. CONTINUES

OBJECTIONS TO THE MERGER OF 1934

THE SOLITARY POSITION OF THE EUREKA CLASSIS — 1934-1939

When the votes of the Classes of the Reformed Church in the U.S. on the matter of union were counted, the majority was so overwhelmingly in favor of merger that none thought final acceptance in 1940, when the old Synods met for the last time, would meet any opposition. This was not the case. The proponents of the merger did not reckon with the solidarity of the western membership of the Reformed Church. From the time that the merger was first proposed, the Synod of the Northwest militated against it, particularly the Classes of Eureka, North Dakota and South Dakota. It soon became evident, however, that the Eureka Classis alone would stand firm to the end. In those crucial years between 1934 and 1939 many Reformed folks in the Midwest realized that there was much more at stake than mere ecclesiastical identity. Soon to be offered up on the altar of union were the precious Reformed doctrines and the Calvinistic heritage which had so long been characteristic of the old Reformed Church. That body had several times before resisted suggestions of merger with the Dutch Reformed, the Presbyterians and various Evangelical bodies. This time, because of increasing laxity of the leaders of the Church in matters of doctrine, the old faith was left behind to follow the siren song of liberalism and the ecumenical spirit of the age. A catastrophe which had been in the making for generations was soon to break forth in full measure upon the Reformed Church.

As we have noted above, the Eureka Classis and its neighbor Classes were already far more conservative than the Eastern sections of the RCUS, indeed that is why the Eureka Classis was founded in 1910. Therefore it is not surprising that as the denominational leaders developed ecumenical relations the Classes in the Dakotas commented negatively on them. We find, for example, that the Eureka Classis in 1924 refused to support a number of agencies of the denomination and retorted to the Synod's suggestion that it support the ecumenical "Church Forward Movement," that the work of the Eureka Classis was to forward the teaching of the Bible. In that year, Rev. John Grossmann, the father of Rev. Walter Grossmann who was to be instrumental after 1934, was President of Classis, Rev. Peter Bauer of Zeeland, North Dakota was Vice President, Rev. J. Klundt of Wishek was Stated Clerk and Rev. P. Schild of Hosmer was Treasurer. It is clear from the minutes of Classis that these men, along with Rev. Henry Treick of Eureka, South Dakota, and

Rev. William Wittenberg, who then served the Kulm, North Dakota charge, were solid in their agreement to hold fast to the old Reformed faith. The same thing was true of the somewhat changed ministerial membership of the Classis in 1932 just before the merger was approved by the General Synod of the RCUS. In this year, Rev. F.A. Rittershaus of Artas was President, Rev. P. Bauer of Leola was Vice President, Rev. W. Schmidt of Zeeland was Treasurer and Rev. F. W. Herzog of Ashley (who shortly returned to Germany) was Stated Clerk, as he had been for several years. This was also the year when Rev. William Krieger, who was to take such a large part in preserving the RCUS, was installed in the Eureka charge. It might well be said that by this time those who were members of the Eureka Classis were serving there just because of its stand for a conservative and strictly Calvinist faith.

Events led in a few years to a change of the personnel who led Classis but not to a change in its stand against the merger of 1934. By the time of a special Classis meeting in October 1935 two pastors, Rev. Thiele and Rev. Herzog, had returned to Germany at the deceptive invitation of the Hitler government to help build a new Germany. Rev. Henry Treick, Rev. Peter Bauer and Rev. Wittenberg had retired, Rev. Rittershaus had left Artas and Rev. Schmidt had left Zeeland. Rev. William Krieger, who had been elected Vice President at the spring meeting of Classis, presided, and Rev. Walter Grossmann was Stated Clerk, a position to which he was elected in the spring of 1935 and which he held without break until his death in 1956. The purpose of this special meeting of the Eureka Classis held at Alpena, South Dakota, is important for our understanding of the stand of the Classis against the merger. The purpose stated in the minutes was fourfold: 1) to settle matters between the Ashley charge and Rev. Herzog, 2) to receive the ministers and charges of the North Dakota Classis as members of the Eureka Classis, 3) to hold a joint session with the South Dakota Classis to discuss serving vacant charges in the Dakotas, and 4) to underwrite the travel expenses of those attending. This meeting was held between the consummation of the E & R merger in 1934 and the final meetings of the old Reformed classes and synods which had been scheduled for 1940. This was, of course, to facilitate merger on the local level. The three Dakota area Classes, however, used these meetings as opportunities to further prepare for final separation from the merger. It is important to note that Rev. K.J. Stuebbe, who in 1935 was pastor at Tripp, South Dakota, and was President of the Synod of the Northwest of the now E & R Church, was also present at this special meeting of Classis. Rev. Stuebbe was later to lead his Manitowoc, Wisconsin, Salem-Ebenezer Reformed Church out of the merger.

It now fell upon two men in particular, Rev. Krieger and Rev. Grossmann, to guide the Classis over the rocky roads ahead, always trying to lead their people along the course of correct biblical faith. The Rev. William Krieger was a native of

Iowa, where he grew up in the German Presbyterian Church. His early education was obtained in the area of Waukon, Iowa, and his theological training at Princeton Seminary in Princeton, New Jersey. Rev. Krieger was educated at Princeton when it was the foremost conservative Reformed seminary in the United States. Rev. Krieger was married to a daughter of Rev. Jacob Stark, a leader of the conservative and Calvinistic Kohlbrueggian school of theology, and so was familiar with the conservatism of the German Reformed in the Dakotas. Probably during the first decade of this century he came to the Dakotas to serve the growing Presbyterian Church there. His associations with the Eureka Classis began quite early for he was a charter member of the Classis at its formation in 1910, when he was serving free Reformed churches at Tripp, South Dakota. Prior to that, he had served the Presbyterian Church at Roscoe, South Dakota, during which time he was a frequent preacher in various German Reformed Churches in the area. He is remembered particularly as having often bicycled some thirty miles to preach in the Glueckstal Reformed Church fifteen miles, north east of Eureka. Rev. Krieger was a man of unusual education and knowledge for those times and places. When in the thirties he came to leadership in the Classis, these talents and associations stood him in good stead. Up until his death in 1948 in California where he had gone for his health, he continued to write and speak against the dangers of the merger.

Rev. Walter Grossmann was a son of the German Reformed Church in the Dakotas. His father, Rev. John Grossmann, was first a pastor in the Reformed Church in Canada where he began his ministry after his immigration from Germany in 1900. He then moved to North Dakota, preached in several charges there and finally to South Dakota where he served Reformed Churches until he died in 1929. The writer's father thus grew up in the Dakotas and was educated at the Mission House Academy, College, and Seminary at Plymouth, Wisconsin. Upon his graduation from the seminary, and due to poor recommendations from the seminary faculty because of his outspoken conservatism, he was forced to work for a year as an engineer until he received a call from the Reformed Church in Hosmer, South Dakota. This call came in 1934, and Rev. Grossmann arrived in Hosmer about one month before the consummation of the E & R merger. Rev. Krieger then served the Church in Eureka, twenty miles to the north, and these two men immediately embarked on a program to keep the Eureka Classis clear of the ever-widening arms of the merger. It can be candidly and honestly said that until 1939 the fortunes of the Classis depended predominantly upon these two ministers, and even after that their influence, along with the faithfulness of many local elders, was essential to keeping many individual congregations of the Classis from defecting into the union.

One of the greatest problems facing pastors Krieger and Grossmann in their work to keep the Eureka Classis free from the E & R was the mediating position of several of their colleagues in the classis. By 1934 there were several crucial vacancies among the congregations of the Classis left by older men who had since retired from the pulpit or passed out of this life. Consequently a number of the smaller vacant churches experienced early difficulties with pressure from the merged Church. This circumstance combined with a weak stand by some within the classis provided an unending amount of trouble in keeping it from succumbing to merger ideology. Because the final acceptance of the union was scheduled for 1940, which would give the various synods and classes ample time to straighten out whatever problems they might have in aligning congregations and individuals on the side of the merger, Krieger and Grossmann were able during those six years to prepare their defenses. There were ministers in the Classis and in other classes of the Northwest Synod who wished to remain clear of the merger, but in time it became evident that by reason of their family ties or because of unsettled convictions they were not willing to stand with so small a minority as the Eureka Classis against the united Church. According to an article in the publication of the Reformed Publication Society, *The Witness* for January, 1945, there was wide and varied opposition in the Reformed Church in the U.S. to the proposed merger in the years up to 1934, but as the time for final ratification approached in 1940, more and more of these opponents moved to support the union. By the Fall of 1940 there were but the Eureka Classis and a few scattered congregations who still held fast to their persuasion to remain Reformed.[16] It seemed unbelievable to the writer's father, as he remarked in a letter to Rev. Krieger in 1937, that so many of the Reformed men could not, or would not, recognize the deviation from biblical teaching that was coming to the surface among the leaders of the merger.

However, indecision alone was not responsible for a desire among some to be included in the Evangelical and Reformed union. First, and quite possibly the most important was the fact that there was among the lay people of the Church a relatively undiscerning Christian faith. Church members in general were not doctrinally aware and certainly were not in a position to be critical of the liberalism couched in glowing terms by the Church's leaders. This was certainly true among the German-speaking congregations of the Northwest Synod, who in any case could not read the English-language materials coming out of the RCUS headquarters on Race Street in Philadelphia. Furthermore, most of the ministers who served these people were graduates of Mission House Seminary, which we noticed earlier was lacking Reformed decisiveness in its preparation of students for the Gospel ministry. The social Gospel and the inroads of liberalism were now being felt. There was therefore a corresponding unconcern among many of the members of the Church for purity of doctrine and adherence to the Scriptures. This was not entirely their own fault, for their pastors were by and large poorly equipped to instruct them. There are to this day (1960 ed.), those who will defend the Mission House and its products.

---

16 "Eureka Classis Merger History," in *The Witness*, Jan. 1945, p. 5.

However, one need only look at their libraries and listen to the sermons of these men to realize that they seriously lack knowledge of some of the most basic principles of Calvinism. Thus, when the move for a union into a "bigger and better" organization was in the making, this was considered by numerous members of the Reformed Church to be very attractive and in keeping with the spirit of the times.

Nationalistic unity among the Germans in the Midwest was strong indeed. In communities all over the country there were few people who came from anything but German stock and any encroachment by outsiders in the life of the Church or in business was not encouraged. Again there is blame for this prevailing situation to be laid at the feet of the leaders of the Church, who should have been able to see the need for the Reformed faith among all Americans, and not just those of German background. Yet for many with such a limited outlook on life in a growing democracy, it became desirable to maintain their peculiar German customs and thus their nationalistic unity. For a large number of these folks the coming merger was an opportunity to both enlarge their Church and at the same time retain their desired German unity. When this aversion to anything "foreign" is coupled with close family ties to members of the Reformed Church outside the Eureka Classis, it is easy to see how many people would not be able to object strongly to the merger.

Another factor contributing to the lack of unity against the merger among the congregations of the Eureka Classis was their wide geographical separation and the relatively small number of large strong congregations. Krieger and Grossmann were separated by only twenty miles, though this distance meant much more twenty five years ago than it does today, and they served the two largest and strongest churches in the Classis. The combination of these two men and their churches was to be a major deterrent to merger within the Classis. They were further augmented in their position by their respective country congregations. Eureka was a two point charge, St Peter's Church in town and Glueckstal congregation fifteen miles to the northeast. Hosmer was a three point charge, being associated with Calvin Church and the Neudorf congregation thirteen miles to the north and northeast. These country congregations contributed significant support to the opposition to union, and remained in the Classis as separate entities until the middle fifties when they amalgamated with their sister churches in Eureka and Hosmer.

Weakness lay, however, in the lack of strong churches elsewhere in the Dakotas. There were several without pastors, for example, Highmore, Heil, Herrick, Delmont, Kulm and Isabel. These were all subject to increasing pressure and inducement from neighboring Reformed churches willing to enter the merger, and in time, most of them were swallowed up by legal process or dissension which divided them from within. For some years several of the smaller ones stayed with the Classis, but came to be disorganized for lack of leadership and eventually dwindled away to non-existence. It was not unusual for the pastors of the Classis to preach of a Sunday in their own congregations and then travel as far as 250 miles to serve a vacancy in the afternoon or evening. This load fell largely on W. Grossmann because he was the youngest of the ministers then in the Classis. The problem was compounded by the demand for both English and German services in many places.

As these various problems became more acute, the supply of pastors was spread more thinly than ever. Many congregations were unable to support their own ministers and had to depend solely on those from other places to serve them. This in turn took valuable time and energy which could well have been spent in organizing opposition to the merger. By 1936 things were well enough defined to indicate that at least the stronger of the Classis' churches were going to see it through. This was the stand of a very small group of Reformed ministers and laity over against a half-million people led by men eager to promote the liberal social Gospel and ecumenicity.

ACTIVE OPPOSITION

Between 1934 and 1940, the Classis was the source of a constant flood of objections to the final fulfillment of the Evangelical and Reformed merger, which as stated, was to come to completion in 1940. Until that year the old Reformed classes and synods were to meet to iron out remaining difficulties, and from that time on the merged Church would be operating under the provisions of the new constitution with Evangelical and Reformed assemblies combined. We shall now consider in some detail the objections that came out of the Classis of Eureka during that interim period. Much of our material will come from letters written by W. Grossmann and W.J. Krieger, and from official resolutions and overtures of the Classis to the Synod of the Northwest and other judicatories of the Reformed Church in the U.S. Articles from *The Witness* and *Reformiertes Gemeindeblatt* will also provide a source of information, though the German paper duplicates much material found in the English publication, and therefore references to the German organ will not be many. The material will be considered in chronological order insofar as is practical to show the development and changes in the Classis' situation.

In a letter to W.J. Krieger, W. Grossmann sets forth certain resolutions for the Classis to consider on the matter of the union.

1. Whereas a union between the Reformed Church in the U.S. and the Evangelical Synod of North America was consummated according to a Plan of Union accepted as such, and this Plan of Union in which various and sundry rights were guaranteed, was arbitrarily disregarded in the formulation of a constitution, which proposed constitution is about to become the fundamental law of

the Church;

2. Whereas the confession of faith of the Reformed Church in the U.S., which is the basis of that corporation, has been made void in the proposed constitution by accepting other differing confessions as equally valid;

3. Whereas the form of church government accepted by the members of the Reformed Church in the U.S. in their constitution has been displaced without the consent of the individual members, who are as stockholders in a corporation and therefore have the right to themselves decide by vote;

4. Whereas the doctrine of the officials of the Church of the union movement, as this doctrine is revealed especially in making the Kingdom of God a social goal, is contrary to scriptural teaching as set forth in the Heidelberg Catechism;

Be it resolved: that we, the dissenting churches, remain organized as the Reformed Church in the U.S. based on the confession of the Heidelberg Catechism, on which this Church is based, and maintain the presbyterial form of church government and thereby contend that that portion of our Church accepting other confessions as equally valid, to have departed from this organization, and thus to have forfeited property and ecclesiastical rights of the Reformed Church in the U.S.

The proposed constitution of the Evangelical and Reformed Church also caused a good deal of consternation among the ministers of the Eureka Classis with respect to their congregation's rights to remain Reformed in their own practices. Once again, a resolution formulated by W. Grossmann on this important matter illustrates their concern.

1. Whereas it is our conviction that the proposed constitution outrageously ignores the provisions of the Plan of Union, safeguarding the interests of the congregations, classes and synods, respecting their positions as judicatories and respecting their doctrinal attitudes; and

2. Whereas the proposed constitution makes provision for the gradual nullification of the effect of the distinctive doctrines by dangerously jeopardizing maintenance of such doctrines by the Placement Committee (the Placement Committee has charge of accepting and placing of pastors in the congregations, ed.)

3. Whereas such nullification of distinctive doctrines has been expressly indicated by the President of the Church as an object to be attained; and

4. Whereas by these facts dissemination among our congregations of the doctrine of the Bible as clearly set forth in the Heidelberg Catechism is gravely endangered; and

5. Whereas it is our conviction that the plan of government provided for in the proposed constitution is flatly contrary to the plan of government taught in the Scriptures; and

6. Whereas we cannot bring upon ourselves the responsibility before the most high Lord Jehovah for supporting and sponsoring such a church government and doctrine;

Be it resolved:

1. That the Eureka Classis rejects the proposed constitution.

2. That the Eureka Classis refers the matter of severing connections with the Evangelical and Reformed Church and of taking necessary and possible legal steps to safeguard their property rights to the individual congregations of the Eureka Classis.

It is important for us to see from the above resolutions that the merged Church took upon itself, without respect to the authority provided by the *Constitution of the Reformed Church in the U.S.*, the assumption that all the bodies of the Reformed Church would automatically become members of the union. The Classis position was that this move stepped beyond the bounds of the rights that rested with the individual classes and congregations to decide for themselves by vote what their status would be with respect to the merger. Two more considerations that are concomitant with the above resolutions are; 1) that the Eureka Classis was of the conviction that the spirit manifested by the authorities in so flagrantly disregarding the Plan of Union boded ill for any contracted rights of any body or member of the Church, and 2) that the intolerant spirit manifested by the supporters of this proposed Constitution in discussing it with opposers was a portent of an arrogant bureaucracy at the helm of the merged Church.

On the topic of litigation over church properties, the case of Watson versus Jones (1871), known as the Walnut Street Case, is of significance for our consideration. This decision of the United States Supreme Court concerning the union of churches put the Eureka Classis in a precarious position. It declared, "The property of every synod, presbytery, and individual church would, the moment the union was consummated, pass under the control of the General Assembly of the united Church." *The Christian Beacon* for 26 October 1939 comments, "This is the leading case and controls the decisions of the courts. Synods, presbyteries and churches that felt in conscience that they could not enter the union, would lose all their property. And those that went in, and felt at any time that conscience called them to come out, would lose all." To this, Zollman, in his *American Church Law* says, "The decision places in the hands of the church judicatories a tyrannical power which is inconsistent with the right of the parties that come before them, and destroys religious liberty *pro tanto*, instead of protecting." Upon considerations such as these, the Eureka Classis gained some measure of success in the courts in contests for church properties, though in several cases demoralizing defeat was the result of litigation.

During the course of the Eureka Classis' contentions against the merger, and particularly the proposed constitution as abrogating important provisions of the Plan of Union, W. Grossmann again filed a paper which makes more explicit objections to the Constitution up for consideration by the E & R. This "Memorandum relative to Church Union" will be self-explanatory.

> In 1934 the General Synod of the Reformed Church in the U.S. adopted a Plan of Union with the Evangelical Synod of North America, in which the following rights were guaranteed the churches, classes and districts; Article V, Section 7, "The General Synod shall promote the reorganization of Classes and Districts into Conferences which shall be constituted on a territorial basis and shall have the same status as Classes or Districts. However, the General Synod shall not have power to unite subordinate judicatories of the consolidated churches except at their request." And Article VIII, Section 1, "the congregations, Classes, Synods and Districts shall continue to exist and to do their work in the way it was done prior to the union; they shall also continue to hold and to supervise whatever property they possess and institutions they control."

> The necessary majority of the Classes and Districts have adopted the Plan of Union, and on the basis of this plan a merger was effected. If the Plan of Union is not merely a scrap of paper, then the Committee on Constitution was fully bound by it. This committee, however, made radical and unwarranted departures from the Plan of Union. Before any departure from the Plan of Union could be made, it would have been the duty of General Synod to take up these changes for reconsideration, and should then again have submitted them to the Classes and Districts for

action. The General Synod failed to do so.

A union based on a federation of confessions is no union at all. It is illogical, indefensible and defeats its true purpose, unity. It is merely an external organization, and as such its existence is unwarranted. And without a definite confession, which, in unequivocal terms, pledges its adherents to all the Scriptures of the Old and New Testaments, as the only rule of faith and practice, it is hardly entitled to be called a member of the Body of Christ. The essential requirements, unity of faith and spirit, are wanting in a federation of confessions.

On June 26th, 1934, at Cleveland, Ohio, the General Synod declared that the Plan of Union was legally adopted. But regardless of the specific provisions of the Plan of Union the Committee on Constitution made, and the General Synod sanctioned violations of the Plan of Union as is evident from the Following:

a) The proposed Constitution of the Evangelical and Reformed Church nullifies the authority of the Heidelberg Catechism as the only standard of our Church, by binding the congregations to standards in many respects contradictory to each other, as Art. I of Part II of the proposed constitution sets forth.[17]

b) The proposed constitution unites subordinate judicatories and eliminates others without their request. (re Art. V. Section 7 of the Plan of Union, "However, the General Synod shall not have power to unite subordinate judicatories of the consolidated churches except at their request"); but Part V, Item 22 of the proposed constitution states: "The Evangelical and Reformed Church consists of ministers and of lay members organized into congregations which constitute Synods; the Synods, through elected delegates, constitute the General Synod."

c) The proposed constitution eliminates classes and synods as they exist, and provides for new divisions contrary to the guaranteed rights provided in the Plan of Union.

d) The proposed constitution takes the control of institutions away from judicatories controlling them and gives it to the General

---

17 This reference reads: "A congregation of the Evangelical and Reformed Church is a body of Christians accepting the standards of faith and doctrine prescribed in the constitution of the Church . . . . a congregation . . . may be admitted into the Evangelical and Reformed Church by the Synod, provided said congregation complies with the requirements of the Church." *Constitution and By-Laws of the Evangelical and Reformed Church*, Part II, Article 1, pp. 6-7.

Synod.

e) The proposed constitution has set up a form of government departing from the historical customs and usages of the Reformed Church in the U.S.

In view of these facts we question the legality of the merger. Two conflicting laws cannot be effective at the same time, neither can several conflicting confessions.

We . . . therefore, respectfully overture General Synod:

1. To revise the proposed constitution in accordance with the guarantees given in the Plan of Union:

2. That congregations, desiring the Heidelberg Catechism as their only confession of faith and presbyterial form of government, shall not be deprived of their rights to continue as, or form, classes and synods in the same manner as provided for in the present *Constitution of the Reformed Church in the U.S.*;

3. That the aforesaid congregations shall not be coerced or permitted to call a minister, holding beliefs contrary to its own confession, and that such rights be safeguarded;

4. That the aforementioned congregations, classes and synods continue to control institutions which have been, and now are under their supervisions; and

5. That General Synod shall see to it that all publications of our Church are in harmony with our confession of faith.

The open and unwarranted abrogation of the Plan of Union by the proposed Constitution of the Evangelical and Reformed Church is clearly set forth above. This illegal procedure prompted several mediating and undecided congregations and ministers to join the Eureka Classis in its stand against the merger.

With passing time it became clear that resolutions to the judicatories of the Evangelical and Reformed Church notwithstanding, there was to be no significant change in either the proposed constitution or the practices of the merged body whereby the all-enclosing arms of the union-octopus would soon envelope even dissenting classes and congregations. Therefore, more positive action had to be taken, and thus in the last months of 1938 matters came to a head with the declaration of the Eureka Classis' intention to continue as the Reformed Church in the U.S., retaining the Heidelberg Catechism as the only confession of the Church.

This definite statement of intention was embodied in two more resolutions, the first of which was sent to the General Synod of the Evangelical and Reformed Church meeting in 1938. This document held that since the Eureka Classis in session at Artas, South Dakota, May 19th to 22nd, 1938, had unanimously resolved to continue existence as the Reformed Church in the U.S., and since the Evangelical and Reformed Synod had officially adopted the proposed Constitution and had thus seceded from the Reformed Church in the U.S., its doctrine and policy, it was resolved by the Eureka Classis that it,

> serves notice on the merged Evangelical and Reformed Church that all properties, holdings and rights of the Reformed Church in the U.S. are now legally vested in the Eureka Classis, and therefore said properties, holdings and rights cannot and may not be diverted or transferred to the new organization called the Evangelical and Reformed Church.
>
> FURTHERMORE BE IT RESOLVED, that the Eureka Classis extend its resolution, adopted at its session at Artas, South Dakota, May 19th to 22nd, 1938, that it also reserves the rights to all properties, holdings and rights of the Reformed Church in the U.S. and if necessary, lay claim to such.

The second resolution here under consideration also made a definite statement to the effect that the continuing Reformed Church in the U.S. remained true to the Scriptures and the interpretation thereof set forth in the Heidelberg Catechism. It was made clear that other bodies which might affiliate themselves with the Eureka Classis would also become members of the continuing Reformed Church in the U.S. Moreover, provision was made

> That the officials of the Eureka Classis (combined Executive Committee and the Board of Trustees, as the case may require) negotiate with the officials of the Evangelical and Reformed Church in regard to coming to a definite agreement regarding properties, holdings and rights of the Reformed Church in the U.S.. Such negotiations must be reciprocated by the officials of the Evangelical and Reformed Church by the 15th of October, 1938, otherwise the Eureka Classis will bring legal action regarding such properties, holdings and rights against the Evangelical and Reformed Church.

In these ways the Eureka Classis struggled to maintain first, its identity as the Reformed Church in the U.S., but more importantly, its adherence to the true teachings of the Scriptures. It was a bitter struggle, one that lasted for years, but one also that was willingly engaged in for the sake of the truth of the Gospel and the Kingdom of God. We can well quote one last resolution from the Eureka Classis to the Synod of the Northwest of the Evangelical and Reformed Church, adopted by roll call vote at its regular annual session at Leola, South Dakota, May 16-19, 1940.

Dear Fathers and Brethren:

Whereas the Eureka Classis has served notice on the General Synod of the Evangelical and Reformed Church, Minutes, Gen. Synod, of its intention to retain its identity as the Reformed Church in the United States, with all its rights, prerogatives and privileges; and whereas the Eureka Classis is firmly convinced that the new merger is not and cannot be conducive for the promotion of the true faith, unity and doctrine, we find it impossible to affiliate with the Evangelical and Reformed Church.

In view of these facts, we the Eureka Classis do now and here resolve and formally declare that we are, and shall henceforth continue to function as the legally constituted Reformed Church in the United States.

(signed) W. Grossmann
Stated Clerk
Eureka Classis

Official seal affixed:
Eureka Classis der Reformierten Kirche in den Vereinigten Staaten
II John 9

With this summary resolution of action that had gone before, the Eureka Classis legally continued to exist as the Reformed Church in the U.S. The break was complete.

THE REBIRTH OF THE EUREKA CLASSIS

Yes, the break was complete, but the struggle was far from over! The Eureka Classis, now officially and legally re-born as the continuing Reformed Church in the U.S. was to be for some years to come hard put to justify its existence and defend its opposition to the Evangelical and Reformed merger of 1934. Criticism and attack came from all quarters, from the union, from other dissenting Churches, but most dangerously and surprisingly of all, from within. There was a variety of criticism that had to be answered, and those who stood solidly on the Scriptures and against the merger once again rose to the occasion. There was a crying need for unity among the congregations of the Classis; disunity could not be tolerated for it endangered the work and principles of a decade of resistance. Individual congregations had internal problems that sometimes led them to the brink of disaster.

On numerous occasions W.J. Krieger and W. Grossmann had been called upon to overcome the attacks of the enemy, and thus far they had proven equal to the demands made upon them. When internal strife threatened the existence of the Classis, these two men had no choice but to join in the fray once more. In late 1940, a particularly grievous situation arose that required quick and decisive action. The Rev. John Bodenmann, pastor of the Wishek, North Dakota, charge, and at that time Vice President of Classis, was encouraged by the Classis to take a stand against the merger and to cooperate with the strengthening of the Reformed stand. His charge was part of the North Dakota Classis that had in 1935 dissolved itself into the Eureka Classis. Bodenmann was known still to be undecided about which side to take, but the Classis was acting in good faith in their conversations with him, giving him every opportunity to learn their position and expecting in turn a definite indication from him of his inclinations. On November 12, 1940, a special session of the Eureka Classis met to consider the question of joining the newly formed Dakota Synod of the Evangelical and Reformed Church. Bodenmann stood at that point for joining this new Synod and wished to present arguments to the classis for doing so. As best we can reconstruct the matter twenty years later, some sort of agreement was reached about a time when written arguments were to be presented to the Stated Clerk and then passed on to the congregations simultaneously. Then just before Christmas of that year and in violation of the agreement made at the special session of Classis, Bodenmann suddenly circulated without the knowledge of the officials of the Classis a letter condemning the stand against the merger. This paper went out to all the churches of the Classis before the anti-merger side had its own arguments ready because they were depending upon Bodenmann to keep the agreement. Following are excerpts from that essay, outlining Bodenmann's position:

> To the congregations of the Eureka Classis,
>
> We were against the church-merger from the beginning and voted against it in the South Dakota Classis. The vote in both Churches (of his charge) . . . produced an overwhelming majority for this Merger. So we had lost, even though we were opposed. We were voted into the Merger. Having been in the pastoral calling for forty years, we had always held that the losing side in a vote must submit to the majority.
>
> The Eureka Classis wants to remain the Reformed Church in the United States. How it wishes to accomplish this, we do not know. A single Classis by itself has never been a church body, but only a judicatory, and in fact the second lowest judicatory the Church . . . . Now the Eureka Classis wants to be an autonomous Church, that has no higher judicatory over itself; it wants to be classis, synod and general synod all in one....

How does it stand with the confession of the united Church? Have we given up anything of our precious faith? Absolutely not! Our Heidelberg is **mutually** recognized in the united Church as an official confession. No one wishes to take the Heidelberg away from anyone. . . .

And so Bodenmann continues for several pages, reproducing all the arguments and guarantees of the Plan of Union of the united Church. The majority rules, the Heidelberg Catechism will be retained, the Placement Committee is not dangerous, and that freedom as well as order is essential. In conjunction with this, Bodenmann claims that in the decade from 1930 - 1940 the Reformed Church in the state of North Dakota had lost more than a dozen congregations while in the same period the Lutherans and Congregationalists had grown, all because they had freedom as well as order, which the Reformed Church did not. And yet, he must have seen, as we have in this discussion, the fallacy of this sort of reasoning. We cannot know exactly what prompted Bodenmann to change banners so suddenly in the midst of the conflict.

Whatever the case may have been, there was but one path left open for the anti-merger side of the Classis, and that was to circulate as quickly as possible its own statement. This was done, in mimeographed form, whereas Bodenmann, having the advantage of surprise, was able to get his essay nicely printed in German.

The answer written by W.J. Krieger and W. Grossmann to Bodenmann's paper came out just after Christmas of 1940 and consolidated in one place the position against the merger as we saw in the last chapter. On the question of the churches of the Eureka Classis joining the Dakota Synod of the Evangelical and Reformed Church, Krieger had this to say:

Does the Dakota Synod (of the E & R) have a written guarantee that it will stay this way (that is, that the Heidelberg will be retained, ed.)? The following church law will certainly be observed: "If one becomes a member of a freely joined religious corporation, one binds himself to all its rules and regulations, and agrees therewith to the carrying out of such authority as is given to its leading officers, and he is bound to the future decisions of those authorities." The Dakota Synod has become a member of the new Church, therefore she is bound to the future actions of the officers of that new Church. And yet it is asserted that one is not bound to all three confessions.

Grossmann wrote in the same paper:

This business concerns itself with one point: **Does one believe the**

Word of God?!! This acceptance of three different confessions in the united Church implies an indifference in relation to doctrine. This indifference is then indifference to a careful attention to the teaching of Scripture. Doctrine, after all, is concerned with **what is actually taught** (in Scripture), and not that one is able to forgive which confession someone might accept. We wish only to bring out some of the least that is taught in the new Church. This teaching can be noticed behind most of the statements of the officers of this Church. It is declared: "The world is not saved through the one cross on Golgatha, but rather through millions of crosses and on each cross a human soul, revealing God's love, because they are reconciled with him." This is certainly manifest and grievous false teaching, for the Bible teaches clearly and distinctly that salvation was completed through one offering of Christ upon the cross. The word of God teaches forcefully that we must test doctrine. John teaches in his second letter that we must not in the least support this kind of false teaching. Paul declares that such false teachers are condemned. John teaches that when we support these kind of teachers **we make ourselves partakers of their punishment**.... The lords of the Church may perhaps allow us to live our faith, but will God uphold our faith if we operate this way?

It is said that we should submit ourselves to the majority (cf. Bodenman's statement above- ed.). This may certainly be the case in ordinary circumstances. But when it comes to opposing the teaching of the Bible, the majority has nothing to vote about. Must one really support false teaching, just because the majority has voted for it? To whom should we give the most obedience, to **God's word** or to the human majority?

Finally, it comes down to this: shall we, because of all kinds of threatened and visible problems — which may never actually appear as facts — operate directly contrary to the admonition of God's word? What Samuel teaches will always be true: whoever rejects God's word, him will **God cast out**.

As the situation developed, a few of the congregations concerned with the matter of joining the Dakota Synod of the Evangelical and Reformed Church did defect from their original stand with the Eureka Classis. Bodenmann's charge at Wishek, North Dakota, was among these. For some time after this particular conflict, W.J. Krieger was actively engaged in circulating several lengthy papers in German on the question of the merger. He did excellent work in presenting arguments on the basis of Scripture against going into a church that had so little doctrinal definition, and partly due to his efforts, several congregations wavering between merger and independence decided to stand with the Classis.

During the early forties, when the stand of the Eureka Classis became clear and more widely known, several other ministers and congregations were attracted to it. Rev. D.E. Bosma, a graduate of the Mission House, in 1943 accepted a call to serve the Eureka charge when W.J. Krieger was forced by ill-health to retire from the pulpit. Rev. Bosma had for many years served Reformed churches in Iowa, and when the dangers of the merger became clear, aligned himself and his congregation against union. He was not a member of the Eureka Classis, and thus for some years was independent of any ecclesiastical affiliation. However, with his coming to Eureka, his former congregation in Iowa decided to join the Evangelical and Reformed Church. Bosma deplored this, and once said to this writer that on a visit to relatives in Iowa he visited the last church he had served there. He was appalled at the changes that had taken place since he had left, "it was like walking into a Catholic Church!"

The Rev. William E. Korn, who has now served the Menno, South Dakota, charge for over twenty years also came into the Classis during this period. He had been born and educated in Germany, then held pastorates in Canada before coming to the Dakotas. He is known as a scholarly man, staunch in his defense of the Eureka Classis and the Reformed faith.

A great amount of good support came from Rev. Kasper Krueger, also from Germany, who served at Ashley, and then Upham, North Dakota, until his death in October of 1957. His close association with W. Grossmann gave the latter cause to take heart in the struggles with the Evangelical and Reformed Church.

In Wisconsin two men, Rev. K.J. Stuebbe and Rev. Emil Buehrer, in the midst of the conflict with the merged Church, concluded that their only right stand could be on the side of the Gospel, so they too left the united Church. The former of these two had been pastor of the Tripp, South Dakota, charge until 1939, when he moved to Newton, Wisconsin, where, at over 70 years of age, he actively served the causes of the Reformed Church in the U.S.

Other men who took a stand with their charges on the side of the Classis were U. Zogg at Sutton, Nebraska, who died in 1954, and Robert Klaudt at Shafter and Bakersfield, California. Rev. Klaudt later served Hosmer, South Dakota, and Sutton, Nebraska, until his retirement in January 1960.

Thus the Eureka Classis continued her existence as the Reformed Church in the U.S., carrying forward the traditional Calvinistic doctrines and a presbyterial form of church government. Many like-thinking people of the Midwest have seen fit to join and so strengthened the position of the Classis. Important in the life of the Classis, as in every Reformed Church, are the doctrines of the Scriptures, as interpreted by the Heidelberg Catechism. It is significant that this little book was a bone of contention between the merged Church and the Classis, and indeed, the strong adherence of the Westerners to that confession lay back of the position many people took against the union in 1934. The survival of catechetical teaching and preaching has contributed largely to the maintenance of Reformed doctrine and the strong desire of the people to stand solely on the Scriptures.

Though the continuance of the Eureka Classis as the only remaining body of the Reformed Church in the U.S. is an indication of the solidarity of the German people of Reformed heritage and an encouraging sign that Calvinism certainly is far from out-moded, many difficulties have been part of the progress of the Church. Every minister who had attended the Mission House faced two problems. One was, of course, his attachment to that school and the constant contact with her graduates that every institution maintains. Therefore pressure to align with the merger was continual from that source. Secondly, there was the realization that the Mission House had not provided what it should have in theological education or evangelical scholarship. Those men who remained Reformed did so in spite of, not because of, the education they received at Mission House. As the writer's father once said, "About the only good I got out of the Seminary at Mission House was some instruction in Hebrew and Greek and a background in dogmatics." Such conditions could only result in weaknesses in preaching and pastoral work.

There remained the problem of serving the widespread pulpit vacancies all over the Dakotas. With the increase in the number of ministers adhering to the Classis' position, this difficulty was somewhat alleviated. There are, however, some congregations which have no ministers of their own, both by reason of a small supply of men and because some of the vacancies are so small they cannot support a pastor of their own. These have been the "home mission" churches of the Classis. One of them, at Heil, North Dakota, organized in 1914 by the writer's grandfather, John Grossmann, has carried on for over forty years without a pastor.

RECENT HISTORY AND CHARACTER OF THE CLASSIS

CONTINUING PROBLEMS, TRIALS AND WEAKNESSES

History shows that every human organization has weaknesses as well as strengths. The Eureka Classis is no exception, and it may indeed seem to those of a pessimistic bent that this small body has had more than its share of problems and weaknesses. On the other hand, the strength of faith and perseverance on the part of those who have maintained the Reformed Church in the U.S. is unmistakable. Our report of the continuing history of the RCUS will focus on both problems and strengths.

The continuing problems of the Classis which confront us are those of losses in property and congregations, and of theological disputes. Litigation over the properties of several churches and charges consumed the energies of the leaders of the Classis for several years. According to the principles of the laws of the land, the position of the Classis was quite precarious. There was little chance that the continuing Reformed Church in the U.S. could retain title to certain buildings and land because of the peculiar situations which arose. In the courts, the Classis contended that in the cases of congregations divided in membership between merger and anti-merger viewpoints, those segments of the people who continued steadfast in the Reformed faith should be allowed to keep their properties and that those who wished to enter the Evangelical and Reformed Church should be willing to forfeit these holdings and rights. This contention we have seen earlier in the resolutions of the Classis to the Synod of the Northwest and to the General Synod of the Evangelical and Reformed Church. With respect to these property questions, churches standing with the Classis sometimes were able to retain their titles, but in others those titles were lost. In A Digest of Legal Investigations Concerning Union of Denominations, prepared by Rev. E. Buehrer of the Reliance Publishing Company, we find on page 7 a consideration based on the laws of the State of Wisconsin that aided the cause of the Classis.

> Where a majority of a religious society has withdrawn therefrom and organized a new church of a different denomination, the minority, adhering to the original society, are entitled to the use and occupation of the church building held in trust for said society, and the new church and its trustees may be restrained from interfering with such use. . . . Neither seceding members, though a majority, nor any majority of a religious society, no matter how fully invested with all corporate powers, have a right to divest its property from the uses defined and limited by the grant of such property to it or the purposes of its organization as regards the particular faith it was organized to promote. The Opinion stated: "Wherefore, it is the opinion that the courts will enforce the use of the church property to the dissemination of the doctrines devoted by its founders, namely in support of the doctrines of the Reformed Church in the United States."

Thus the property of the Salem-Ebenezer Reformed Church, rural Manitowoc, Wisconsin, was never disputed; it remained with the congregation. However the picture was quite different in South Dakota. Here, for example, the Marion charge was forfeited to the majority of the members who voted to enter the union. Even in the case of the church at Scotland, the property ended up in the hands of the minority that wished to join the merger. The South Dakota Supreme Court ruled that the RCUS was Presbyterian in church government, and therefore that the property was controlled not by the local congregation, but by the higher ruling bodies in the Church. This question was solved by the Classis for future situations by amending the *Constitution of the RCUS* to provide that local property was always to be disposed of by local authority.

The next problem we will discuss is that of providing pastors for the churches. The Classis imported two men from Germany and sought to educate one Classis prospect through parsonage training. In the late forties, W. Grossmann undertook to educate Mr. Hermann Mensch in the principles of Reformed theology. Mensch was a mature man, with a family, some of whom were already students in high school when he decided to enter the ministry. For some two years Rev. Grossmann instructed Mensch three times a week in doctrine, catechetics and the original languages of Scripture. After this, Mensch attended the seminary of the Protestant Reformed Church (PRC) in Michigan, and in due time was ordained to the ministry by the Classis. He was to take charge of two congregations, Leola, South Dakota, in the central part of the state, and Isabel, in the western part of the same, as well as to serve Heil, North Dakota, when able. At first he was well liked, being a vigorous preacher and seemingly sound in teaching. After a short time however, it became evident that he differed with the whole tenor of Reformed teaching and he came to have serious personal difficulties with other pastors in the Classis. At the height of the crisis, Mensch had publicly distinguished between the reprobate members and those in grace in the Leola congregation. The reprobate were certainly condemned to hell from the pulpit, and indeed, had different sermons preached to them than those heard by the saved!

Eventually, Mensch succeeded in so dividing the membership of both the Isabel and Leola Churches that both were in grave danger of imminent disintegration. The Executive Committee of Classis held several meetings with the Leola Congregation and eventually dissolved the pastoral relation and reprimanded Mensch. The Isabel congregation did not consent to the actions of the Executive Committee and was stricken from the roll of Classis. It later joined the PRC. The Leola Congregation was divided, with a smaller part establishing a Protestant Reformed Church in Forbes, North Dakota, and the remaining congregation at Leola continuing in the RCUS to this day. Many years later Mr. Mensch expressed repentance for his actions and requested to be reinstated as a minister of Classis. Forgiveness was granted but he was not able to sustain a theological examination for reinstatement.

Late in the forties there was presented to the Eureka Classis the opportunity of inviting two men from Germany to serve the Church. Rev. Fred Herzog, who with his father the earlier Rev. Fred Herzog had returned to Germany, was one of these men. He was educated in Germany and Switzerland (having lived in Karl Barth's home for a year). Then after the war, with the hard times in occupied Germany causing the Herzogs considerable difficulty, the Classis undertook to assist Herzog and his sister Hannah to migrate to the United States. This was brought about by the generosity of several congregations, and Herzog was installed in the Ashley charge. He soon ran a foul of W. Grossmann who strongly opposed his neo-orthodoxy. The two had protracted correspondence and long discussions, concerning in particular the solitary position of the Eureka Classis and its determination to stay out of the Evangelical and Reformed merger. Herzog held that this was wrong, he said he felt "like a Reformed pillar saint" outside the E & R. He claimed further that the Reformers were in error for leaving the Roman Catholic Church. To summarize the situation, let us quote from a letter by W. Grossmann to Rev. William Korn November 16, 1951. Concerning Herzog he says: "He writes that Calvin initiated an error when he separated himself from the Roman Catholic Church. If I understand his writings correctly, Calvin should have remained in the Roman Catholic Church in order to reform it. Then he writes that Christ did not step out of the Church. He writes further, toward the end of this part of his treatment 'And thus He gives us the great example rather to die than to leave the church. At His death false doctrine was at its peak. And yet He did not secede. His martyrdom in the church was the salvation of the church.' Then in reference to 2 John 9-11, he writes on another occasion: 'Yet as to the problem of reforming the church, I would rather be rebuffed by the Apostle John for receiving a false teacher into my house in order to preach unto him God's judgment than slam the door in the wicked man's face and afterwards in heaven get a medal hung around my neck with the inscription "Defensor Fidei." This pretty much gives the basic tenor of his whole writing, of course one would have to read the whole letter . . . ."

The crux of the discussion soon focused on Herzog's dialectical ideas of Scripture and inspiration. When it became evident to him that he could not reform the stand of the leaders of the Classis, he sought refuge elsewhere. He joined the E & R and eventually became professor of Systematic Theology at the Mission House Seminary. In January of 1960 he accepted a position on the faculty of the Divinity School at Duke University.

Rev. F. Lierhaus was a case similar to Herzog's, and again W. Grossmann had to combat certain leaders in the Classis who favored this man's ministry at Artas, South Dakota. However, matters came to a sad and abrupt conclusion when Lierhaus and another minister visiting from Germany were killed in an auto accident near Rapid City, South Dakota, in 1951.

Another problem of continuing concern was the depopulation of the farming areas of the Dakotas. As a result of the Great Depression and the second World War, thousands of people moved off the land, many of them finding work in the cities. Often Reformed people would become entangled with liberal Lutheranism or Methodism, and even Pentecostalist organizations. For this reason a mission was begun in Aberdeen, South Dakota, by W. Grossmann and D.E. Bosma in 1948. Aberdeen was then the second largest city in the state and many Reformed people lived there without a church of their own. The mission there held worship services in the YMCA building for about five years before organizing in November 1953 and calling a pastor in 1958, the Rev. Calvin Stuebbe. At the same time the Calvin country congregation of the Hosmer charge disbanded and sold their building to the Aberdeen congregation.

Attempts have recently been made to begin a work in cooperation with the Orthodox Presbyterian Church in Pierre, South Dakota, the state capitol. However, there has not to date been enough support for this project and it is now at a standstill. But, the future for that city looks promising.[18]

Speaking of missions brings up the matter of foreign missions which have not been supported until recently by the Eureka Classis. Two things make progress slow: one is the small size of the Classis (some 2500 members) and the other is a de-emphasis on foreign work by some pastors. These say that we have enough trouble supplying our vacant home missions congregations and that it costs too much money to support a foreign work.

We turn briefly to a combination of two related negative aspects of church life in the RCUS in recent years. The first of these is the common tendency to separate life from doctrine. Many in the Church have been instructed in the doctrines of the Catechism but have failed to apply them consistently to their lives. This seems also to have been a result in part of a Neo-Kohlbrueggian influence in the Classis. Complicating this is the second negative tendency which arises when a church continues to preach and teach in a language foreign to the language of daily life. While a simple German is still used in some homes and in greetings on the streets of many German-Russian towns in the Dakotas, English is the language of business, education and social life for most people, especially the younger generations. When these generations are forced to carry on their worship services and religious instruction in another language, religion and life often become separate compartments of existence. As a result, for too many of the people in the Church, religion is too much a "Sunday morning" affair.

POSITIVE ASPECTS

On the credit side of the ledger we find the first and foremost strength in the Eureka Classis to be the strong desire for truly Reformed doctrine and

---

18 An RCUS congregation, Hope Reformed Church, was founded at Pierre in 1963, with Rev. Robert Grossmann as its first pastor.

preaching. Though there are some shortcomings in this desire and the fulfillment thereof, the fact that commitment to the Scriptures and the Heidelberg Catechism have remained at a high level gives great encouragement. In the last analysis, the Bible alone can serve as the reliable ground for faith and life. This is recognized by all concerned, and by God's grace will in the future, as it has in the past, protect the Classis from liberal error and the possibility of becoming enmeshed in the ecumenical octopus of the modern day.

There have also been recent gains in the size of the Classis. Churches in Garner, Iowa, and in Bakersfield and Shafter, California, have become official member congregations of the body. This lends considerable financial support as well as numerical strength. In this way the Reformed witness also is solidified and carried over a wider area. The field in almost all of the State of California is wide open, and it is hoped that there can soon be additional churches there outside the German community (which migrated from the Dakotas before World War I, and also during the Great Depression).

Our investigation of the stand of the Eureka Classis of the Reformed Church in the U.S. has covered two centuries of history. It is necessary that we take into account all that history of the Church in order to properly understand how the present situation came to be. We have tried to show how the Mercersburg Theology and the liturgical controversy of the nineteenth century in the Reformed Church in the U.S. laid foundations for the Evangelical and Reformed merger of 1934. In spite of these influences, the Church in the Midwestern part of the United States was able to maintain relative purity both in doctrine and practice. The steadfastness of this community in the things of the Word and its adherence to the Heidelberg Catechism were at the heart of this consistent position. For this also, may the Lord be praised!

Our God's providential care over his children provided the necessary leaders in crucial years, and by His power alone they were able to persist in the life-and-death struggle against a liberal union of two mediating ecclesiastical bodies.

We have tried to be as honest and candid as possible in our appraisal of the various stands and teachings of the Eureka Classis. The author has profited immeasurably from this study, and it is hoped that it has contributed to a wider understanding of the Classis' stand for the Church of Christ.

We rest on the motto of the Eureka Classis, 2 John 9:

"Whosoever transgresseth, and abideth not in the doctrine of Christ hath not God. He that abideth in the doctrine of Christ, he hath both the Father and the Son."

Peter Grossmann, April 1960

C H A P T E R   F O U R

The History of the RCUS Since the 1934 Merger

Rev. Robert Grossmann

HISTORICAL REVIEW

T he Reformed Church in the United States (RCUS) has a history going back in North America to 1725 when the first three permanent congregations were founded under the leadership of Rev. John Philip Boehm at the villages of Skippack, Whitemarsh and Falkner's Swamp in the Colony of Pennsylvania.[1] The history of the RCUS prior to its establishment in North America goes back to the Reformed Reformation in Switzerland and Germany, when and where the specifically Reformed doctrines of the Protestant Reformation were discovered in the Bible and taught by preachers such as Ulrich Zwingli, Martin Bucer, Henry Bullinger, John Calvin, Zacharias Ursinus and Casper Olevianus. These teachings were also defended to the death by kings such as Frederick the Pious and his grandson Frederick V of the Palatinate, as well as several of the Princes of Brandenburg-Hesse.

German Reformed people who had fled their homes in the Palatinate of Germany, also home of the Heidelberg Catechism, were the people who made up

---

1 For a detailed account of this history see James I. Good, *The History of the Reformed Church in the U.S. 1725-1792*, (Reading, PA: Daniel Miller, 1899), or Robert E. Grossmann, *Outline History of the Reformed Church in the U.S. 1725-1995*, (Garner, Iowa: Elector Publications, 1995).

these early Reformed Churches in North America.[2] These folks fled their homes because of persecution and the devastation wrought on the Palatinate during the Thirty Years War (ended with the Peace of Westphalia in 1648), and the French and Austrian military campaigns that followed.

It is important to understand not only the facts of this early background of the Reformed Church in the United States, but also the profoundly Reformed theological convictions of the earliest members and leaders of this Church. This theological background is especially important today because the element of the Reformed Church in the United States that continued after 1934 is far more representative of the Church's theology in 1725 than it is of the general theology which dominated the Reformed Church in 1934. While it could claim a continuing organizational heritage, the Church which in 1934 merged with the Evangelical Synod of North America to form the Evangelical and Reformed Church (E & R) was doctrinally quite removed from its roots in the 1700s. It has, of course, been the general trend in most church denominations in the United States, that they have left their strictly Bible-based doctrines to include a much broader idea of Christianity as a religion of "love" and social progress. The theological currents which drew the leadership of the RCUS to carry out the E & R merger of 1934 are much more those of the modern liberal ecumenical movement than the strictly Reformed theological convictions that led to the formation of the denomination's first churches in 1725, and which undergirded its first national assembly in 1747. (We use the word "liberal" here and elsewhere below to refer to those who emphasize the human rather than the divine element in Scripture and who therefore do not receive the words of the Bible as the very words of God, inerrant in their writing and infallible in their teaching.)

How it came to be that in 1934 a small group within the Reformed Church in the U.S. held a theology similar to that of the Church in the 1700s while the rest of the denomination around them was quite different is a fascinating story. We do not have space for the whole story, but it is important to have at least a brief outline of it if we are to understand the continuing Reformed Church in the U.S. at the end of the twentieth century. Several elements in this story may be outlined to give us the overall picture. These elements include periodic immigrations, theological importations, and the general secularization of western society in the nineteenth and twentieth centuries.

---

2 These German Reformed Churches began the RCUS, a denomination. Not to be confused with the Reformed Church in America (RCA). This is an entirely different church of Dutch background begun already in 1628 in the Colony of New Amsterdam (later named "New York" when the British drove out the Dutch in 1664).

THEOLOGICAL IMPORTATIONS

Since its beginning as a national denomination in 1747, the "High German Reformed Church," as it was called in those days, faced a formidable task in securing educated and qualified ministers. This particular need for ministers was paramount in the Church's early relationship with the Dutch Synods of North and South Holland and the Classis Amsterdam, as cumbersome as communication across the Atlantic Ocean was in those days. This relationship was one in which the Dutch assemblies searched Europe to provide qualified ministers for their daughter Church in North America, and also provided funds to help pay their salaries. Interestingly, the ministers provided by the Dutch were all German and Swiss, none were themselves Dutch. The positive result of this relationship was that even though a number of early ministers sent by the Dutch did not turn out well and left the service of the Church, the majority of them labored faithfully and strenuously to found a truly Reformed denomination in the New World.

Following the governmental separation of the German Reformed in North America from Dutch oversight, which was accomplished after the Revolutionary War when the German Coetus declared itself a Synod in 1792, the need for ministers continued to increase because of continued German Reformed immigration to the newly founded United States of America. Over the next forty years some seventy-five ministers were trained by older pastors in more or less formal "parsonage-training" programs. The quality of training here of course varied with the quality of the leading teacher, but many of these men also rendered admirable service to the Church. Nevertheless, from 1792 on there was a desire among many in the Church to found their own seminary.

The founding of the Seminary at Carlisle, Pennsylvania, was a traumatic event in the history of the RCUS. A decision to found the Seminary at Fredericksburg, Maryland, was taken by the Synod of 1820 and actually resulted in a split in the Church which lasted until 1836. While meaning well, the Synod in 1820 declared that no more parsonage-training would be allowed. In addition the Synod decided to offer the position of professor to Rev. Philip Milledoler, a Dutch Reformed minister who had been born German Reformed, at the then princely salary of $2000 per year. This, along with the Seminary's proposed location, was unpopular among many ministers. As a result, about one-fourth of the ministers left the old Synod in 1821 to found the "Free Reformed Synod of Pennsylvania." This Synod rejoined the old Synod in 1836.[3]

---

3 The history of the Free Synod is chronicled in H.M.J. Klein, *The History of the Eastern Synod of the Reformed Church in the United States*, Lancaster, PA: Published by the Eastern Synod, 1943), chapter VII.

The Seminary was finally opened at Carlisle, Pennsylvania, in 1824 with the Rev. Lewis Mayer as its first professor. Rev. Mayer turned out to be an effective and solidly Reformed teacher who labored in difficult financial circumstances. However, as the years went by the Synod imported professors from Germany and the New School party in the Presbyterian Church who laid foundations for liberalizing the teachings of the RCUS. In 1838 the Synod engaged Dr. Frederick Rauch to teach in the Seminary and serve as its president. While it is difficult at this distance to determine a great deal about Rauch's theology, especially because of his short time at the Seminary, there were complaints about his use of terminology and concepts common to the rationalistic theologies then spreading across Germany. In God's providence this professor became ill and died in 1842, only four years after beginning his labors.

To replace Rev. Mayer, the Synod sent a committee to Germany to engage the services of the world-renowned Reformed professor Dr. F.W. Krummacher. When Krummacher turned them down because of his age, the Committee took the advice of a number of German theological conservatives and invited the Rev. Philip Schaff to become their new professor. Schaff came to America in 1844 and was soon embroiled in controversy. His very opening speech at his inauguration as professor was entitled, "The Principle of Protestantism," and raised a storm of protest about his sympathy for Roman Catholicism and his use of the "thesis, antithesis and synthesis" historical scheme of the German rationalist philosopher G.W.F. Hegel.

To replace Dr. Rauch, the Synod of the German Reformed Church now engaged the services of Dr. John Williamson Nevin, a Princeton Seminary graduate. Dr. Nevin had been terminated at the Presbyterian college in Allegheny, Pennsylvania, because of his support for New School Presbyterianism during the time the Old School Presbyterians had taken over their General Assembly and had excised nine synods(!) from their denomination. Both Dr. Nevin and Rev. Schaff were brilliant men, and it was not long before they developed a close friendship and working relationship. It turned out that their theological sympathies also moved in the same directions, directions which led them away from historic Reformed orthodoxy toward a semi-sacramentalist view of the Church and salvation. They also introduced a highly liturgical form of worship which had much in common with Episcopal and Roman Catholic practices. Indeed, several of their students eventually left Protestantism for the bosom of the Roman Church.

The Synod of the RCUS now entered a stormy period in which many charges against these new professors were brought, and a magazine war erupted between the old Reformed and the new "Mercersburg" sides of the controversy. The new movement was called "Mercersburg Theology" because during this period the

Seminary had been moved to the city of Mercersburg in central Pennsylvania.[4] This controversy resulted in compromise between the two parties, with the old Reformed party loosing the most ground. The Synod almost annually dealt with complaints against the professors and their teaching, often restating historic Reformed views of certain issues, but always refusing to reprimand or dismiss the professors who kept right on teaching their novelties, many of which simply contradicted Reformed orthodoxy. The result was internal strife which only ended with a compromising peace in which a mediating *Directory of Worship* was published in 1887. In this Directory, Lutheran and Episcopalian views, particularly of baptism and confirmation, and a weakening of the vows of officers to the Scriptures and Heidelberg Catechism are found.[5]

There can be little doubt that the weakening of Reformed commitment and the compromise with sacramentalist theology which now became the norm in the Reformed Church in the U.S. were precursors and preparation for the later entrance of complete theological liberalism and ecumenism into the leadership of the Eastern part of the RCUS. This liberalism and relaxed relationship with Lutheran influences are what made it possible for the RCUS to enter into a merger with the Evangelical Synod of North America, which was basically a Lutheran denomination of German background. Indeed, the later life of Philip Schaff demonstrates his own commitment to liberalism, for he retired from the RCUS Seminary and later became a professor at Union Seminary in New York, the only seminary in American history to be established for the specific purpose of teaching theological liberalism.

By 1900, the strict historic Calvinism of the early fathers of the RCUS had long been left behind and actually held sway only in a few isolated congregations. Most of the conservative element in the Church was content with a more or less biblical evangelicalism rather than a positive Calvinism. The only organized exception to this rule in the RCUS was the Calvinism of its most recent immigrants, the German-Russians of the Dakotas and Nebraska. The book, *A History of Mission-House Lakeland*,[6] contains a most interesting footnote which illuminates this situation. This footnote concerns Rev. D.W. Vriesen, who agreed with these

---

4 The Mercersburg Theology and the battles it aroused are chronicled in James I. Good, *The History of the Reformed Church in the United States in the Nineteenth Century*, (New York: Board of Publications of the Reformed Church in America, 1911), and in *The Mercersburg Theology*, edited by James Hastings Nichols, (New York: Oxford University Press, 1966). A book-length critique of the Mercersburg Theology was written by J.S. Schneck, an early supporter of Philip Schaff, who later changed his mind. This book is entitled, *The Mercersburg Theology Inconsistent With Protestant and Reformed Doctrine*, (Philadelphia: J.B. Lippencott and Company, 1874).

5 Portions of this *Directory of Worship* demonstrating these points are quoted below.

6 Edited by Eugene C. Jaberg and Roland Kley, (Philadelphia: The Christian Education Press, 1962), p. 92.

Calvinist German-Russians. Vriesen was pastor of Ebenezer Reformed Church at Newton, WI, and for many years a professor of preparatory studies for seminary students at the Mission House. The footnote reads, "Vriesen was a Kohlbrueggian; that is, a follower of the extreme Calvinism of the Dutch theologian Herman F. Kohlbruegge (born 1803). The Kohlbrueggians gained some following among the German pastors, particularly in the Dakotas, and at the Northwest Synod of 1906 accused one of the Mission House professors (H.A. Meier) of heresy." This action at the Northwest Synod in 1906 was perhaps a precursor of the refusal of the Eureka Classis of the Dakotas to enter the less than Calvinist Evangelical and Reformed merger of 1934.

PERIODIC IMMIGRATIONS AND THE MAKEUP OF THE RCUS

As noted above, the founders and first generation of Reformed Christians who made up what later came to call itself "The Reformed Church in the United States" were predominantly from the Palatinate of Germany, an area which had moved from being a cradle and stronghold of Reformed teaching to being a devastated land of persecution for believers of this persuasion. This first generation of Reformed people held the common Reformation conviction that the Bible is literally God's word, and that whatever it teaches is true, whether it be the central message of God's creation and salvation, or the number of soldiers in David's army. The idea was that as a result of its inspiration by the Holy Spirit the Bible had to be considered without error in every part even though in putting it down on paper God used the writing styles, theological convictions and historical memories of fallible human beings.

As John Calvin remarked concerning 2 Tim. 3:16, one of the apostle Paul's great statements concerning inspiration, "So, the first point is that we treat Scripture with the same reverence that we do God, because it is from God alone, and unmixed with anything human."[7] Anyone familiar with Calvin will realize that this does not mean that Calvin believed a "mechanical inspiration" as some would charge, but rather that God so used the human writers with all their human characteristics in such a way that they wrote the very words of God. Nor is this a new idea at the time of the Reformation; this very Protestant sounding view of the Bible was sounded one thousand years before Calvin by one of the early bishops of Rome who claimed a special title among the leaders of the Church as "pope." Gregory the Great (died 604 A.D.) held that if we know the true author of each work (book of the Bible) and we understand what He says to us, why should we be curious to learn what pen

---

7 Quoted in *Calvin: Commentaries*, edited by Joseph Haroutunian, (Philadelphia: Westminster Press, 1958) p. 85.

imprinted the divine words on the page.[8]

This Reformed respect for Holy Scripture also meant that the founders of the RCUS were robust Calvinists. John Philip Boehm, Michael Schlatter and the other ministers, as well as all the Elders who attended the first meeting of the coetus in 1747, signed the Heidelberg Catechism and "all the acts of the Synod of Dort of 1618-19" with "heart and soul." One minister, Rev. Bartholomew Rieger, hesitated briefly and then agreed to sign because he was at first "not sure of the article of predestination according to Calvin." This carefulness on the part of Rieger as well as of the other men demonstrates a clear and conscious adherence to the teachings of the Reformed creeds.

What followed in the years after 1800 made the RCUS all too typical of American Protestant churches during their second century of existence. After the Revolutionary war in which her people gave a patriotic account of themselves, the German Reformed severed their earlier (1727-1792) connection with the Dutch ruling bodies in Holland, the Classis of Amsterdam and the North and South Synods of Holland. Following 1800 they were swept up in the great controversies concerning modern "excitement" methods of evangelism and the desire to fit in well with the broadening American Christian community. The evangelism practiced by Charles Finney and others preached an anti-church, anti-doctrine Gospel which generally produced a negative attitude toward an educated and teaching-centered ministry. It often destroyed local churches in the name of "evangelism," so much so that the four great American cults grew up in New England in the areas of this kind of preaching.[9] Thus the Reformed Church, like many others, began to lose some of its earlier commitment to specifically Reformed principles and practices.

About this time, which was also when the "German Reformed Church in the United States" was beginning its first seminary (1824), there came a second great immigration of Germans to North America. The Palatinate Germans had settled along the Eastern seaboard of North America, some in New York, Virginia and the Carolinas, but most in Pennsylvania. By 1830 the borders of the "free land" which could be homesteaded had moved west to Illinois, Wisconsin and Missouri. These new Germans homesteaded land in these western states. Homesteading was a method by which land could be removed from government ownership into private hands by any able-bodied family head who would occupy it for five years and improve it through farming. This was an enlightened program if ever a government had one, and quite the opposite of modern schemes to place more and more land under government control. The Homestead Act had a large part in providing the

---

8 Quoted in *Scripture and Truth*, edited by D.A. Carson and John Woodbridge, (Grand Rapids: Zondervan 1983) p 205.

9 These cults are: Mormonism, Seventh Day Adventism, the Jehovah's Witnesses and Christian Science.

opportunity for individuals upon which the prosperity of America grew over the last 150 years.

These new immigrants came from all over Germany as a result of over population, and as the result of a new movement for consolidating and confusing the Protestant churches in the various parts of that European country. In 1817 William, King of Prussia, had ordered the Reformed and Lutheran Churches to combine under one administration, a move which caused great distress among people in both communions who wished to maintain their doctrinal distinctives. Ruling princes in other provinces of Germany soon followed William's lead, and the result was a new flow of doctrinally conservative Lutheran and Reformed people to the United States, the home of religious liberty. The large German populations of St. Louis, Missouri, and Milwaukee, Wisconsin, are the direct results of this emigration which lasted some thirty years.

Among these many new German Americans were not only the ancestral founders of the American beer brewing industry, but also many people of Reformed persuasion who soon joined the German Reformed Church in the United States. Many of them also fought on the side of the Union in the Civil War. These new RCUS people had not participated in the theological and social currents that had already affected their new denomination and they tended to be old-fashioned conservative Reformed, though generally not as specifically Calvinistic as the Church's founders had been 100 years earlier. These new Reformed Germans in America were quite devoted to the Heidelberg Catechism and continued the tradition of complete trust in the Bible as the written word of God. Because of theological developments in the Eastern section of the Church, and because of the great distances involved, these Wisconsin and Missouri German Reformed were soon founding their own college and a seminary at Plymouth, Wisconsin. The college was founded in 1860 and was called "The Mission House." Today it continues as Lakeland College of the United Church of Christ while the seminary has been merged into a UCC institution.

As the Eastern portion of the RCUS moved in a less doctrinal, more ecumenical and more secular theological direction (not without resistance from many), the new immigrants on the Western frontier held more to the old faith. Fifty years later, and even as the newer and less specifically Reformed ideas moved west, there came a third and final great immigration of Reformed Germans, this time from the country of Russia. The total of German immigrants to North America over the whole period from 1650 to 1950 has been over 50 million. Many of these, especially those coming after World War II, were far less committed to a particular theological position than were the earlier immigrants. This was not true of the "German-Russians." These immigrants were descendants of Germans who had moved to Russia beginning in 1760 at the invitation of the Czarina Catherine the Great, who was herself a German princess before marrying the Czar. The German-Russians were staunch members of the doctrinal traditions of their home churches in Germany, whether they were Roman Catholic, Lutheran, Reformed, Congregational or Mennonite. This was because they been insulated from the so-called "Enlightenment" philosophy, having spent the nineteenth century in Russia, which was even then an insular country. Thus they had escaped the replacement of the Christian faith with rational philosophy, something that had happened among the churches in their homeland.

Thus there arrived in the United States just at the end of the nineteenth century a whole new group of Christians who found their way into the Reformed Church in the United States because of their common European heritage. It was not long however, before these new immigrants realized that they were old Reformed believers in a church denomination that was far down the road to liberalism and ecumenism. They began considering various alternatives by which they could maintain their traditional Calvinism and appreciation for the teachings of Herman F. Kohlbruegge.

Kohlbruegge was an old-fashioned Calvinist who also had a few interesting twists in his understanding of the Bible's teaching. His main concern was to enforce the teaching of total depravity and he therefore denied that even Christians are anything but totally depraved in all respects. While this teaching did not lead him to antinominianism, he was careful to maintain that "the Ten Commandments are not abrogated but are given to us to teach us how to think and act,"[10] some of his followers developed a Neo-Kohlbrueggianism which did move in that direction. Nevertheless these German-Russian immigrants were the only real Calvinists of any consequence left in the RCUS, and they numbered only one percent of the congregations and less than one percent of the members of the denomination.

After some searching, the conservative Calvinist pastors of the Dakotas discovered a provision in the Constitution of the RCUS by which they might be able to establish a specific language classis. In 1910 they presented a petition to the Northwest Synod of the RCUS to constitute them as a separate classis to exist on the same geographical area as the North and South Dakota Classes but to be a specifically German-speaking Classis. This petition was granted and when the Classis met for the first time in June of 1911 at Scotland, SD, they immediately chose the name "Eureka Classis" for their new body to reflect the meaning that they had "found it," that is, they had found a way to maintain their conservative theology in a liberal denomination. The Greek word *eureka* means, "I have found."

---

10   Herman F. Kohlbruegge, *Erlaeuternde und befestigende Fragen und Anworten zu dem Heidelberger Katechismus*, (Elberveld, Germany: Verlag der niederland-reformierte Gemeine, 1894), p 181.

In this way there developed within the Reformed Church in the United States in the early part of the twentieth century, a ruling assembly over a group of churches which had far more in common with the teachings held by the earliest founders of the denomination than they had with the current leadership. Indeed, it can be said that the leadership and much of the RCUS was out of touch with the theology upon which the Church was founded, just as the Eureka Classis was out of touch with the theology and aspirations of the great majority of the Church around them. The interesting thing is that without being very much aware of it, the theology of the Eureka Classis, except for a few specific tenets of Kohlbrueggianism, was quite in harmony with that of John Philip Boehm and Michael Schlatter who had in 1747 founded the first Coetus of the German Reformed Church in North America. In the amazing providence of God this small group of committed Calvinists was destined to continue the name and testimony of the Reformed Church in the United States long after the vast majority of the RCUS had ceased to exist by merging itself into the Evangelical and Reformed Church, which itself later merged with congregational churches to form the United Church of Christ.

Along with the Eureka Classis there were a number of individual congregations around the United States that were quite conservative and also a number of pastors who held Kohlbrueggian viewpoints. These congregations were scattered from Wisconsin to California but all consisted of people and pastors who were part of the later two immigrations of German Reformed people to the United States. Even though some of the congregations and pastors in the East were quite conservative in their view of Scripture, none of the churches in the older part of the RCUS were as strictly Calvinistic as were the Eureka Classis and the congregations that held to a Kohlbrueggian theology. All of this led to a continuing Reformed Church in the United States that is quite different from where the majority of the Church stood just before the merger of 1934. By 1925 the Eureka Classis consisted of twenty-nine congregations, all in North and South Dakota.

ANTECEDENTS OF THE EVANGELICAL AND REFORMED MERGER

Ecumenical interests had long been a part of RCUS thought and life. Not only had the Church begun under the auspices of the Dutch Reformed in Holland, but throughout the nineteenth century strong ecumenical relations were conducted with the Dutch Reformed Church in America, which today is known as the "Reformed Church in America." Notwithstanding the fact that the early leaders of the RCUS, in particular John Philip Boehm, had resisted an early attempt by the Dutch to merge them with the Presbyterians and had successfully fought off an attempt by the Moravian leader Count Nicholas Ludwig von Zinzendorf to gather all German churches in America into one organization regardless of their creeds, the

German Reformed always maintained cordial relations with their neighbors who held to similar doctrines. The German and Dutch Reformed had exchanged synodical delegates as early as 1809 and had held triennial meetings from 1816 until the Dutch cut off all ties in 1858 as a reaction to the influence of the quite unreformed Mercersburg Theology mentioned above.

As the leadership of the RCUS became more and more liberal toward the end of the nineteenth century, it also became more and more interested in the modern ecumenical movement. This movement believes that the church must act as a political force in society and that it can only do this if it gathers as many people and churches as possible into large super-denominations. This belief in the "clout" of large interest groups is founded on the liberal "social Gospel" which had replaced the old salvation-gospel in most large Protestant churches in the United States by 1900. The social Gospel teaches that this world is far more important than whatever other worlds may or may not actually exist, and that therefore the church, as well as government and all other institutions, ought to be dedicated to the betterment of man in this life. In this view the "betterment of man" is focused on economic equality and license to live a man-centered life without regard to God's commandments. Because of their common interest in these ideas, the leaders of the RCUS were deeply involved in the formation of all of the modern liberal ecumenical organizations.

The RCUS was a charter member of the Federal Council of Churches founded in 1908, which in 1950 became the National Council of Churches. Dr. George W. Richards, for many years the president of Lancaster Seminary, played an important part in the founding of the World Council of Churches at Amsterdam in 1948. The first World War created a crisis for America, but once it was past, especially the modernist churches looked forward to moving their "Christian" vision (which by now in the RCUS included some distinctively socialist ideas among some leaders) across the world.

We should not be surprised that the social Gospel produced these kinds of results in North America; after all the liberal social Gospel produced in Karl Marx the foundations of Communism[11] and in Adolph Hitler the foundations of Nazi

---

11 Marx was a German, educated in the theologically liberal universities of the early nineteenth century there. He studied under the radically rationalist theologian Bruno Baur for a time. Baur called the Gospels "forgeries." Marx was also Hegelian in his thinking for a time and one can see this influence in all of his writing about history (as one can see with no less a Reformed writer than Philip Schaff!). Marx also built his atheism on Ludwig Feuerbach's idea that religion is what is holding people under submission to authorities, and thus keeping them from true "progress."

Socialism for Germany.[12] Therefore it should not be surprising that the modern liberal and ecumenical churches in the United States have been in the forefront of supporting Communist movements all over the third world. It needs to be understood in this connection that people who believe the social Gospel also believe that they know better what is good for people than the people themselves ever could. Besides which, socialism as a system that confiscates the product of one person's labor and gives it to another is by this very action always dictatorial. From a conservative biblical point of view, all of this amounts to nothing more than a violation of the Eighth Commandment and of the personal stewardship of earthly goods required by it.

The Synod of the RCUS formed a "Forward Movement" in 1919 to advance the Church on all fronts of endeavor, and in particular to forward the social Gospel agenda. The Interchurch World Movement, of which the RCUS was a participant, sought to "overcome the overlooking and overlapping" that existed in American Protestantism. A reawakened interest in Mercersburg liturgy also prepared the church for eventual merger with a Lutheran body, even though that was not particularly in view in 1900. It should be understood that a large segment of the RCUS, including its official historians, always had viewed the Mercersburg movement in a positive light.[13] There were, as mentioned above, strong reactions against Mercersburg during its rise but by 1900 the only objections were found in the books of James I. Good. Good had discovered in Holland the original records of the coetus and had become a defender of the old Reformed faith as being the genius of the RCUS, even though he himself was not strongly predestinarian.[14] Good's book, *The History of the Reformed Church in the United States in the Nineteenth Century*, in which there is a detailed criticism of Mercersburg Theology, was published not by the RCUS, but by the Board of Publications of the Reformed Church in America, a Church of Dutch heritage.

By 1930, three years before the Reformed Church in the U.S. merged with the Evangelical Synod of North America, the Reformed Church consisted of 1685 congregations in 58 classes which all told included 348,189 members. The

---

12 Hitler's system was also socialistic, NAZI stands for National Socialist Party. The idea that Hitler was "right-wing" is the figment of American newspeak. Hitler much admired the German philosopher Nietzsche who was the son of a Lutheran minister and a part of the liberal and rationalist German educational establishment.

13 Joseph Dubbs concludes, "We have no hesitation in affirming that the period of 'the Mercersburg movement' was not a time of retrogression but of genuine advancement." *Historic Manual of the Reformed Church*. Published by the General Synod of the RCUS in 1885.

14 This writer has in his possession an original letter from Professor Good to a Rev. Kieffer in which Good claims that he is of "the school of Saumar" (usually called Amyraldianism, and which holds to a hypothetical universal atonement) and that he does "not believe in any limited atonement."

denomination supported at least eight colleges and three seminaries, as well as numerous orphanages, hospitals and homes for the infirm elderly. She had been carrying on her own foreign mission work since 1866, especially in the near East (modern day Iraq), Japan and China.

THE EVANGELICAL AND REFORMED MERGER OF 1934

THE PLAN OF UNION

By the early 1920s, voices were heard throughout the eastern wing of the RCUS calling for union with any one of a variety of Protestant bodies, from Presbyterian to United Brethren to Reformed Church in America. By 1926 the General Synod had established a Commission on Closer Union which was in communication with several groups, particularly the United Brethren (the old Moravians) and the Evangelical Church (the product of a 1922 merger of Evangelical [Lutheran] churches). In 1928 the Commission on Closer Union prepared a Plan of Union for the uniting of the RCUS with the United Brethren. While this was passed by the General Synod of the RCUS in 1929, it was not received enthusiastically by the classes. Furthermore, it was not approved by the synod of the United Brethren.

Negotiations were reopened with the Evangelical Synod of North America in February 1932 (it almost seems the men were determined to merge with somebody) and by the time of their respective general synods, a new Plan of Union was ready for consideration. By this time the negotiators had realized that denominational differences could not easily or quickly be overcome by direct negotiation and the conclusion was taken that such differences were simply to be ignored. Carl Schneider says, "Without defining or establishing a consensus of beliefs or the extent of agreement or disagreement, a unity in spirit was affirmed as a sufficient basis for the steps now to be ventured. The Plan of Union thus lost the aspects of a contractual merger and was thrown into area of faith." The Plan of Union simply swept differences in doctrine and practice under the rug (here euphemistically called "the area of faith"), at least until after union could be accomplished.

In 1932, the General Synod of the RCUS approved this Plan of Union with the Evangelical Synod of North America. Then in 1933, the Evangelical Synod of North America approved as well, and by that time the necessary majority of the 58 Classes of the RCUS had approved. The union forming the Evangelical and Reformed Church was consummated in a meeting at Cleveland, Ohio, on the night of June 26, 1934.

The Eureka Classis and the Merger of 1934

The ministers and elders of the Eureka Classis were of course aware of the general tenor of theology and life in the broader RCUS and their own differences with this direction. A brief selection of decisions of the Eureka Classis at its 1924 meeting will make this evident. The Classis met at Zeeland, North Dakota, on the evening of May 14, and it is probably significant that the opening sermon by the President, Rev. John Grossmann, was based on 2 Pet. 1:19, where the written word of God is heralded as a "light shining in a dark place." The Classis in 1924 was in receipt of a variety notices from the Synod of the Northwest and from the General Synod of the RCUS which included matters from a list of excused and unexcused absences from Synod's previous meeting to a request from the Council of Churches in Christ in America encouraging support for the entrance of the United States into a World Court Tribunal. On the latter matter, the Classis reported succinctly, "As Classis we are opposed to United States membership in a World Court Tribunal."

Concerning a request for financial help for needy persons and diaconal institutions in Germany, Classis decided to adopt this notice and encourage its congregations not to become weary in loving our neighbors. Concerning the celebration of the 200th anniversary in 1925 of the founding of the Reformed Church in the U.S., Classis decided to adopt this point and instruct its officers to include this celebration in its program for worship services during the 1925 session of Classis and that this be included in the schedule for the congregations in 1925.

Concerning an admonition that Classis was behind in its support of denominational causes, Classis wrote, "The Eureka Classis, as it has in the past, will support denominational causes through freewill collections." Concerning questions about the constitutionality of certain of its actions, Classis replied, "We do not accept the answer of the Synod through its Justice-committee because their explanation is in conflict with the spirit and thought of Articles 20 and 94 of the Church Order. Concerning General Synod's request for the introduction (into Classis) and strong support for the "Church Forward Movement," Classis replied, "That on the basis of grounds given earlier, the Eureka Classis cannot participate in the Forward Movement. Synod has not refuted these grounds by pointing out that other synods and classes, within and without the Church, have joined the Forward Movement. The Eureka Classis will only be convinced by the Scriptures." On a number of matters ranging from requested votes on constitutional amendments to further disagreements with Synod and General Synod, Classis simply "took note." Classis referred reports about the discarding of German language teaching, of the teaching of evolution and of the accreditation of the Mission House to its Committee on Education. Finally, the Classis made provision for the public printing of a report by Rev. Ulrich Zogg about the influence of liberalism in the RCUS, especially through a Dr. Truxal, who was a member of the denominational Board of Trustees. It also adopted a series of resolutions seeking to defend their churches from this influence. The resolutions had previously been adopted by the South Dakota Classis and along with Rev. Zogg's report had been sent as official business to the Eureka Classis.

From this brief digest of classical business, it becomes clear that the Evangelical and Reformed merger of 1934 came as no surprise to our fathers, nor was their rejection of this merger to be unexpected, based on their earlier decisions and attitudes. It would be surprising if no one in the rest of the denomination had joined many in the Eureka Classis in breathing a sigh of relief when this "thorn in the side" finally did separate itself from the rest of the Church after 1934.

Prior to 1933 the Eureka Classis had voted, along with three others, to express opposition to any proposed merger with churches of non-reformed character. Many local congregations across the United States. also viewed the merger with dismay, but there was no way to stop approval of a measure that was planned by eastern leaders and approved by the vast majority of educators, institutional board members and synodical leaders throughout the denomination. The Eureka Classis itself consisted of little more than 1% of the churches of the RCUS and about one-half of one percent of the members.

POST-MERGER STRUGGLES TO MAINTAIN THE RCUS

The Eureka Classis rejected the merger and voted in 1938 that it could in no wise participate but would firmly continue as the Reformed Church in the United States. The Rev. William J. Krieger, a leader in the battle to continue as Reformed, and a charter member of the Eureka Classis, was from 1932 pastor at Eureka, South Dakota, and continued there until his retirement in 1943. He served as president of Classis from 1936 to 1943. Rev. Krieger was a "German Presbyterian," having graduated from Princeton Seminary. He was also the son-in-law of Rev. Jacob Stark, a leading Kohlbrueggian theologian and founding editor of the very conservative church paper, *Der Waechter*. In his retirement, Rev. Krieger lived with family in Lodi, California, but he continued to have influence in the Eureka Classis, which now continued and had incorporated itself as the Reformed Church in the United States. Rev. Krieger died in 1948, and was buried at Eureka, South Dakota.

In 1934, Rev. Krieger was joined in the battle to maintain the Reformed Church by newly ordained Rev. Walter Grossmann, whose father John Grossmann had been a pastor in the RCUS from 1910 to his death in 1929, and had served in the Eureka Classis from 1922-1924. Rev. Walter Grossmann graduated from Mission House Seminary in 1932, but was unable to find a field of service because of poor recommendations from faculty members who were put off by his outspoken conservatism. Rev. Grossmann served the three congregations of the Hosmer charge until 1952, and served as Stated Clerk of the Eureka Classis from 1935 until his death in 1956.

Upon these two men, the experienced theologian and the novice pastor, fell much of the burden of maintaining the ministry of the Gospel among the numerous churches of the Eureka Classis as well as leading the classical organization. This was because only a few pastors continued to serve the Classis churches, including retired men who preached on a part-time basis. In 1944 Classis listed four ministers, one retired, to serve twenty churches with 1380 members. Rev. D.E. Bosma was at Eureka, having replaced Rev. Krieger who was in retirement, Rev. W. Grossmann served the Hosmer Charge and Rev. Erwin Pfeiffer was missionary-at-large residing at Herried, South Dakota. The three active pastors lived within forty-five miles of each other, but the churches of Classis were spread over an area 400 miles North to south and 200 miles east to west.

During the late 1930s and the second World War years, churches at Highmore, Alpena, Isabel, Trail City, Herried, Artas, Greenway, and Leola, South Dakota, and at Heil, Ashley, Venturia, Lincoln Valley, and Upham, North Dakota, were maintained by faithful elders who read sermons for morning worship. These churches were often served at evening services led by a pastor who had driven forty to 200 miles on Sunday afternoon to be present.

At the 1936 session of Eureka Classis, the North Dakota Classis dissolved, and its pastors and churches joined the Eureka Classis (some later left — the Zeeland, North Dakota congregation, for example, joined the E & R and then returned to the RCUS from the UCC in 1971). Unfortunately several of the pastors from the North Dakota Classis later joined the E & R (some to maintain interest in the Church's retirement fund) and two of them, Rev. Thiele and Rev. Herzog, returned to Germany at the misleading invitation of the NAZI government. At its 1938 and 1939 meetings the Classis dealt with the question of the merger most carefully, and decided that it could in not participate in any way, but that it must continue as the RCUS.

At its meeting in 1945, the Eureka Classis voted to incorporate in the state of North Dakota as the Reformed Church in the United States. Since the merged church was not concerned to keep this name, this action of the Classis was not challenged in the ecclesiastical or civil courts. Meanwhile the Synod of the Northwest continued to report the 1935 statistics of the Eureka Classis churches as part of its statistics up through the second World War.

DISPOSITION OF CHURCHES AFTER 1934

Not surprisingly, since there was not a unified conservative movement in the RCUS before the 1934 merger, a number of churches slowly died off or made their way out of the E & R. St. Matthew's Reformed Church in Philadelphia simply died off after its pastor, Rev. Silvius, who served them 50 years, retired, and a suitable replacement could not be found. A number of congregations joined the Reformed Church in America and as late as 1960 a congregation in downtown Manhattan, New York, joined with the Moravian Brethren.

Several other congregations with previous ties to the Eureka Classis became more or less independent and eventually joined the Eureka Classis during the 1940s and 1950s. Among these (dates of joining in parentheses) were Newton (Manitowoc), Wisconsin (1958), Garner, Iowa (1959), Menno, South Dakota (1945), Hope Church of Sutton, Nebraska (1945), Shafter, California (1960) and Bakersfield, California (1960).

Salem-Ebenezer at rural Manitowoc, Wisconsin, had been the church served by Rev. D.W. Vriesen, the outspoken conservative and Kohlbrueggian Calvinist who had taught at the Mission House from 1875 to 1888. Rev. Vriesen thus formed a strong connection to the conservative movement among the Reformed pastors in the Dakotas. Rev. Vriesen's later successor, the Rev. K.J. Stuebbe was in contact with the Eureka Classis and along with Rev. Emil Buehrer of Green Bay, Wisconsin, often visited Classis meetings during its years of struggle.

Peace Reformed Church at Garner, Iowa, also had an early pastoral connection with the Eureka Classis through a retired minister, the Rev. William Wittenburg living there. Wittenberg had been a charter member of the Classis when it was formed in 1911. Also the Rev. Robert Stuebbe, second son of Rev. K.J. Stuebbe, was ordained by the Eureka Classis upon his graduation from Mission House in 1944 and served both Peace Reformed in rural Garner, which stayed out of the merger, and Zion Reformed in Garner, which had joined the merger.

Zion Reformed Church in rural Menno, South Dakota, was made up of German-Russian people, many of whom had relatives among Eureka Classis Churches at Eureka and Alpena, South Dakota, and at Upham and Lincoln Valley, North Dakota. Zion Church at Menno had also been a congregation of the South Dakota Classis, among whose pastors and churches there was also a strong reaction against the liberalism and ecumenism which gripped the RCUS during the early part of the twentieth century. Zion's pastor, the Rev. William E. Korn had immigrated to the United States from Germany through Canada, and was a close friend of the Eureka Classis leaders. In 1965 Zion Reformed Church moved to a new building in the town of Menno where there already existed the Menno United Church of Christ, a Reformed congregation that had joined the merger in 1934. To complicate matters further, a portion of Zion UCC in Menno left that congregation and the UCC in 1978 to found a new congregation, Peace Christian Reformed Church, which is a member of the Christian Reformed Church in North America.

Hope Reformed Church of Sutton, Nebraska, was being served by Rev. Ulrich Zogg at the time it joined the Eureka Classis in 1945. Rev. Zogg was a conservative Kohlbrueggian pastor who was well acquainted with the ministers of the Eureka Classis. The people of this congregation were also German-Russians who had maintained their conservative Reformed heritage after coming to the United States.

The Reformed Churches at Shafter and Bakersfield, California, were also made up of German-Russian people, most of whom had migrated to California from Menno, South Dakota, and its surrounding area during the Teens and Twenties of the twentieth century. By 1960 when these congregations joined the Eureka Classis, they had been served by Eureka Classis ministers for a number of years; Shafter by Rev. Walter Grossmann from 1952 to 1956, and Bakersfield by Rev. Robert Stuebbe from 1951.

There was a fairly large and widespread group of conservative Reformed churches within the E & R at first, but liberal seminary education soon infected all but a very few of them with the progressive spirit. Of these conservative E & R churches, some died off and a few finally left after the UCC merger of 1957. Included among those that left the UCC and joined the continuing RCUS (dates of joining in parentheses) were Zeeland, North Dakota (1971), Emmanuel at Sutton, Nebraska (1969), Peace at Napoleon, Ohio (new church organized out of UCC 1972), and St. Paul's at Hamburg, Minnesota (1992). Included among the more conservative elements in the E & R must be the Magyar (Hungarian) Synod, which refrained from joining the 1957 UCC merger and continues as the E & R. Its position, however, is to the left of the continuing RCUS.

THE E & R MERGES INTO THE UCC

The congregations of the RCUS that were in the E & R after 1934 again had an identity change in 1957. In that year the Evangelical and Reformed Church merged with the Congregational Christian Churches and a few other smaller congregational denominations to form the United Church of Christ.

As early as 1941, committees of the E & R recommended talks with other churches which might lead toward union with them. These talks led to a merger proposal with the Congregational Christian Churches and by 1944 had produced a procedure for merger. By 1947, a final text of a "Basis for Union" had been proposed to the ruling bodies of the Denominations involved and approved by them. However, a "small" group within the Congregational Christian Churches forced the adoption of a series of "Interpretations" of this plan to be passed at the General Conference of 1948. These were in turn approved by the General Synod of the E &

R in 1949 and then by 33 of its 34 synods.

The uniting General Synod was to be held June 26, 1950 but a court challenge by a Congregational Church to the authority of the General Council of that body to conclude a merger held up the action for four years. Then, after court approval in 1953, more negotiations ensued, finally culminating in a Uniting General Synod at Cleveland, Ohio, June 25-27, 1957. The second General Synod of the UCC in 1960 adopted a new Statement of Faith, which was added to earlier confessions. Two Hungarian Reformed Synods had existed within the old RCUS and in the E & R but now came to different conclusions. As noted above, the Magyar Synod refrained from joining the UCC merger and continued as the only synod of the Evangelical and Reformed Church. The Calvin Synod, also Hungarian, joined with the UCC merger but continues today as a relatively conservative group within that denomination. The Calvin Synod has in recent years been noted for its resistance to the approval of various liberal agenda items in the UCC, such as the ordination of homosexuals, and has helped various non-Hungarian groups to remain conservative while remaining in the UCC.

THE CONTINUING R.C.U.S.

THE SECOND WORLD WAR YEARS

The next great struggle for the continuing existence of the RCUS came with the United States' entrance into second World War. While RCUS young men went off to fight the second World War with the rest of the American youth, the Eureka Classis fought to maintain its existence. The need for pastors was acute for many years, yet no young men were found to enter seminary. Eureka Classis churches were a far-flung domain covering North and South Dakota, with one congregation in Nebraska joining in 1945. As noted above, in 1944 there were as few as three active pastors in Classis to serve twenty churches whose charges were flung across 8,000 square miles of the old Dakota Territory. Not only were pastors circuit riders in their home charges, they spent most Sunday afternoons driving hundreds of miles to serve vacant congregations, often across gravel roads which were death on the low-quality war tires. Carrying two spare tires became standard operating procedure. Rev. Krieger and later Rev. Bosma served two congregations in the Eureka Charge, Rev. W. Grossmann served three congregations at Hosmer and Rev. Pfeiffer had five congregations in the Odessa Charge, centered at Artas, South Dakota. Nor were these small charges. The Eureka Charge reported 282 communicant members in 1944, while Hosmer Charge reported 325 in the same year.

The lack of pastors during these years can also be laid to the other facts besides the world war. Many of the conservative pastors were older men by 1940. Some stayed in the E & R to receive the pensions they had paid for, others simply had to retire, as G. Zenk, W. Krieger. After the end of the war, a few men from Classis churches went to Mission House Seminary which was now in the E & R, but they left the Classis and joined the E & R These included Melvin Vilhauer of Hosmer and Howard Kusler of Eureka.

Later, a couple of men were imported from Germany, Rev. Frederick Herzog (son of the Pastor F. Herzog who had returned to Germany in the thirties) and Rev. Frederick Lierhaus. Rev. Lierhaus served the Odessa Charge at Artas and Herried, South Dakota, and Rev. Herzog served the Ashley Charge at Ashley and Venturia, North Dakota. Both of these men turned out to be less than conservative Reformed. Herzog left for graduate studies and greener pastures in the E & R and Rev. Lierhaus was killed in a tragic automobile accident in 1954.

Rev. Herman Mensch was parsonage trained and then attended the Protestant Reformed Seminary. He came out to split one church and take another into the Protestant Reformed Church. He was deposed, and later asked forgiveness, which was granted. Eventually he requested to be examined for re-instatement but was unable to sustain the exam.

Finally in about 1952 the Classis men decided to try Westminster Theological Seminary in Philadelphia. Lloyd Gross began attendance there in 1955, and 1955 graduate Norman Hoeflinger was recruited for our ministry. This began a relationship with Westminster Seminary which became the only approved seminary of the RCUS for the next twenty years. We will have opportunity to speak more about Westminster below.

ECCLESIASTICAL SURVIVAL DURING AND AFTER SECOND WORLD WAR

In the providence of God, the Evangelical and Reformed Church never questioned the right of the Eureka Classis to the name "Reformed Church in the U.S.," although they did attempt to regain some local church property (see below). Eureka Classis churches were continued on the roll by the E & R throughout the second World War by simply listing the statistics from their last reports, some as old as 1933. In 1945, the Classis took the important step of incorporating under the laws of North Dakota as the Reformed Church in the United States and after that had a protected legal claim to their continuance as the RCUS.

In 1945, the *Reformiertes Gemeindeblatt* (literally "Reformed Congregation-sheet," now the *Reformed Herald*) was begun with the Rev. William Korn as editor. This publication explained the position of the Eureka Classis as the continuing RCUS, and began to weave a web of information and interrelatedness among the churches. Over the years the editorship of this important publication in the life of the RCUS has passed from Rev. Korn to Rev. Norman Hoeflinger, Rev.

Melvin Nonhof, Rev. Norman Jones, Rev. Steven Demers, Rev. Peter Grossmann and Rev. David Dawn. Each editor has made a large contribution to the life of the Church and each has strengthened one or another aspect of its unity as a continuing denomination of Christians.

In 1950 a Eureka Classis edition of the Heidelberg Catechism was printed in German and English (it could be had in either or both languages). This edition sought to return to the earliest text of the Catechism in German (though it did correct the very colloquial German of the 1563 editions) and to provide a most careful and direct translation of the same into English. The Catechism in use among RCUS churches since 1863 had been the Tercentenary edition edited by Philip Schaff. Interestingly, while all original Eureka Classis churches switched to the new edition, several congregations which were now in membership but had not been part of the original Classis resolutely clung to the Tercentenary edition.[15]

This new edition of the venerable Heidelberg was financed by a Mr. William Krueger of Baxter, Iowa, and like other RCUS materials, was published by Reliance Printing at Green Bay, Wisconsin, Rev. Emil Buehrer (1889-1972) proprietor. Rev. Buehrer had been pastor of the Reformed Church at Green Bay, from 1918 until he was forced to retire in 1938 by the E & R authorities because of his continuing objections to the merger of 1934. He joined the Eureka Classis in 1946 and his company became the unofficial printing house of the continuing RCUS. Rev. Buehrer and Reliance printing were most generous with the RCUS, providing books and other printed materials at very little profit, depending upon other printing work for their livelihood, including for many years the printing of the programs for the Green Bay Packer football organization.

SOCIAL AND NATIONAL EFFECTS ON THE RCUS

The continuing history of the United States, especially the second World War, provided other influences and concerns for the RCUS. German Americans had integrated into the life of citizenry in the United States with little problem even early on. Immigrants from the 1840s already served in the Union army during the Civil War. This was true of German immigrants and their descendants during the First World War, even though in some communities there was hearty distrust and hate for Germans during that war. In fact, certain states attempted to outlaw the use of the German language during the First World War (Iowa was one), and names of places were sometimes changed. For example the name German Township in Hancock County, Iowa, was changed to Liberty Township during this war.

Little of such rancor seems to have occurred for German-Americans during

---

15 J. I. Good complains of some slanted translation in the Tercentenary. Good, *History of the Reformed Church in the United States in the Nineteenth Century*, p. 405.

second World War. Germans in South and North Dakota continued to hold worship services in German without molestation. Thousands of young men of German descent participated in the Second World War on the American side, including hundreds from the Eureka Classis. Many of these young men were quite fluent in German and thus found use as interpreters. Others found their facility in German a curse as they not only heard, but also understood, the dying cries and curses of the enemy soldiers. Yet the patriotic pride in years, wounds and lives given to the American cause runs extremely high in the German-Russian communities comprising most RCUS locales.

Nevertheless, there were RCUS folk who found their loyalties split. As mentioned above, two pastors returned to Germany at the call of the government there for godly men to help build a new Germany. While most remaining RCUS ministers were completely opposed to the German cause, Rev. D.E. Bosma, who took the Eureka charge in 1943, often praised the Third Reich, also in print in *The Witness*, a theological paper published by the conservative Reformed Kohlbrueggians through their Reformed Publication Society.

As mentioned above, the war almost totally cut off the supply of men entering seminary and candidating for the ministry. During second World War, the Eureka Classis ordained but one man, Rev. Robert Stuebbe, who was then a member of Classis, but was serving the Garner congregation which did not join Classis until 1959.

During the war another American phenomenon began to affect the RCUS. As a result of the great depression, thousands of farm families and young people began moving to the cities. This began depopulation of the rural areas, particularly in the Dakotas, but it also opened possibilities for beginning congregations in the larger cities. In 1948, the Revs. W. Grossmann and D.E. Bosma began evening services in Aberdeen, South Dakota, which resulted in the establishment of a congregation there. This work progressed quite slowly and Aberdeen was not organized as a congregation until 1953. Aberdeen was without a pastor until 1958 when the Rev. Calvin Stuebbe, eldest son of Rev. K.J. Stuebbe, began serving it and the Leola, South Dakota, church some forty miles distant.

During the winter of 1945-46, a property rights suit was heard by the Supreme Court of South Dakota in which the Dakota Synod of the E & R sued the congregation of Bethany Reformed Church at Scotland, South Dakota, for its property. The Congregation had voted by a majority of 65% to leave the E & R and join the Eureka Classis. The court found in favor of the E & R citing the organization of the RCUS as basically "Presbyterian" in government, and pointing out that the congregation had earlier peacefully joined the merger in 1934.

There was a different outcome to a somewhat similar case in Iowa. In 1951, after Rev. Robert Stuebbe had left Peace Reformed at Garner, to pastor Bakersfield, California, officials of the E & R sought to gain control of the property of that local church. Here the court found in favor of the congregation and demanded that the E & R never again attempt to meddle in the congregation's affairs. Following these developments, the Classis amended the *Constitution of the RCUS* to declare with certainty that property of congregations is held in trust for them, and not for the denomination.

During these war years the now independent congregations at Newton, Wisconsin, Garner, Iowa, Menno, South Dakota, and Shafter, California, maintained friendly relations with the Eureka Classis but did not join. This weakened the hand of the Classis somewhat, but these congregations were doubtful about denominational entanglements and some among them were reluctant to join what they thought might well be a dying cause.

A final matter of historical interest during this period were the brief relations of the continuing RCUS with the Protestant Reformed Churches. During the second World War years, the Eureka Classis began a brief series of meetings with the Protestant Reformed brethren aimed at seeking closer cooperation between the two groups. These meetings ended abruptly in 1947 when none of the PRC men appeared for a meeting scheduled at Waukon, Iowa. When the RCUS men found out that the reason for this absence was the sickness of only one of the PRC men, their leader the Rev. Herman Hoeksema, they broke off further discussions. Contacts were continued during these years however as the RCUS thought of looking to the Protestant Reformed seminary as a training ground for ministerial students. This too came to a bitter end when the Rev. Herman Mensch, who had studied at the Protestant Reformed seminary, turned out to be a proselytizer for them, and was found guilty of schismatic activity and deposed from the ministry. It was not without influence in this bitterness that Rev. Mensch had been actively supported in his efforts by PRC minister Rev. Lubbers.

One more meeting was held between Protestant Reformed and RCUS ministers in about 1970 at the instigation of Rev. Mark Hoeksema, grandson of Herman. Rev. Mark Hoeksema and a fellow pastor who served what were formerly RCUS people at Forbes, North Dakota (near Leola, South Dakota) and Isabel, South Dakota (the two churches involved in Rev. Mensch's schism), had found friendly fellowship among RCUS ministers in the Dakotas and recommended that a meeting be held to improve understanding and perhaps reconcile old differences. These meetings were held in a friendly atmosphere over several days at a retreat center, with the above-mentioned Rev. Lubbers present, but nothing further developed.

THE WESTMINSTER PERIOD

It cannot be doubted that the decision made informally but firmly by pastors William Korn and Walter Grossmann to send students for the ministry to Westminster Theological Seminary in Philadelphia, and recruit graduates from there for our ministry, was one that guaranteed the continuing existence of the RCUS as well as its continuing adherence to Reformed orthodoxy. There was by no means a universal agreement on this among Classis pastors. Rev. D. E. Bosma, who served as Classis President, continued to support the Mission House, now in the E & R. He encouraged two young men, Melvin Volhauer and Howard Kusler, to attend there with the result that they entered the E & R upon graduation. Bosma's position was supported by Rev. F. Herzog, who also soon left the RCUS, joined the E & R and taught briefly at Mission House.

Through his scholarly pursuits, Rev. Korn had become aware of the writings of Dr. Edward J. Young of Westminster. Following up on these, he and Rev. Grossmann accumulated and appreciated the works of Cornelius Van Til as well. These writings convinced the two men that while Westminster was Presbyterian, it was truly Reformed and especially, its view of Scripture was that of the historic Reformed faith. Eureka Classis ministerial student (now Rev.) Lloyd Gross was pre-enrolled at Mission House Seminary of the E & R when in 1953 his former pastor, W. Grossmann, virtually coerced him to choose Westminster. This began a trend that continued for the next twenty-five years, so much so that men seeking to attend other seminaries were heartily discouraged from doing so.

Westminster turned out to be conservative indeed, but much more than that it provided what was probably the best Reformed theological education available in the United States at the time. While its graduates lacked something in pastoral training and preaching skills, they were very well trained in Reformed teaching and biblical exegetical skills. This turned out to be a boon for the Eureka Classis whose pulpits were now more and more filled with Westminster men. These men also had been imbued with a full-orbed view of Reformed teaching, having been thoroughly introduced to the world of Dutch and Scottish Calvinism, as well as its roots in the Swiss and German Reformations. Their theological and historical training allowed them to understand the totalitarian nature of Calvinism, as well as its developments and implications for life. The names of professors John Murray, Cornelius Van Til, Edward J. Young, Paul Woolley, and Ned Stonehouse now became honored and beloved by ministers in the RCUS as well as those of the Orthodox Presbyterian Church and many in the Christian Reformed Church. The RCUS now began to look outward as well as inward to preserve its faith.

Though not the primary reason for sending men to Westminster Seminary, the presuppositional apologetic of Cornelius Van Til became an important tenet of

RCUS thinking. Having been converted through Van Til's teaching to the necessity of the absolute authority of the "self-authenticating word of God" in the Bible, these men, whether they were sons of the RCUS or came to it from other backgrounds, were now truly prepared to carry on the conservative Calvinism of the founders of the Eureka Classis, even though they generally found some of Herman Kohlbruegge's ideas somewhat off the beaten track of Reformed theology.

Beginning in the early 1970s, some questions about teaching at Westminster Seminary on the part of its second generation of professors arose among RCUS pastors due to our students being sympathetic toward infant participation in the Lord's Supper. Several young men under care of Classis ended up leaving the ministry of our churches as a result of these differences. With the establishment of Westminster Seminary in California, more of our students have attended there, although theological questions about the church growth movement and lack of adherence to Van Tilian apologetics have also been raised about its teachings.

The provision of new conservative pastors for the RCUS soon had a settling and strengthening effect on the denomination. Statistics in 1960 showed that the now more stable continuation of the RCUS consisted of twenty congregations with 2419 communicant members and a total baptized membership of 3371. By the end of the year fourteen pastors served these churches. It is of note that three of the pastors were Westminster graduates, newly ordained and installed: Rev. Thomas Beech at Ashley-Venturia, North Dakota, Rev. Peter Grossmann at Hope Church in Sutton, Nebraska, and Rev. Hessel Stevens at Hosmer, South Dakota.

ECUMENICAL RELATIONS WITH OTHER REFORMED CHURCHES

1960 was also significant because in that year the RCUS established fraternal relations with the Orthodox Presbyterian Church (OPC), also a conservative Reformed remnant group. These relations have been close and happy for now 35 years. Many cooperative ventures, from foreign missions to youth camps and pastors' retreats, have resulted.

Learning from the practices and principles of our OPC brethren has influenced the RCUS over these years. Several items in our Directory of Worship and Constitution have been taken over from OPC materials. A number of ministers of the OPC have transferred to the RCUS and several men from the RCUS have transferred to the OPC. The former include Rev. Melvin Nonhof (1957), Rev. Howard Hart (1970), and Rev. Robert Sander. The latter include Rev. William Warren, Rev. Roger Gibbons and Rev. Sam Bacon.

During the 1960s fraternal relations were also opened with the Christian Reformed Church in North America (CRC). In 1965, feeling a kinship with the staunch Calvinism that had historically characterized the CRC, the Eureka Classis agreed to establish relations with them and became a "Church in Correspondence." Many in the RCUS had listened with great profit to pastor Peter Eldersveld on the original Back-to-God hour radio program, and several churches used CRC Sunday School materials during the 1950s. Classis voted to dissolve these relations just a few years later when the ecumenical relations committee of the CRC synod proposed "actively seeking organic union" as one of the rules for churches in correspondence. The appearance of pictures of Christ in CRC Sunday School material and the outcome of the controversy surrounding Calvin Seminary professor Harold Dekker's teachings concerning a "universal love of God" were other factors in this decision.

MISSIONS IN THE CONTINUING RCUS

Fraternal relations with the Orthodox Presbyterian Church were begun in the same year that the RCUS began a twenty-six year period of cooperation with that denomination in the work of foreign missions. The procedure was for the OPC to recommend a prospective missionary who would be examined by the Eureka Classis and sent out with its support but under the oversight of the OPC Committee on Foreign Missions. Later the Classis adopted a procedure for officially "Commissioning a Missionary" of the RCUS to formalize this arrangement. This arrangement was the suggestion of Rev. John Galbraith, Executive Secretary for OPC foreign missions. The first missionary sent out was the Rev. Harvey Conn, who proved to be an extraordinarily effective missionary in Korea.

This step on the part of Classis rounded out the vision and work of the continuing RCUS to include, along with home missions, the full work of a church denomination. In this respect the OPC with its brotherly concern has been a challenge and inspiration to the RCUS to move forward on the path of serving her Lord. Following the resignation of Rev. Conn from missions to teach at Westminster Seminary, the Rev. Lendall Smith was commissioned by the Classis to work in the OPC mission to Taiwan, free China. This arrangement ended in 1986 due to dissatisfaction on the part of the RCUS brethren with the approach to missions by the Taiwanese mission of the OPC. There was disappointment on both sides with these developments but the OPC and RCUS have continued their cordial relations.

In the field of Home Missions, the RCUS has worked long and hard with mixed results. As noted above, services were held as early as 1947 and after 1949 on a regular basis for Reformed people who had moved from the German-Russian farming communities of the Dakotas to Aberdeen, the "Hub-city of South Dakota." In 1958 the Rev. Calvin Stuebbe, who had been serving the Emmanuel E & R of Sutton, Nebraska, but who had formerly served a student summer at Eureka, South Dakota, was installed as pastor of the newly created Aberdeen-Leola joint charge. This church continues today.

A new congregation was begun in the South Dakota capitol of Pierre in 1961 with area pastors serving in winters and student Robert Grossmann serving in summers until 1963, when he was ordained and installed as mission pastor. This church has had ups and downs but continues today. Subsequent missions were begun in the next few years at Minot, North Dakota (also continuing), Hastings, Nebraska (since dissolved), Bismarck, North Dakota (dissolved) and in 1975 at Mitchell, South Dakota (which prospered so a new church was built in 1985 and paid off in early 1993), and Kansas City, Missouri (where a small group still struggles to maintain itself).

In all of these works the RCUS folk have labored faithfully, if not always wisely, and various lessons still need to be learned about starting churches and faithfully using God's appointed means of building His church, namely, the preaching of the Gospel. Nevertheless, while there were seventeen churches in the Eureka Classis in 1934, today there are forty, over half of them having been begun as missions (many of the original seventeen were country or very small town churches and have dissolved to join congregations in larger towns and cities).

ADDITIONS FROM OUTSIDE OF THE DENOMINATION

In 1968, the Eureka Classis session was visited by representatives of two groups of General Association of Regular Baptist (GARB) background. The original group from Faith Community Church at Anderson, California, which was also the mother of the second, came only to observe (but joined the RCUS the next year). The second, American Reformed Church of Fort Collins, Colorado (which later moved to Loveland), made application and was received as a member congregation of the RCUS.

These people had traveled a long theological road under the leadership of Rev. Jefferson Duckett, for over twenty years a GARB pastor. Rev. Duckett had come to a Reformed position through the writings of Cornelius Van Til and eventually left the GARB to form Faith Community Church. Pastors C.W. Powell, Dorman Savage and Roger Gibbons were spiritual sons of Rev. Duckett. Rev. Gibbons and Rev. Savage, who had met at Bob Jones University, had moved to Colorado and begun what they called "American Reformed Church."

Over the next ten years all of these men served pastorates in the RCUS with Rev. Duckett retiring and Rev. Gibbons transferring to the OPC. Churches at Sacramento, CA, and Karval, CO, can also be attributed to their work in and for the RCUS. Following Rev. Duckett's missionary vision, a number of RCUS congregations have been founded in Northern California. Rev. Duckett himself founded Sacramento Covenant Reformed Church.

A RE-FORMED DIRECTORY OF WORSHIP

Following the Mercersburg controversy of the nineteenth century, a compromise directory of worship was adopted by the General Synod of the RCUS in 1884 and approved by two-thirds of the classes by 1887. This Directory is one result of the "peace movement " in the RCUS which sought to bury the hatchet of controversy over the Mercersburg Theology. Collage pictures of the members of the "Peace Commission" can still occasionally be seen in churches or books.[16]

Like most compromises, this Directory avoids controversial terms. In this case terms such as "altar" and other Lutheran phrases are left out even though Mercersburg advocates spoke openly of a "service of the altar." Nevertheless it contains a number of Lutheran elements, such as the naming of the child at baptism and the laying on of hands in confirmation. It also contains a specifically Lutheran reference to baptism in the formula for confirmation, namely, "In this sacred ordinance, you on your part renew and ratify the promise and vow made in your baptism. . . ." It is here referring to the vows and confession of faith made on behalf of the child by the sponsors in Lutheran baptism, an element foreign to the Reformed use of the sacrament.

With these problems in view, the Eureka Classis in 1965 erected a committee to revise the *Reformed Directory of Worship*. This Committee reported first in 1966 with a directory to be used provisionally for a year, then again in 1967. At the 1967 meeting the proposed directory was carefully corrected by the Classis meeting as a committee of the whole, and several new members were added to the Committee.

The final report of the Committee was adopted in 1969 and the newly re-formed *Directory of Worship of the RCUS* bears the publication date of 1970. This directory attempts to be thoroughly Reformed and utilizes not only the regulative principle (see the preface and first chapter on the Public Worship), but also reflects careful study of other Reformed and Presbyterian forms, particularly those of the OPC (from which the questions for profession of faith and confirmation were derived).

THE RECONSTITUTED SYNOD OF THE RCUS — 1986 TO THE PRESENT

At the 75th, or 1985, meeting of the Eureka Classis at Aberdeen, South Dakota, there was not only a Diamond Jubilee celebrating this important birthday, plans were also made to lay this historic body to rest. At the direction of Classis a

---

16 In 1995 this author found one hanging in the unused balcony of St. Matthew's UCC in Bridgewater, Virginia.

book celebrating its 75th anniversary was prepared by the Rev. Norman Hoeflinger and Rev. Robert Stuebbe. This book, *History of the Eureka Classis 1910-1985*, provides an introductory chapter on the European roots of the RCUS and centers around a series of brief descriptions of each of the annual sessions of Classis from 1911 to 1985. It also contains a digest of the pastors and churches of Classis and thus serves as an important resource for those interested in the continuing RCUS.

At the 1983 meeting of Classis, a new Constitution had been adopted by the Eureka Classis which also received from its Committee on Constitutional Revision a recommendation to reinstitute a synod for the RCUS. At its 1985 meeting, Classis decided to move forward on this recommendation, adopted geographical borders for the new classes, and voted to reconstitute as a synod after the opening session of Classis in 1986. Thus plans were made to lay the Eureka Classis to rest with its fathers. The Classis was full of years and had served her Lord and His people well. She had been approved by the Northwest Synod in 1910, had been organized in 1911, and had carried out her purpose of maintaining a conservative Reformed theology in a liberalizing Church. In God's providence she also served as the vehicle for continuing the RCUS when the majority of the denomination entered the E & R merger of 1934. Not only that, the Eureka Classis had served a growing national Church organization for many more years as its only major assembly and judicatory. She had engaged in home and foreign missions, and had become an "Adullam's cave," of twentieth century Reformed Christians who had fled to her for refuge from the widespread unbelief and false teaching that gripped the old Protestant denominations in North America. Readers will remember that the future King David and his men used Adullam's cave in the mountains of Judah as their base of operation, a place which became a refuge for all those in Israel who sought escape from King Saul. The Eureka Classis was only one of several such remnant refuge Churches in the United States during the latter part of the twentieth century.

As planned in 1985, the Eureka Classis was called to order once more at Menno, South Dakota, on May 6, 1986. Classis immediately dissolved itself to form the Synod of the Reformed Church in the United States. The four classes planned in 1985 met separately and then together reconstituted the Synod of the RCUS. The plan went off without a hitch and Synod and each of the Classes have met in each of the following years. Teething problems have arisen in some of the smaller classes but over the years each has gained a sense of its own identity and Synod has continued faithfully to attend to the work of the whole denomination.

MISSIONS IN THE RCUS SINCE 1984

At the 1984 session of Classis at Bakersfield-Shafter, California, the Rev. Aaron Kayayan, French minister of the Back-to-God Hour of the Christian

Reformed Church, presented the cause of the need to organize a Reformed Church in Zaire. Classis approved this as a mission project and gave its Foreign Missions Committee authority to formulate plans and begin this work. By the end of 1984, Rev. Paul Treick had traveled to Zaire with Rev. Kayayan, and the two men had examined and ordained a number of elders and one minister, thus founding the Reformed Confessing Church of Zaire (ERCZ to reflect its French name).

Throughout the years since 1984, the RCUS has supported several preaching elders in Zaire who function as part-time ministers and evangelists. RCUS representatives have traveled to Zaire on several occasions for teaching sessions, to help with broader assemblies and to help in getting the ERCZ approved as a church by the government of Zaire. Recognition was finally accomplished through seven years of work and financial aid, and the Church now operates legally in the country.

In December 1986 members of the Zaire Administration Committee of the RCUS met in Chicago with representatives of the Reformed Churches in the Netherlands (Liberated) (GKN [Librated]) to work out cooperative agreements for mutual work in Zaire. This relationship has continued to the present and both churches continue helping the ERCZ even though political unrest in Zaire has made matters exceedingly difficult in recent years, with foreigners having to flee the country temporarily on more than one occasion.

The GKN (Liberated) and RCUS have cooperated in founding a seminary in Zaire and in providing diaconal help to the churches and people there. The GKN has sent men for both works and the RCUS has provided funds for a central building for the ERCZ and for pastoral support.

The synod and classes of the RCUS have also continued to carry out a large number of home mission projects considering the number of supporting congregations. As noted above, not all home mission works have resulted in thriving churches, nonetheless, this is not for lack of trying. During the 1980s churches begun earlier at Hastings, Nebraska, Bismarck, North Dakota, Mobile, Alabama, and Miami, Florida were dissolved after valiant struggles to become self-supporting churches. A work attempted at Fargo, North Dakota, also failed to establish a viable organization. Nevertheless new works continue to be started with some success. Among these are Modesto, Yuba City, Chico and Willows, and Lodi, California, and Sioux Falls, South Dakota. Attempts have also been made at Minneapolis, Minnesota with limited results. At Rapid City, South Dakota, worship services were begun in 1992, and a new church was founded there in 1993 with Rev. Dorman Savage as pastor.

Several congregations have also been begun in recent years as self-supporting works from their inception. Among these are Arvada, Colorado, (since disfellowshipped by the South Central Classis over the issue of serving communion to young children), Karval, Colorado, Rock Springs, Wyoming, and Carbondale, Pennsylvania. One congregation, St. Paul's Evangelical Reformed Church at Hamburg, Minnesota, has returned to the RCUS from the UCC during this period.

The RCUS continues its zealous attempts to spread the Gospel and begin churches wherever prospects seem positive. Many congregations have regular outreach programs through radio and other means. Ebenezer Reformed Church at Shafter, California, has developed a prison ministry in the maximum security facility at Corcoran. Rev. Gene Sawtelle of First Reformed Church at Yuba City, California conducts a similar ministry at Folsom Prison. The Shafter prison ministry has resulted in a number of conversions, regular Bible studies within the prison walls by pastor Vernon Pollema, and membership in Ebenezer Church by several long-term prisoners.

EDUCATION AND NEW INTERCHURCH RELATIONS

As a result of travels by representatives of the RCUS and Reformed Churches in the Netherlands (Liberated) or "GKN (Liberated)," in each other's countries, there has been much contact between these two conservative Reformed church bodies. Finding a great unity in doctrine between the two Churches, they began to speak about a formal interchurch relationship. The GKN (liberated) suggested working toward "sister-church" relations which were established by the General Synod of Leeuwarden, Holland, in 1990 and confirmed by the Synod of the RCUS at Garner, Iowa, at its next meeting in 1991. As a result of its relationship with the GKN (liberated), the RCUS has also become a member of the International Council of Reformed Churches (ICRC) which is an association of over a dozen conservative Reformed Churches from around the world and which holds meetings every four years.

During the period of the reconstituted synod, the RCUS has used several seminaries for ministerial training. These include Westminster in Philadelphia, Westminster in California, Reformed Seminary in Jackson, Mississippi, and Mid-America Reformed Seminary at Orange City, Iowa. In addition, a number of graduates of Covenant Seminary in St. Louis, Missouri, and Reformed Episcopal Seminary in Philadelphia have entered the RCUS ministry. Presently (1996) the two Westminsters and Mid-America Reformed Seminary are approved for students from the RCUS. Westminster in California and Mid-America are seminaries included on the RCUS synodical guidelines for giving.

During this period, two RCUS men have served as professors at RCUS approved seminaries. Dr. John Zinkand was ordained by the Eureka Classis in 1965 to serve as an associate professor at Westminster Seminary in Philadelphia. He had been professor of biblical languages at Dort College and a member of the CRC previous to that. Dr. Zinkand returned to Dort College after a few years and some years after that transferred his membership back to the Christian Reformed Church. While in the RCUS he often served churches during the summer months. In 1986, Rev. Robert Grossmann began teaching Ministerial Studies and Church History at Mid-America Reformed Seminary after serving twenty three years in various pastorates of the RCUS. In 1993 Rev. Grossmann left Mid-America seminary to return to an RCUS pastorate.

The Reformed Church in the U.S. has pursued Christian education for its children and youth beyond the Sunday School and Catechism class. Several congregations or their members have been involved in beginning and/or supporting Christian day schools for elementary and high school students. Such associations are found in Anderson, California, Mitchell, South Dakota, Carbondale, Pennsylvania, Yuba City, California, and Sutton, Nebraska. One pastor, the Rev. C.W. Powell, has taught in Christian schools almost continuously for the past twenty years, even though he has always been pastor of a church during those same years. Also, a fair percentage of Reformed Church families engage in home-schooling their children, including several pastors' families.

Since the early 1960s, the Reformed Church has supported Dordt College at Sioux Center, Iowa, and in recent years has had approximately twenty students in attendance each year. A good number of students also attend other Christian Colleges.

The Reformed Presbyterian Church in North America (RPCNA), an historic Covenanter and exclusive Psalm-singing church of Scotch-Irish background, has had fraternal relations with the RCUS since 1975. In spite of differences in practice, the RCUS has been comfortable with this fraternity as it stated upon entering the relationship, "because of your commitment to the Word of God and your firm stand in the Reformed faith."

The RCUS has had sporadic relations with the Independent Presbyterian Church of Mexico. Through the efforts of Rev. John Paul Roberts, contacts were established in 1991 between the RCUS and the Independent Presbyterian Church of Mexico (this is one of several splinter groups; at least one other has the same name). These contacts involved meetings with seminary faculty members in Mexico and several trips and shipments of aid to the Mexican church people. This relationship has not been unbroken, but California RCUS Churches have attempted to maintain contact.

RETURN TO THE THREE FORMS OF UNITY

Sometime during the years from approximately 1800 to 1850, the High German Reformed Church gave up the Belgic Confession of Faith and Canons of

Dort as creeds. How or why this happened is a matter for conjecture and perhaps an educated guess. Though diligent searches have been made, so far no record of synodical or classical action, or in fact of any kind of action, which would date and explain this significant change has come to light. We do not even know if the change was sudden or occurred over a period of time. We know that John Philip Boehm in 1725 founded the first three German Reformed Churches in Pennsylvania with the Belgic Confession and Canons of Dort as well as the Heidelberg Catechism as creeds. We know also that the coetus was founded with all three creeds in 1747 and that this adherence was reiterated in 1752.

It is known from the records of the Coetus of Pennsylvania that as late as 1790 the coetus clearly declared that the "Netherlands confession of faith and church formulas" were "implicitly" a part of the "doctrine, customs and ordinances of the Reformed Church." We know further that in the report of a committee of the Synod of the Reformed Church in 1817 to explain the reasons for the 1793 separation from Holland, that neither doctrine nor creeds are mentioned. We also know that in 1820 when a group in the Synod was dissatisfied with the plans for a theological seminary, they threatened to withdraw and join the Reformed Dutch Church. This move would have placed the ministers clearly under subscription to both the Belgic Confession and Canons of Dort as well as the Heidelberg Catechism, a fact known to them without a doubt. However, neither of these latter two facts contain positive information about actual adherence of the Church to these creeds at this time.

In 1846, early in the Mercersburg Theology years, the Synod of the Reformed Church declared adoption of a constitution which included only the Heidelberg Catechism in its section on creeds. Certainly from this time forward the Reformed Church in the U.S. operated with only the Heidelberg Catechism as its creed. The Eureka Classis was founded as a conservative classis in 1910 with mostly German-Russian people as church members. These people also held only to the Heidelberg Catechism as their creed.

A new awareness of the biblical character and usefulness of the Belgic Confession and Canons of Dort became part of the thinking of Reformed Church ministers, and a number of elders and lay people during the Westminster period mentioned above. As a generation of pastors with roots inside and outside of the RCUS who were educated at Westminster and were exposed to these creeds as well as the Westminster Standards, they became convinced that the giving up of the Belgic Confession and the Canons of Dort by the RCUS was a mistake. The entrance of people of Dutch Reformed background and of others of who had been exposed to these two creeds added numerical strength to those who held this conclusion.

During the decades of 1970 and 1980, two major attempts were made to readopt these creeds and add them to the Heidelberg Catechism as confessions of the Reformed Church in the U.S. In both cases the matter was laid on the table in order to avoid so offending the minority that opposed this measure that it might have split the otherwise solidly united denomination. It needs to be noted that the opposition was not essentially doctrinal. All of the ministers and elders held to all the points of teaching in these creeds even though there was a question raised about the wording of one article of the Canons of Dort. The opposition seemed to center most on the idea that adopting these additional creeds would somehow denigrate the Heidelberg Catechism from its place of high esteem or even dilute the Church's adherence to it.

Readoption was finally accomplished in 1995. At the 1993 Synod meeting of the Reformed Church in the U.S., the matter of adopting the Belgic Confession and Canons of Dort was again proposed, on this occasion by the Standing Ecumenical Committee of Synod. This matter was postponed until 1994 and the Executive Committee of Synod was charged with submitting recommendations to the 1994 Synod on the "implementation and implications" of such adoption.

At the 1994 Synod meeting, the matter was presented by the Executive Committee and passed on a roll call vote by more than the two-thirds majority required. The vote was 39-13. Before the vote on adoption was taken the Synod had adopted several minor wording amendments to the Belgic and Canons, including one which changed the wording previously found offensive in the Canons of Dort. The matter of adopting these additional creeds was then submitted to each of the four classes for ratification, also a requirement of the *Constitution of the Reformed Church in the U.S.*[17]

The 1995 Synod of the Reformed Church in the U.S. declared on the basis of majority votes in three of the four classes and a tie vote in one of them, that the Belgic Confession and Canons of Dort were once again the official creeds of the Reformed Church in the United States. In answer to a complaint about the tie vote in the Covenant East Classis, Synod agreed with its Judicial Committee that a tie vote does not amount to a rejection, which the *Constitution of the RCUS* calls for if constitutional amendments are to be rejected (Article 104), and thus the tie amounts to tacit approval of the issue placed before the Classes by Synod.

SUMMARY OF THE RCUS TODAY

In doctrine, the RCUS continues to the present day (1996) to maintain a strong adherence to the infallibility and inerrancy of Scripture, and to the historic

---

17 Article 104.

Reformed faith. The RCUS holds to the Heidelberg Catechism, the Belgic Confession and the Canons of Dort as its official creeds, and demands strict subscription to the creeds on the part of its ministers. Doctrinal emphases include a continuance of the Reformed regulative principle[18] of worship, including the rejection of pictures and images, a rejection of modern feminism, and adherence to the biblical teaching of the Divine creation of the heavens and earth in six ordinary days of light and darkness.

Adherence to the historic Calvinist teachings of double predestination, the unity of the covenant and the application of Scripture to all of life are also strong emphases. In line with the latter teaching, the ideas of Theonomic Reconstructionism and a modified Post-Millennialism have caused some controversy within the Church. The RCUS also continues a strong emphasis on covenant catechization and practices the rite of confirmation as subscribed to by John Calvin.[19] Covenant children are required to learn and pass examinations on the history of redemption and memorization of the Heidelberg Catechism prior to making profession of faith in confirmation.[20]

Geographically, the Reformed Church in the United States exists in four classes combined under one synod. There are about forty congregations with a total of some 3200 communicant and 4200 baptized members. The classes with the locations of their congregations are listed below:

1. **Covenant East Classis** with congregations at Carbondale, Pennsylvania, Napoleon, Ohio, Manitowoc, Wisconsin, Hamburg, Minnesota, and Garner, Iowa. A new congregation, Deaf Reformed Church of Bowie, Maryland, is in the process of being accepted into Classis as this is being written.

2. **Northern Plains Classis** with congregations at Aberdeen, Artas, Eureka, Herreid, Hosmer, Leola and Pierre, South Dakota, and Ashley, rural Denhoff, Minot and Upham, North Dakota. This Classis founded a new mission work at Watertown, South Dakota during 1995.

3. **South Central Classis** with congregations at Colorado Springs, Loveland and Karval, Colorado, at Kansas City, Missouri, Rock Springs, Wyoming, at Lincoln and Sutton (two congregations), Nebraska, and at Menno, Mitchell, Rapid City and Sioux Falls, South Dakota.

4. **Western Classis** with congregations at Anderson, Lancaster, Bakersfield,

---

18 The Reformed or "Regulative" principle of worship holds that man may worship God "in no other way than He has commanded us in His Word" (Heidelberg Catechism 96).

19 Calvin, John, *Institutes*, Book 4, Chap. 19, Section 13.

20 See *Constitution of the Reformed Church in the United States*, Article 192.

Lodi, Modesto, Sacramento, Shafter, Willows, Chico, Grass Valley and Yuba City, California.

Ecumenical interest in other Reformed bodies and Christians of a conservative stripe runs strong, and the synod of the RCUS continues official relations with the OPC, the Reformed Presbyterian Church in North America, and the Reformed Churches in the Netherlands (liberated). Exploratory talks are under way toward formal relations with the Canadian Reformed Churches. The Synod has been received into membership in NAPARC (North American Presbyterian and Reformed Council) and the ICRC (International Council of Reformed Churches) within the last few years.

Bibliography

Bosma, D.E., Korn, Wm., and Hieb, Henry, *Fiftieth Anniversary History of the Eureka Classis, RCUS.* Green Bay: Reliance, 1960.

Dubbs, Joseph, *Historic Manual of the Reformed Church in the U.S.* Lancaster, PA: 1885.

Dunn, David, *et al., A History of the Evangelical and Reformed Church.* New York: Pilgrim Press, 1990.

Good, James I., *Historical Handbook of the RCUS.* Philadelphia: Heidelberg Press, 1901.

Good, James I., *History of the Reformed Church in the U.S. 1725-1792.* Reading, PA: Daniel Miller, 1899.

Good, James I., *History of the Reformed Church in the Nineteenth Century.* New York: Board of Publications of the Reformed Church in America, 1911.

Grossmann, Robert E., *Outline History of the Reformed Church in the U.S. 1725-1995.* Garner, IA: Elector Publications, 1995.

Harbaugh, Henry, *The Life of Rev. Michael Schlatter.* Philadelphia: Lindsay and Blakiston, 1857.

Hincke, William, Ed., *Minutes and Letters of the Coetus of the German Reformed Congregations in Pennsylvania.* Philadelphia: Reformed Church Publications Board, 1903.

Hoeflinger, Norman & Stuebbe, Robert, *Seventy-fifth Anniversary History of the Eureka Classis of the Reformed Church,* Green Bay: Reliance, 1985.

Jaberg, Eugene C. and Kley, Roland, editors, *A History of Mission House Lakeland.* Philadelphia: Christian Education Press, 1962.

Klein, H.M.J., *History of the Eastern Synod of the Reformed Church in the U.S.* Lancaster, PA: Eastern Synod of the RCUS, 1943.

Nichols, James Hastings, *The Mercersburg Theology.* New York: Oxford University Press, 1996.

Reformed Church Publications Board, *Addresses on the Life and Theology of Henry Harbaugh and Emmanuel Gerhart.* Philadelphia, 1918.

Richards, George Warren, *History of the Theological Seminary of the Evangelical and Reformed Church.* Lancaster, PA: Rudisill, 1952

Russell, George B., *Creeds and Customs of the RCUS.* Philadelphia: Reformed Church Publication Board, 1869.

Schneck, B.S., *Mercersburg Theology Inconsistent With Protestant and Reformed Doctrine.* Philadelphia: Lippencot, 1874.

1977 EUREKA CLASSIS SESSION—EMANUEL, SUTTON, NEBRASKA

First row: Albert Koerner, Leopold Dockter, Rev. M. Koerner, Rev. D. W. Treick, Marvin Bender, Rev. Steve Demers, Rev. H. Hart, Alfred Feil, Walter Springer, Rev. V. Pollema. Second row: Rev. C. W. Powell, Rudolph Opp, Don Monteath, Rev. R. Grossmann, Rev. C. Ploeger, Rev. Wm. Traub, Rev. N. Jones, Rev. R. Gibbons, missing. Third Row: Rev. N. Riffert, Rev. C. Stuebbe, Rev. H. Van Stedum, Alvin Mettler, Rev. L. Gross, missing, Rev. N. Hoeflinger, Jake Fisher, Stanley Peter, Rev. P. Treick, D. Dockter, Rev. Steve Schlei, Rev. J. Zinkand. Fourth row: Rev. J. Duckett, Kenneth Armbruster, missing, Don Greimann, Rev. S. Work, Edgar Dewald, Alvin Reichert, missing, missing, Elton Hackmann.

CHAPTER FIVE

The German-Russians and the Influence

of Dr. H. F. Kohlbruegge

Rev. Norman C. Hoeflinger

Some years ago at an adult Bible study I gave a lesson on "How the Christian Church became German." In a German Reformed Church that might seem a bit "chauvinistic." What I had in mind was the invasion of the Roman Empire by the Germanic tribes beginning in 376 A.D. when the Goths crossed the lower Danube and culminating with the fall of Rome in 476. But while the Germans conquered the Roman Empire, the Christian Church converted the Germans. And it was no less a German than Martin Luther who reformed the German church, or one might say the church as a whole (Protestant). It's not my task to trace how a portion of that German church became Reformed, but we are all familiar with the story of the Elector Frederick III, Olevianus and Ursinus and our beloved Heidelberg Catechism. Most of us who read this have cut our Reformed teeth and were made to chew on this meaty instructor in the German Reformed Church in the U.S. But among those of us in the Reformed Church in the U.S. who were nurtured on the Heidelberg, a considerable number are not only German but are known also as German-Russians. And that's the story of this chapter: How the German Reformed Church became German-Russian.

Of course not all German-Russians are Reformed. We wish that they were, seeing that in the 1970s according to the estimate of Richard Sallet there were

303,532 first and second generation German-Russians in the U.S.[1] North Dakota led the way by far with approximately 70,000 while South Dakota and Kansas each had less than half that amount with Nebraska and Colorado numbering a little over 20,000 each. When we subtract the 37,000 Volhynian (Polish) and Lithuanian Germans spread throughout the U.S. there were 266,000 Black Sea and Volga Germans. Of these 67% were Evangelical, that is, Lutheran, Reformed, Congregational, etc., while 21% were Catholics and 12% Mennonites. How many of the German-Russians were Reformed? It's hard to say. In the 1897 census in Russia 3.6% of all the German-Russians were Reformed.[2] If we use 3% for the 1970s in the U.S. we get about 9,000 Reformed, but RCUS statistics just before the merger in 1934 show about 5,000 in the Classes Nebraska, South Dakota, North Dakota and Eureka.[3] The Eureka Classis in 1915 showed 1186 confirmed members and in 1935 1406. No doubt almost all of these were German-Russians. Today the RCUS shows a confirmed membership of 3160. Of these I would estimate that 58% are German-Russians.

The Eureka Classis was the one classis in the Reformed Church in the U.S. that did not go into the Evangelical and Reformed merger of 1934 nor the United Church of Christ merger in 1957. Why? Undoubtedly it was because the Eureka Classis organized in 1911 on dogmatic or doctrinal grounds. "Wir haben uns dogmatisch organisiert" (We have organized ourselves doctrinally), is the way one of the founders of the classis expressed it. And what was that doctrine? It was the Calvinistic theology of Dr. H. F. Kohlbruegge (Kohlbrügge). His distinctive teaching so impressed certain Reformed pastors that it united them in the conviction that this is the true doctrine of the Reformed Faith. And it was some of these pastors who labored among the German-Russian congregations of the Eureka Classis convincing them to maintain their doctrine and their congregations against the compromising unionism of the mergers. So it was the German-Russians who were Kohlbrueggians who maintained and saved the Reformed Church in the U.S. And that's what this chapter of our celebration volume is all about.

GERMANS TO RUSSIA

The name German-Russians is convertible. It can even be more accurately Russian Germans, or the name that perhaps says it best:

---

1 Richard Sallet, *Russian-German Settlements in the United States* (North Dakota Institute for Regional Studies, Fargo, 1974), p. 112.

2 Karl Stumpp, *The German-Russians* (Edition Atlantic-Forum, Bonn-Brussels-New York, 1967) p. 20.

3 David Dunn, *et al, A History of the Evangelical and Reformed Church* (The pilgrim Press, New York, 1990), p. 340.

Germans from Russia, as in the "Germans from Russian Heritage Society" at Bismarck, North Dakota, and the "American Historical Society Of Germans from Russia" at Lincoln, Nebraska. One thing about these German-Russians: there is very little Russian about them, though they were in many ways model citizens in Russia for a hundred years. But they were not Russians in politics, language, culture and religion. They not only came from Germany, but they were Germans all the way through. So faithfully had they maintained their heritage that in the 1940s when some returned as refugees to Germany the native Germans said of them. "They are more German than we are.[4]

When I came to South Dakota in 1955 as pastor of the Reformed churches at Artas and Herreid, I found out how German they still were. I was expected to preach occasionally in the German language. However, with my German preaching their English improved so rapidly that the German soon became unnecessary! Of interest though, our children, at least on one occasion, played with children who spoke no English, and the "congress" in the town store was conducted in German except when the minister was there. (That was before TV and the leveling, or should I say mongrelization, of all cultures in America and the even more horrible modern "Multi-culturalism.")

But the story of the German-Russians is well-known, appearing in the celebration booklets of our churches in Nebraska and the Dakotas. Also the centennial volumes of the various communities in North and South Dakota, for example, Menno, Tripp, Eureka, South Dakota, all repeat the German-Russian saga.

It is a tale of two continents, or as T. C. Wenzlaff titled his work, *Pioneers on Two Continents,*[5] using a phrase in James Griess' *The German-Russian Those Who Came to Sutton;*[6]a tale of two continents, not, *A Tale of Two Cities.* As Dickens began that work with the familiar words, "It was the best of times, it was the worst of times," so in God's providence it was the worst of times in Germany that made emigration attractive to these solid German farmers and burghers to leave their homeland and go to the bleak steppe of Russia, and then a century later when they saw their situation in Russia worsening that they looked to another great plain for a homeland. And it was the best of times for them to establish themselves first in their own dorfs on the vast steppe that isolated and insulated them from the rest of society:

4 Edward C. Ehrensperger, Ed., *History of the United Church of Christ in South Dakota* (Pine Hill Press, Freeman, SD, 1977) p. 203.

5 T. C. Wenzlaff, *Pioneers on Two Continents* (Service Press, Henderson, NE, 1974).

6 James Griess, *The German-Russians Those Who Came to Sutton*, (Hastings, NE, 1968) p. v.

. . . They sit, as it were, alone on the lonely steppe. Mingling in closer association with other nationalities has served to erase the differences among the Germans themselves; yet the German cares not for an intimate association with the filthy, degenerate Tartars, Bulgarians or Jews. He stays in his own village and only maintains a limited contact even with the nearest German colony; often only a mile (five English miles) wide field on the steppe separates a neighbor, but is a formidable obstacle for any contact. This, then, is how the colonist lives his lonely existence in his colony on the endless steppe to which broad plain no sound from the outer world penetrates[7].

Then, when again in God's providence it seemed time to move on, it was the best of times because the American west was opening up, and the German-Russians found the "endless prairies of the northern Great Plains, North and South Dakota, Nebraska, Kansas and Eastern Colorado, much like the landscapes they had abandoned in South Russia."[8]

Why did these folks go to Russia to begin with? War, famine and pestilence can be mentioned: the Thirty Years' War (1618-48), the Seven Year's War (1756-73) and the French Revolution and Napoleonic Wars (1789-1816) all contributed to the devastation of South Germany. The disruption and destruction of war, plus occasional crop failures and unemployment, and the resulting social stress made many feel the need to move out. For whatever reason one hears the common German complaint, *"Wir sind bis zur Stunde ein volk ohne Raum,"* — a people in need of room. During the late eighteenth century and through the nineteenth many Germans emigrated. And early on the push was eastward to Russia, a land of opportunity.

Catherine II of Russia made this an attractive move. In order to bring Russia into the Western World and at the same time buffer her eastern frontier against the wild Siberian tribes, she sought European farmers, particularly Germans, to settle along the Volga River. She particularly sought after Germans as she herself had been a German princess of the House of Anhalt-Zerbst. After she married Peter (Peter the Great's grandson), he despised her and she in turn conspired to have him deposed. He was later murdered! Catherine the Great, as she is known, issued a proclamation in 1763, encouraging the colonization along the Volga River with promises of religious liberty, tax exemption up to thirty years for farmers, exemption from military service and cash grants for buildings and livestock. Along with these and certain other privileges was the freedom to leave Russia at anytime.

7 *Ibid.*, p. 32, quotation from Hermann Dalton.

8 R. Sallet, *op. cit.*, p. 5.

By 1768, 103 colonies were established on both sides of the Volga, containing about 23,000 Germans from Hesse, the Rhineland and the Palatinate. Sixty-five of these colonies were Evangelical and thirty-eight were Catholic.

Certainly some of these Volga Germans were Reformed. A number of the Volga German-Russians later settled in Nebraska, temporarily in Sutton, but more so in Lincoln and Hastings, working for the railroad. I do not know whether or not any of the congregations of the Reformed Church in the U.S. were made up of Volga River Germans.

However the other major settlement of Germans in Russia, in the Black Sea area, has provided the Reformed Church in the U.S. with that corps of people who made up the Eureka Classis, who are most of the people in the congregations of the continuing RCUS. The grandson of Catherine the Great, Alexander I, furthered the plan of his grandmother by sending agents into troubled southwest Germany. In 1803 he promised the settlers free acreage in addition to those former promises made by Catherine. But he required that the immigrants must be families worth no less than 300 guilders — a sizable amount — and he wanted no singles — adventurers or drifters — but farmers and craftsman who could serve as models to the Russian citizens.

While most Black Sea Germans say they are from Odessa, there were actually only a very small number who were from that seaport city on the Black Sea. There was a Reformed Church in Odessa itself. In 1843, forty-two members separated themselves from the Lutherans in the Evangelical Church, and the group quickly grew to seventy voting members and 200 souls. By 1865 there were 138 voters and 514 souls.[9] However the German-Russians in the Reformed Church in the U.S. came not from Odessa but from its vicinity, from the villages of Rohrbach, Worms, Johannesthal and Waterloo in the Beresan Group (by the Beresan River between the Bug and Dniester rivers in the southern Ukraine). These were from Wuertemberg, the Palatinate and Baden in Germany. The Glueckstal group was made up of the villages of Glueckstal, Neudorf, Kassel and Bergdorf. These came from Wuertemberg, Alsace, Baden and the Palatinate. The Reformed from Alsace organized a number of villages.[10] In all the German immigrants established 214 colonies and 1000 daughter colonies in the Black Sea region.

LIFE IN RUSSIA

At the beginning life was extremely difficult for these colonists. There first homes were dugouts, though eventually they had homes of brick and stone quarried

---

9 Hermann Dalton, *Geschichte der Reformierten Kirche in Russland* (Gotha, 1865), p. 186.

10 George Rath, *The Black Sea Germans in the Dakotas* (Pine Hill Press, Freeman, SD, 1977) pp. 4, 5.

or made locally. Diseases, such as cholera, were a threat to the whole community; and robbers were always a danger. And as an agricultural people they constantly faced the problems of natural disasters of one kind or another causing crop failures. But another hazard is reported in the colony Rohrbach; not just poor farming but an unchristian life style. There was a lack of the fear of God; immorality was unchecked and applauded by those who sat idly in the shade of the whiskey taverns unconcerned about the welfare of their families. Village officials didn't seem to care and the education of the youth was neglected. But then a change took place:

> A new era was ushered in with the year 1824. God had mercy on us in every respect and in His discerning design sent us Johannes Bonekemper, a serious minded preacher of the Gospel, whose labors were blessed.... His twenty-four years work with us will long be remembered."[11]

In 1865 Pastor Hermann Dalton of the German Reformed Church in St. Petersburg wrote in his "History of the Reformed Church in Russia" after visiting the Reformed colonies, "All Other interests yield to that of religion. Politics, literature, commerce, art, in so far as they can relate to a rural population, have entirely receded to the background, while all church and religious questions occupy most of the colonists in their leisure hours."[12] Another report states that Sundays especially were devoted to religious interests: Sunday morning worship and Sunday afternoon Bible study - with a nap in between. Preparation began already Saturday with regular work stopping at 6:00 P.M. and the cleanup begun for Sunday so that by 9:00 o'clock everything was ready and everyone waited for Sunday. On Sunday the mood was festive. No one worked. The only wagon driven Sunday morning was the one that brought the minister. Everyone went to church. The report concludes, "The German settlements in foreign countries were recognized for their diligent labors on workdays and as being a haven of rest for the residents on Sundays."[13]

THE GERMAN REFORMED

The people in the colonies had a strong religious background, and the Protestants had a Reformation heritage. This was true of the Reformed. It can be illustrated by the Ochsner family. Johann Nikolas Ochsner had emigrated from Edenkoben in Germany in 1809 to South Russia and helped to found the colony of Worms. Cleon Ochsner reported at the Ochsner family reunion in 1994:

---

11 T. C. Wenzlaff, *Heritage Review* (Germans from Russian Heritage Society, Bismarck, ND), Vol. No. 2, May 1988, p. 30, 31.

12 H. Dalton, *op. cit.,* p. 201, Trans. *Heritage Review* 1974, No. 9, p. 32.

13 *Heritage Review* (Bismarck, ND), Vol. 21, No. 3, p. 27.

According to church records, Felix Ochsner was married by the Swiss Reformer, Ulrich Zwingli. It is safe, therefore, to assume that the Ochsners were very early involved in the Reformation movement. When Jacob "Jaegli" emigrated from Witikon, Switzerland to Edenkoben in 1656, he chose to go to the Palatinate, where in 1563, under the sponsorship of Elector Prince Frederick III, the Heidelberg Catechism was published. We know from the history of the time, that the citizens of a particular principality were expected to embrace the religion of the ruler and Frederick embraced the Reformed movement whole-heartedly. As far as we can determine, the Edenkoben Ochsners were all baptized, married and buried in the Reformed Church there.[14]

So from this we see that Nikolas Ochsner came from a long and strong Reformed background. We are not surprise to hear him mentioned as being present at the farewell sermon of Johannes Bonekemper which he preached on March 25, 1848 at Rohrbach. He was no doubt a friend of this staunch Reformed pastor.

Johannes Bonekemper came to Rohrbach in 1824 from the Mission House at Basel, Switzerland. He lived at Rohrbach and preached there, and at Worms and Johannesthal, and later also in Gueldendorf and Waterloo. His main pastoral concern was to strengthen the Reformed consciousness of his people by arranging classes for Reformed instruction and by teaching the young people the Heidelberg Catechism.[15] Dalton reports of him that he was accused of being a hyper-Calvinist,[16] and he refused to conduct worship and communion according to the new church regulations of the Consistorium in Odessa in the Lutheran form. He opposed liturgy, ritual and candles. In the Evangelical Church the Lutheran and Reformed worshiped together, and the Lutherans had been satisfied with Bonekemper's Reformed worship. But now there was trouble, and the upshot of it was that separate worship services were ordered to be held for each. Bonekemper's own conscience and his Reformed convictions no doubt led to this separation. At a later date the Reformed in Rohrbach and Worms were organized as a separate parish, calling its own Reformed pastor.

But Bonekemper had another problem. He was not only Reformed, but he was an ardent pietist. Now pietism emphasizes the personal experience in the life of the Christian; the experiential above the doctrinal and confessional aspects of church life. Due largely to the dead orthodoxy in the Lutheran Churches at this time, pietism made its appeal throughout Europe. Three groups made an entrance into

---

14 Cleon Ochsner, *Jacob and Klara Ochsner Family*, Ochsner Family Reunion (Hastings, NE, 1994).

15 G. Rath, *op. cit.*, p. 365.

16 H. Dalton, *op. cit.*, p. 225.

Russia: the Stundists, Separatists and Chiliasts. The Chiliasts were the most extreme and were those who looked for Christ to return in 1836 on Mt. Ararat in the Caucasus Mountains of South Russia. Disastrous journeys were made by many German emigrants to be present for this event, journeys on which a great many of them lost their lives because they were unprepared for the hardships and disease. Less radical than the Chiliasts but still withdrawn from society were the Separatists who had lost faith in both government and the established church. Johannes Bonekemper certainly avoided these extremes, but he was an advocate of the Stunden. Bonekemper introduced the "Erbauungstunde" (hour of devotion). These hours of prayer and study were something like our present day home Bible study groups of prayer gatherings, though they did not militate against the organized worship of the church but were supportive of it. Nevertheless they had the unfortunate result of separating the congregation into the "converted" and the "unconverted," or the "children of God" and the "world."[17]

A further complication developed. A further development that eventually brought an end to Bonekemper's ministry was the bizarre activities that began in 1847. Among the children and young people of the parish, repentance took the form of bodily convulsions and shivering. Some screamed out loud or groaned and beat themselves so that their hands bled, pulling on their clothing and hair. They became stupefied. Some shouted, "Get away, devil... I have obeyed you long enough...." Some jumped up and smiled and said, "Only a little bit more of faith," and others shouted, "Jesus lives... I've got the Savior." This was all reported by Bonekemper himself in his diary. His son, Carl, later wrote in the margin of the diary, "peasants", indicating his disapproval. He also noted that the young school teacher, Jacob Orth, who later became the first minister among the German Russians in America was as a child among these religious fanatics.[18]

The Lutheran authorities objected to this phenomenon and informed Bonekemper to "regulate more carefully the ways of true Christian salvation by prayer and sane exploration...." But Bonekemper defended these activities as the work of God because those who "engaged and praised divine grace for the forgiveness of sins showed themselves from that day on to be decent Christians."[19] Now, though he had served for twenty-four years, he realized he could no longer remain as the pastor at Rohrbach and resigned, intending to go to America with his friends; but he never made it.

Bonekemper's son, Carl, had already gone to America. On his trip to the United States he experienced a severe storm on March 20, 1848 that produced such

17 G. Rath, *op. cit.*, pp. 365, 366.

18 *Ibid.*, pp. 32-34.

19 *Ibid.*, p. 38.

a spiritual awakening in him that he decided to become a minister. He studied at the Theological Seminary at Mercersburg in Pennsylvania. After that he was ordained and organized the Zion Reformed Church in Philadelphia. He returned to Europe in 1855 and studied at the University of Berlin. He was then a teacher for seven years at Pilgermission in Basel before returning to South Russia to undertake pastoral labors in the Rohrbach-Worms Reformed congregations where his father had served so long. It seems that he shared his father's theology and pietism without the extreme physical manifestations of previous years. He was a very learned man of whom it was said that he could preach in seven languages or be silent in seven languages. In Rohrbach he also introduced preaching in Russian to the farm laborers and was largely responsible for bringing the Gospel to the Russian and Ukrainian people.[20]

GERMAN-RUSSIANS TO AMERICA

But the times were a changing in Russia. Tsar Alexander II, introducing a more liberal policy, freed the Russian serfs in 1861 and introduced some self-government. But in so doing he sought to make all citizens equal and so revoked the privileges given the German colonists in the Volga and Black Sea areas. All schools and local government had to be in Russian, and universal military conscription was instituted in 1874. The "forever" privileges promised the German colonists were interpreted by the Tsar to mean a century. The colonists were given ten years to decide whether or not they wished to remain in Russia or emigrate.

Already in 1849 one group from Odessa left Russia for the United States. Among them was Ludwig Bette and A. Scheller. Some of this group settled in Ohio. Scheller and Bette ended up on Kelley's Island in Lake Erie where they operated very successful vineyards. A German Reformed Church was organized there in 1865. Ludwig Bette anglicized his name to Lewis Beaty. He made a trip back to Russia in 1872 to visit his relatives, and talked up the advantages and opportunities of America so freely that the authorities sought to arrest him. He had to get rid of his American top hat and suit for a colonists cap and clothing to escape detection. Bette's relatives decided for the U.S. and left in 1872. There were three groups who first came, for a total of 121 persons. These were from the Odessa area: Johannesthal, Rohrbach and Worms.

These first groups came to Sandusky, Ohio, where there was a German population and a Reformed Church since 1853. From there they sent scouts to the surrounding states but could not find what they were looking for: "We want to be

---

20 *Ibid.*, pp. 368-372.

together and have our church and school."[21]   So they looked further, to Iowa, Nebraska, Minnesota and the Dakota Territory. In this last they found what they were looking for; the land, a steppe, similar to the one in Russia. When they visited Yankton, the city of entry, "They were most pleasantly surprised for they found in ill-reputed Dakota the most pleasant spring weather," and they thought they were back in Russia. When the families arrived in April, they found deep snow lying in the fields! But they stayed anyway.[22]

In 1873 fifty-five families of about four hundred individuals left Worms and Rohrbach for the U.S. This group was led by Johann Grosshans, who had married J. Bonekempers widow, and Heinrich and Michael Griess and Heinrich Hoffmann. They came through Burlington, Iowa, where there were some earlier settlers from the colonies, and then on to Lincoln, Nebraska. They moved on to Sutton where twenty-two of the families bought land from the Burlington Railroad. The rest of the group decided in favor of the Dakota Territory. Yankton was the "Mother City of the Dakotas" at that time, and the German-Russians came there in 1873. However they didn't stay there but began a settlement, which they called Odessa, southeast of present Scotland, South Dakota. The laws passed by congress enabled these immigrants to acquire homesteads cheaply in South Dakota whereas the lands owned by the railroads in Nebraska were higher priced. From then on the German-Russians continued to pour into the countryside through Yankton, among them were those by name of Neuharth, Koerner, Goehring, Aman, Nuss, Becher, Hoff, Bentz. P. F. Neuharth reported,

> First we began to look for land. There was enough of it at that time. All that was necessary was to wish to settle on it and to choose a suitable place. We found such a suitable place forty miles north of Yankton, in Hutchinson County. Then we had to fix us an abode. In the beginning tents were built. Thus my father built one size 10x12 with the help of planks. We children had to sleep on the floor. Of course we did not have a door in our tent. My mother simply hung a blanket over the entrance and that was it. Besides us, two other families were in this region. We were the only ones as far as one could see."[23]

In 1874 the first settler in Menno was Ludwig Mehlhaf. The settlers north of Menno were from Kassel, so that's what they named their settlement. When some moved from there north of Freeman that was called KleinKassel (Little Kassel). In the Tripp area the first settlers came by ox cart from Yankton in 1875, others in

---

21 *Ibid.*, p. 68.

22 *Ibid.*, pp. 70, 71.

23 *Ibid.*, p. 87.

1879. There were also settlements in the Marion, Delmont and Emery areas where Reformed congregations were established. Of the one hundred or so families in the Menno, Scotland, and Tripp area, about half were Reformed.

THE REFORMED CHURCH

In Russia it was the custom for the Lutheran and Reformed congregations to worship together in one parish without stressing the differences in confessions. We remember that there were exceptions to this as in the case where separation occurred in the Worms Rohrbach parish where J. Bonekemper was pastor. But the practice of combined worship did not continue in this country. One Reformed elder reports:

> But we remembered the prayer meetings which we had over there
> and began to gather in the larger homes to hear God's Word in
> order to strengthen our faith and to get consolation for our poor
> heart. Soon a minister of a Lutheran church found us and threw out
> his net, but it was (done) awkwardly and clumsily. He taught us
> that the only right and true church was the Lutheran Church
> Missouri Synod, that the ministers of all other churches were
> fanatics and heretics. The prayer meetings which we held he called
> foolish humbug, which had to come to an end. That was too much;
> we did not want to listen to him any more. . . . Thus we were
> without a religious leader; but God in His mercy thought of
> our need and sent us in Jacob Orth a capable and faithful pastor.[24]

Jacob Orth was born in Worms, South Russia, in 1837. He grew up under the instruction of Pastor J. Bonekemper and became a teacher in the Reformed school. There he served for seventeen years before coming to this country in 1874 to homestead near Lesterville, South Dakota. In Russia the school teacher was also the minister's assistant. He often conducted worship and carried on the religious instruction — since most of the education was religious in character: catechism, Bible History, reading from the Bible, plus writing and arithmetic. So the neighbors of Jacob Orth, being dissatisfied with the Lutheran pastors, asked him to be their spiritual leader. He consented and began holding reading services. Soon there were some from farther away who asked him to do the same for them.

In the providence of God, the Rev. Carl Kuss, who had known Jacob Orth in Russia, was sent out by the Mission Board of the Reformed Church to bring aid to the German-Russian immigrants struggling with the drought and locusts and to help them in their spiritual needs. Rev. Kuss went around with Jacob Orth and

---

24 *Ibid.*, 24.

visited various congregations gathered in overcrowded homes. He preached every day in the week, sometimes three times. He also informed the people on the practices of the Reformed Church. These congregations were then organized into churches, and many are still in existence today.

Rev. Kuss recommended to the Mission Board that $50 be given to Jacob Orth to travel to Sheboygan, Wisconsin, to be examined, licensed and ordained by the Sheboygan Classis. It was given, and he went and attended a few classes at the Mission House Seminary and copied in his notes the *Dogmatics* of Dr. H.A. Muehlmeier. He also became acquainted with the practices of the Reformed Church in the U.S. The Mission Board also offered $500 to the Reformed congregations in South Dakota, but they turned it down for fear of too much influence from Synod! These Dakota congregations were organized into the newly created Nebraska Classis, and later transferred to constitute the Dakota Classis.

After his ordination, Pastor Orth was called by both the Friedens Charge of Tripp and the Kassel Charge of Menno. He chose the Friedens but ended up serving Kassel as well. Congregations organized by him included Scotland, Menno, Tripp, Delmont, Cassel, Marion and others.[25] An example of the stand he took recalls what occurred possibly in the Johannesthal congregation. The group assembled in the house was Lutheran but had diligently attended services though they seemed hesitant to come over to the Reformed side. Orth was somewhat reluctant to go in but was urged to do so. His texts for that day were 1 Kings 18:21, "How long will you halt between two opinions?" and 1 Corinthians 11:19, "For there must be heresies among you. . . ." A few weeks later a Reformed congregation was organized there.[26] Jacob Orth was ordained at age 37 and labored as a pastor for eight years, serving as many as 240 families spread over the area. His estimation of his work, shortly before he died at the age of 46, "I have worked myself to death."[27] Pastor Orth encouraged the reading of sermons by the elders in each congregation on the Lord's Day when there was no minister there. In that way regular worship was encouraged.

In the meantime, the Reformed German-Russians in Sutton, Nebraska, also obtained a pastor. As we mentioned, the widow of Rev. J. Bonekemper (his third wife) had married the teacher Johann Grosshans. They were among the group that came to Sutton. On the trip from Russia to the U.S., while in Hamburg, Germany, Grosshans and H. Hoffmann made the trip to Barmen where William Bonekemper, the son of J. Bonekemper and his third wife, was studying at the Mission House to be a missionary to China. They petitioned the school to send William to the U.S.

25 *Ibid.*, p. 375-377.

26 *Ibid.*, p. 173.

27 *Ibid.*, p. 377.

when he finished his education. This was agreed as long as the group would pay his travel expense. So in 1876 William Bonekemper came to Sutton and was ordained as a Reformed minister. The next week the Immanuel Reformed Church was organized in Sutton, and Pastor Bonekemper served the parish for thirty-two years.

In 1897 a group withdrew from the Immanuel Reformed Church and organized the Free German Reformed Salem Church, calling Rev. Michael Hofer from Menno, South Dakota, to be its pastor. Rev. Hofer served this congregation for thirty-one years, until his death in 1929. Since that time, this congregation has continued to read over again and again in the German language 275 published sermons of the more than 800 he preached.[28] This congregation is aptly referred to as the "Hofer Church." In recent years many of the younger families have joined Immanuel or Hope churches in Sutton. Hope Reformed Church was also organized by a group that withdrew from Immanuel Church. Seventy-one members organized the church in 1908. Rev. U. Zogg was its first pastor. Hope Reformed Church was independent until 1937 when it joined the Nebraska Classis of the Synod of the Northwest. But it withdrew again in 1942 and in 1945 under the second pastorate of Rev. Zogg, the congregation united with the Eureka Classis, RCUS. The Immanuel Reformed Church went along with the mergers, though maintaining the Heidelberg Catechism and its Reformed stance. In 1969 Immanuel withdrew from the United Church of Christ and overwhelmingly voted to rejoin the Reformed Church in the U.S., Eureka Classis.

In the Dakotas the German-Russians, including the Reformed, moved northward in 1884 and 1885. In central South Dakota there were congregations at Alpena, Wessington Springs and Highmore. West of the Missouri there was a church at Herrick. But the main movement was to the northern counties, Edmunds, McPherson, Walworth and Campbell. Most of the Reformed settlers there came from the Menno area. In 1887 the railroad terminated at Eureka, and Eureka was for a while the "Wheat Capital of the World." It really seemed that the community had "found it," since that's the meaning of the name. The Rev. Frank Grether, a Reformed Church missionary to the Dakotas, visiting at the time was present at the meeting when the name was being considered. He suggested "Eureka" - "I have found (it)." This Greek word was reportedly said by Archemides when he found out how to refine gold.[29] The Eureka Classis founded in 1911 was given that name for the same reason, having nothing to do with the town of Eureka, but indicating that they had truly found a way to maintain their Kohlbrueggian theology in the less-than-sympathetic RCUS.

Congregations were also numerous in the areas surrounding Artas, Herreid,

28 T. C. Wenzlaff, *Pioneers on Two Continents*, p. 46.

29 G. Rath, *op. cit.,* p. 118.

Hosmer and Leola. In 1887 the South Dakota Classis was organized with four ministers, twenty-nine congregations, 1145 confirmed members and 1400 unconfirmed. Rev. Walter Odenbach has said the obvious, "The need for German speaking ministers was great in the Dakotas, lack of whom considerably hampered the growth of the Reformed church. Congregations were organized but there were too few pastors to serve them."[30]   And again, "It seems likely that the Reformed Church in the United States missed a great opportunity to gain more strength in South Dakota because it failed in any strong missionary effort to organize more congregations and have more pastors available to serve them. The availability of pastors was the major problem."[31]   Language too was a problem since as one elder said, "Unser Gott is ein Deutscher Gott" (Our God is German).[32]

A great many German Russians entered North Dakota. Early Reformed settlements were in the area of Streeter and Medina in Stutsman County, served by the traveling missionary Rev. Peter Bauer, and in the Ashley-Wishek area, under the ministry of Rev. H. W. Steinecker. Congregations were also established at Upham, up north, and at Heil, out west river. Also there were a number of congregations in the Goodrich area, again served by Rev. Bauer. Very interesting reading is his booklet, *Experiences From My Missionary Life in the Dakotas*.[33] Also very inspiring are the spiritual pilgrimages of Johannes Bonekemper, Carl Bonekemper and Michael Nuss found in the *Heritage Review*.[34]

A number of the early pastors who contributed much to the life of the Reformed Church in the Dakotas came from South Russia: Carl Bonekemper, Peter Bauer, Michael Nuss and Michael Hofer. Other ministers who played an important part were F.A. Rittershaus, A. Steinecker and Ulrich Reue. (No doubt others could be mentioned.) Michael Hofer was the most controversial of these. He had been a missionary worker in India. When he came to Scotland, South Dakota, in 1883 he claimed he was ordained but had no papers to prove it and the authorities in Russia said that he never had been ordained. He refused to be examined, licensed and ordained by the Classis but let his church elders ordain him. The Reformed Church therefore erased his name for its roll of ministers. Thereafter he pastored the Reformed Zion Church (Kassel), north of Menno, and led it out of the bounds of the

30 W. Odenbach in *History of the U.C.C. in S.D.*, p. 206.

31 *Ibid.*, p. 214.

32 *Ibid.*

33 Peter Bauer, *Experiences From My Missionary Life In The Dakotas* (Germans from Russia Heritage Society, Bismarck, ND).

34 *Heritage Review*, (Germans from Russia Heritage Society, Bismarck, ND).

RCUS.[35] Later, as we have seen, he went to the Free Reformed Church near Sutton, Nebraska. The Zion Reformed Church, sometime later, returned to the RCUS, joining the Eureka Classis in 1944. On the whole these pastors were dedicated servants of Christ, and to read of their lives and labors is truly edifying and inspiring. In many ways the Reformed Church in the U.S. today is a living fruit of the labors of Johannes Bonekemper. As it was said of him in 1848, "For a long time this blessing which he left will be with us, a memorial which he established by his activities of twenty-four years."[36] Professor Rath goes on to say with regard to the continuing Reformed Church, "The pietistic inclinations of Bonekemper were quenched during the years but not the Reformed convictions."[37] How did that happen? Enter Dr. Kohlbruegge.

WHO IS KOHLBRUEGGE?

Who was Dr. Hermann Friedrich Kohlbruegge, that he made such a lasting impression on the German-Russians in the Dakotas? He was not a German-Russian, and he never came to America. For that matter neither was he ever in Russia. His life span though was during the same period that most of the fore bearers of our Dakota German-Russians were in Russia. His dates were 1803 - 1875, and our German-Russian Reformed began settling in the Odessa area in 1804 - 1805 and started to leave around 1874. While they may have been contemporaneous, there was no personal connection.

Actually Hermann Friedrich Kohlbruegge was born in Amsterdam, the Netherlands. As a child he acquired from his grandmother great enthusiasm for "church, Netherlands and Orange,"[38] this last being the House of Orange, the ruling family of the Netherlands. On his deathbed he said, "Cut me up and you will find nothing but Orange."[39] His mother was Dutch, Petronella Terhuis, but his father, Hermann Gerhard, was a German immigrant from Osnabrueck in western Germany. Hermann Friedrich was baptized in the Westerkerk Reformed Church, but his parents left that congregation because of its liberalism and joined a "*Hersteld*" (Restored) Lutheran Church, a group which had separated from the more liberal Lutheran congregation to restore original Lutheranism.

After the time of Luther a number of controversies raged among the Lutherans. While we think generally of the differences between the Reformed and Lutheran on the Lord's Supper, relating also to the person of Christ, these were by

---

35 G. Rath, *op. cit.*, p. 177.

36 *Ibid.*, p. 289.

37 *Ibid.*

38 H. K. Hesse, *H. F. Kohlbruegge* (Emil Muellers Verlag, Wuppertal-Barmen, 1935), p. 25.

39 *Ibid.*, p. 26.

no means the only areas of discussion and disagreement among Lutherans. Luther had raised the basic issue of how a man can be righteous before God, and thereupon founded the Reformation on the biblical doctrine of justification by faith. Or as is frequently stated, by faith **alone**. Virtually no one denies the role of faith in justification; it's the "alone" part that creates the controversies.

In the Majoristic Controversy, it was charged that George Major omitted the word "alone" in the phrase justification by faith alone. He later denied this but said, "I will teach all my life that good works are necessary for salvation."[40]   In the course of the controversy Amsdorf over-reacted by writing a pamphlet, "Good Works Are Injurious to Salvation: This is a correct, true, Christian proposition taught and preached by St. Paul and Luther."[41]   A further issue growing out of this controversy was the place of the law in the life of the Christian — the Antinomistic Controversy. Some held that there is no use of the law in the life of the Christian, who should simply remain in faith. The Synergistic Controversy dealt with the question of the freedom of the will and man's cooperation in conversion, that is, "Man must do his part." In attempting to defend genuine Lutheranism, Flacius went so far as to say that not only is man dead in sin but that the image of God has been replaced by the "true and living image of the devil."[42]   Then there was the Controversy with Osiander who said that Christ's righteousness was infused into the believers for justification rather than accounted to them as the forensic (legal) ground of their acceptance with God. These and others were the battle grounds between the Philippists, defenders of certain positions attributed to Philip Melanchthon, Luther's aid and successor, and the *Gnesio* Lutherans, or "original, genuine" Lutherans, who claimed to be going back to Luther. The issues raised in these controversies certainly had some bearing on the questions that Kohlbruegge wrestled with later on.

So it was in the Hersteld Lutheran congregation that Kohlbruegge grew up and received his catechetical training. As a child he entered whole soul into the Bible stories his grandmother told him, and as a boy he didn't care much about playing. He gave himself to learning Greek, Latin and Hebrew, and in time Syriac and Arabic. Books were his joy and pleasure. At the age of twenty he attended the theological lectures of Professors Hengel and Bendinger for three years, after which he became a vicar in his home congregation and thus a candidate for ordination in the Lutheran church. Meanwhile his father's business, a soap factory, failed and so did his health with it. "Now I die in peace," he said on his deathbed when his son

---

40 *Book of Concord*, (Concordia Publishing House, St. Louis, MO, 1922), p. 115.

41 *Ibid.*, p. 122.

42 *Ibid.*, p. 144.

promised to continue his studies until he received his Doctor of Theology degree.[43]

REVIVAL AND CONVERSION

Revival was sweeping across Europe at this time, especially among the Reformed. Called *Le Reveil*, it began in French Switzerland, and spread through France and settled in Holland to produce among other things what we know as the Christian Reformed Church. Kohlbruegge delved into this movement in Holland and associated with its leaders; the Reformed Bilderjik, a famous poet, and his disciple, the converted Jew, Isaac Da Costa, who became the leader of the movement. Kohlbruegge met with these and other intellectuals in the stimulating gatherings in their homes. Yet it seems he saw this as an indulgence in mysticism. A life of uninterrupted prayer and contemplation of God is not healthy. One day he heard a voice ask, "What are you worshiping — God or yourself?" He confessed that he worshiped himself; that he had brought God down out of heaven and into his heart. "Then he lost and condemned mysticism."[44]   So in his first sermon he stood before the Hersteld congregation as one who was not a mystic nor a poet, but as one who had lost all possiblity of saving himself and cast himself into the arms of grace by which God saves the godless. "As far as virtue and works are concerned, we are done for — faith alone justifies. Only by this will we enter the kingdom of heaven. Only by this can we stand before God."[45]

In 1825, "In fear of hell, I had the Bible before me. . . in a moment something penetrated my heart that I cannot describe. . . . I heard the words of Isaiah 54:7-10. A cloud of deep peace was in me and around me, and all my sins were gone from me. And from that hour I spoke another language."[46]   This continued until 1833. This first conversion occurred as he was preparing a sermon on Romans 5:1. Later he was to experience a second conversion when he was preparing his famous sermon on Romans 7:14.

Though he got a good response to his sermon from some, it did not go over so well with the powers that be. Liberal tendencies were now felt in the Hersteld congregation too. Pastor Uckermann was of that mind and he persuaded the church consistory: "He had committed a mortal sin; he had brought unrest to the congregation; he couldn't stay." In Kohlbruegge's own words, "I threw the match into the powder keg." He told the congregation, "What I preached to you I have

---

43 H.K. Hesse, *op. cit.*, p. 35.

44 *Ibid.*, p. 54.

45 *Ibid.*, p. 55.

46 *Ibid.*, pp. 55, 56.

learned from the Lord. It came out of my heart. . . "[47]   So Kohlbruegge was deposed from his position in the Hersteld church but later declared that it was "the true church (that) was excommunicated out of the fellowship."[48]

Kohlbruegge was now jobless and down to his last penny, but he remembered the promise to his father and moved from Amsterdam to Utrecht where a stranger befriended him and gave him housing. There he pursued his doctoral studies and chose for his dissertation Psalm 45. In this he defended the orthodox view as over against the view that Uckermann held. After receiving his doctorate he got married to Catherina Louisa Engelbert, an orphan, and a member of the Hersteld congregation. But her grandmother forbade the marriage until she knew that Kohlbruegge was defending the view of Psalm 45 that it was about Christ and His bride![49]

CONVERSION TO CALVIN

Surprisingly now we find that the Kohlbruegges sought to have their first child baptized in the Reformed Church in Utrecht. In his soul searching study of the prophets he became convinced of the sovereignty of God and His election, and he concluded that Calvin and the Reformed church best understood this. Also he remembered his roots in the faith of his grandmother, as well as the historic, stalwart stand of the Dutch Calvinists. So Kohlbruegge became a Calvinist, though he didn't give up Luther. In fact he read more of Luther than Calvin, but the clear explanation of Scripture by Calvin deeply impressed him. And he gladly embraced the teaching of Olevianus in the Heidelberg Catechism.

So Kohlbruegge stated, "I could no longer, as an honest man, accept an office in the Lutheran Church. . . ."[50] But now when he applied for membership in the Netherlands Reformed Church, he was rejected and told by the president of the Classis, "We must have peace in our church." Kohlbruegge was considered a troublesome agitator. But still he felt his was a happy situation because he took it as a "powerful proof of the truth."[51]

Kohlbruegge turned to his friends in the *Reveil* movement for support, but their individualism and differences of opinion proved no help. He was desperate, yet

---

47 *Ibid.*, p. 68.

48 *Ibid.*, p. 78.

49 *Ibid.*, p. 89.

50 Eric Bristley, *An Historical Comparison of the Interpretation of Romans 7:14-25 in Augustine, Luther, Calvin and H.F. Kohlbruegge* written in 1981 at Westminster Theological Seminary, Phila., PA. Mr. Bristley was a licentiate of the Eureka Classis, RCUS in 1984. He very graciously sent me this paper and other information which was very helpful to me. p. 29.

51 Hesse, *op. cit.*, p. 106.

the dregs of the cup were not yet drained, his beloved wife died of a fever leaving him with two small children. Then the news reached him that his dear brother had died at sea. Truly the shadow of death hung over him; yet he wrote "The Lord is with us. . . . He is our portion. He leads us in the narrow way to glory. . . ."[52]

FINAL CONVERSION

When he was thirty years old, Kohlbruegge's doctors advised him to take a cruise down the Rhine for the sake of his health. As he made his way he looked for those who "understood the language of Canaan," or as some would say today, who "really know the Lord." His journey took him to the Wuppertal Valley, where at an earlier date revival had come. And now the fire had been rekindled by the Reformed pastors Gottfried Daniel Krummacher and his nephew, Friedrich Wilhelm Krummacher, at the Reformed Church at Elberfeld. Kohlbruegge was welcomed here and even asked to preach. Sixteen times in one month he gave witness to the all sufficient grace of the Gospel of Christ. He proclaimed the inability of man, even the pious man, and God's justification of the ungodly.

On July 29, 1833, Kohlbruegge spoke at the Mission House in Barmen on the text Romans 7:14, explaining it in the traditional manner: "I am fleshly, that is, as much as I am fleshly, I am sold under sin." When he arrived home he had a request from G.D. Krummacher, who was sick, asking him to preach for him on Wednesday evening. Kohlbruegge asked God for a text and then settled on the text Romans 7:14. As he thought on the text,

> . . . he noticed something which he never noticed before, and this changed the whole sense of the entire chapter, and everything came in a new light. In the Greek text there was a comma after the word "fleshly." This caught a hold of him and shook him up - it was an enlightenment to him. Hence, not only "as far as I am fleshly, I am, Paul, sold under sin." No. "I Paul as Paul am fleshly; I Paul am, as I am, sold under sin; I also as the regenerate man am opposed to the law." And this sudden insight did not distress him but rather it made him drunk with comfort. He had to praise the mercy of God.[53]

This date, July 31, 1833 was a very special date in Wuppertal, but also in the life of Kohlbruegge. A second conversion of Kohlbruegge had taken place. "I don't know that in my whole life anything has gripped me more than the seeing of this comma." That even the regenerate (those born again) stand under the judgment,

52 *Ibid.*, p. 123.

53 *Ibid.*, p. 151 & Bristley, p. 35. But there were no commas at all in the earliest Greek manuscripts, *ie*. the uncials (ed. note).

"I am flesh, sold under sin." Thus for the regenerate also Christ alone is wisdom, righteousness, sanctification and redemption. Kohlbruegge intends from now on to proclaim that God justifies the godless, and that Jesus Christ as the one made sin by God coming in the flesh is the only Savior. He says, "I am fleshly. — notice what we read. Paul does not say . . . I was previously — but I **am** fleshly." This was now Kohlbruegge's message to all, and the emphasis that would dominate his preaching and the preaching of the Kohlbrueggians. It is that God justifies the ungodly, and that includes the believer as well; "I am fleshly, sold under sin."[54] Was this a second conversion of Kohlbruegge? Rightly understood, it was a conversion of his conversion.[55]

With this very special day in the spiritual pilgrimage of Kohlbruegge, we will break off following the details of his life except to give a brief summary. He was asked to continue in the Reformed Church at Elberfeld, but he was unable to be licensed to preach because the Prussian government viewed him as an opponent to their proposed union of the Lutheran and Reformed churches.

He returned to Utrecht and remarried. Because of the poor health of his wife some time was spent at Godesburg in Germany. Many gathered on Sundays to hear him open the Scriptures to them. At Elberfeld a battle over the union and a new liturgy caused a group of twenty-nine to leave the Reformed Church. Daniel and Carl van der Heydt were its leaders. In 1846 they sent a call to Kohlbruegge to come and be their pastor. He accepted and sought ordination, but neither the Reformed Church in Elberfeld nor the Reformed Church in the Netherlands would ordain him. So the congregation of fifty-three decided to ordain him themselves. In the meantime the church was organized as the Niederlaendisch Reformierte Gemeine with the Belgic Confession, the Scotch Confession and the Heidelberg Catechism as its doctrinal standards. It was recognized by the Prussian state, and in 1848 Kohlbruegge was ordained by the elders of the congregation which had grown to 696 members. While Kohlbruegge was considered controversial, and there was much opposition to the church, in time there was acceptance and Kohlbruegge was fairly well received in the Reformed Church in Germany and in his native Holland. He was a friend of the famous Dr. Abraham Kuyper in the Netherlands and was invited to preach in his church in Amsterdam. He continued to serve the independent Elberfeld congregation until his death on March 5, 1875. Kohlbruegge's sermons and writings were widely distributed among the Reformed in Europe and to some extent here in America, including among the German-Russians. And that's our story — but first a look at the theology of Dr. Kohlbruegge.

54 Hesse, *op. cit.*, pp. 151-153.

55 *Ibid.*, p. 156.

THE THEOLOGY OF KOHLBRUEGGE

Life's experiences help to forge one's faith and theology. It's true in the Bible. God touched the lives of His people with His redemptive revelation. But it's also true in our lives; and as we have seen, the life situation of Hermann Friedrich Kohlbruegge largely directed and drove him to his theological conclusions. To some extent his was a theology of reactions. He not only spoke to his generation but in many ways he spoke against it. And not just against the rationalism and liberalism which was rampant in the nineteenth century, but also against the pietistic reaction to them. Kohlbruegge saw both the liberalism of his day and its pietism as man centered. He saw the focus of the Gospel elsewhere, and in his own catechism, *Die Lehre des Heils* (The Doctrine of Salvation) the three parts are — I. I am man and nothing more; II. That God is God; III. God also fulfills His promises to me. This could be summarized, "Let God be God," and that certainly is not a foreign theme to Reformed thinking.   At one time Kohlbruegge began translating Bunyan's *Pilgrim's Progress* but gave it up in favor of writing what appears to be a more autobiographical "conversation between two pilgrims on the journey to eternity" entitled *Die Sprache Kanaans*. This title was taken from Isaiah 19:18, "The Language of Canaan," and Kohlbruegge takes it to mean the conversation of the redeemed. In this allegory the pilgrims are tempted by various religious groups: free-thinkers, moralists, rationalists, revivalists, liberals, skeptics, quietists, pietists, anti-nomists and separatists (these were Kohlbruegge's conflicts in Holland); then the unionists, orthodox glad-hearers, peace preservers, enthusiasts, planners and sentimentalists (with these he struggled in Germany). But none of these could help the pilgrim find the King, "I was concerned about the city, that I might behold the king in His beauty, but they were concerned only about the temple, 'I'. . . .they were all united in this out of eagerness for their own glory. . . . They had the words of truth, but not the truth of the words."[56]

Then in contrast to all the others there is True-Work who said, "I have sinned against the king, and truly against better knowledge and conscience. I am utterly lost." Nothing could console him until one morning he said, "I have found the King, and grace in His eyes. He told me Himself that He has paid everything for me, and that His Father and God is my Father and God and will remain so forever."[57]   Here then we see something of Kohlbrügge's themes: I am nothing (more than man), God is God, and He fulfills His promises to me.

---

56 Edward Martin Huenemann, *Hermann Friedrich Kohlbruegge* (Doctoral Dissertation submitted to the Faculty of Princeton Theological Seminary, Princeton, NJ, 1961) This dissertation was sent to me by Dr. Huenemann's nephew, Lynn Huenemann. It has been very useful to me as I have followed much of Dr. Huenemann's outline. p. 26.

57 *Ibid.*, pp. 28, 29.

We notice, too, the statement about those who had "the words of truth." These were no doubt the orthodox, confessional churches, whose confidence was in believing the right things and maintaining the confessions - but who suffered perhaps from dead orthodoxy. On the other hand there were those who did not have "the truth of the words" because they were trusting in their own religious experience, whether mystics, or the pious, whose confidence was in God's work in them rather than the finished work of Christ.

If then God's grace is not received by merely orthodox belief nor by pious subjective experience, how does one live by grace? By a life out of God. In his *Erlaeuternde Fragen und Antworten Zum Heidelberger Katechismus* (Questions and Answers Explaining the Heidelberg Catechism) he says in regard to Question 8 of the catechism that we need to learn of our depravity,

> To bring us to the conviction that we are truly lost, however virtuous, however pious, however upright we may be, if we are not born of God. So the knowledge of our misery shall drive us to seek life from God, to seek to be justified in Christ. The catechism leads us to a new creation of grace.[58]

This life from God, this life of grace, comes by the Spirit. Kohlbruegge says in regard to the life of thankfulness of the believer,

> Christ has risen from the dead and purchased the Holy Spirit. In His resurrection rests a power of grace for all God-pleasing walk, and His Spirit keeps us in the freedom wherewith Christ has made us free from devil, sin and world. God works with this power and with this Spirit in the believers. . . [59]

But God's free grace operates not in our "God-likeness" but in our "God-forsakenness." Nevertheless there is a real personal encounter with the Lord:

> However dark it appears, before long a guiding star will rise for one; however forsaken one walks along, before long he will surely encounter a companion, who does not, like so many, plague us with a speech which flesh and blood inspire, but encourages us with the words of the Holy Spirit, that through Him we become newly aware from God Himself that it is nevertheless the good way.[60]

This good way is out of the Word of God, law and Gospel. This is one

---

58 *Ibid.*, p. 33.

59 *Ibid.*

60 *Ibid.*, p. 36.

word of God's grace. This Word is Christ in the Scriptures,

> Who can raise up a spirit that is cast down? Only the Word of
> God, yet not the word in itself but united with the Spirit who
> makes alive, who glorifies the grace of Jesus Christ in the soul; the
> letter, we know kills. Only through the Spirit of the Lord are the
> words of the Lord spirit and life to us.[61]

For Kohlbruegge the Bible is the Word of God, self-validating and verbally inspired. He states, "What a presumption and want of understanding, what lack of attention, what deplorable blindness and ingratitude is manifest when a person questions the verbal inspiration of the Holy Spirit."[62] It is to be noted that Karl Barth was influenced by Kohlbruegge. He considered him the one truly Reformed theologian of the nineteenth century. The Barthians endeavor to find in Kohlbruegge a forerunner of their dialectical and existential theology. But our fathers in Eureka Classis understood Kohlbruegge's view of Scripture to mean not only that the Bible is the Word of God, but that the Word of God is the Bible.

For Kohlbruegge the Bible, law and Gospel, is all Christ. The law was preached throughout the Holy Scriptures but its full spirituality is revealed in the New Testament and is fulfilled in Christ. The law must prevail for both unbeliever and believer. Romans 7:14 is central here, "For we know that the law is spiritual; but I am fleshly, sold under sin." The law is misused when the Christian seeks either to use it legally as a means of justification, or subjectively as a measure of his sanctification. The believer when he sees himself in the light of the law can only see his own death. "The law is the commandment which kills while the Spirit makes alive."[63] The law itself is good, but man uses it wrongly because of sin.

> Therefore it was not that which is good in itself, but I myself, who
> made use of the good in such a way that thereby I brought death
> upon me: and because I brought death upon me by that which is
> good, it had to become clear that that sin had become sinful
> beyond measure through the commandment.[64]

When the Heidelberg Catechism asks in question 3, "From where do you know your misery? Out of the law of God," Kohlbruegge uses this as the place to bring in the Ten Commandments and prayer; but primarily (as Luther) to reveal man's sin in contrast to the optimistic view of man in that age. So Kohlbruegge

---

61 *Ibid.*, p. 38 & Kohlbruegge, *I Believe in the Holy Spirit* (Reliance Printing Co., Green Bay, WI, n.d.) p. 6.

62 Kohlbruegge, *I Believe in the Holy Spirit*, p. 5.

63 Huenemann, *op. cit.*, p. 66.

64 H.F. Kohlbruegge, *Romans Seven* (Reliance Publishing Co., Green Bay, WI, 1951), pp. 25,26

entitles the first section of his catechism, "I am Man and Nothing More." He then asks, "What are you saying when you say you are human? That I am subject to vanity, that I am evil and sold under sin."[65] But isn't man made in God's image? Yes, this is the effulgence and reflection of His glory, to which He gave a form which is the image in which man is made.[66] Kohlbruegge understands man's sin as being that like Adam he does not accept God's word but desires to know good and evil. Man's inability then is his passion to have his salvation in his own hands.[67] This is the great temptation of the third use of the law as the standard of the Christian life. If Christ has fulfilled the law, then man cannot take into his own hands to add to the finished work of Christ. It is here that he must learn that he is flesh and nothing more, and must seek his life from God. It is the law of God's grace that condemns him because he is unwilling to live by every word which proceeds out of the mouth of the Father as a word of promise but seeks to take the law in his own hands. Man knowing himself as a sinner is not just the first step in the right relationship to God, it is the continued walk of the Christian who in Christ is *simul just et peccator* - at the same time righteous and sinner.[68]

The second part of Kohlbruegge's catechism is "That God is God." This means that, "When I confess to being a man, a sinner, I leave to God the honor of being none other than the one who has made Himself known to us in His Word."[69] This revelation of God is in the Mediator, the only begotten and well-beloved Son, Jesus Christ our Lord in whom God did "establish His law, remove the barrier of sin and present man to Himself in righteousness."[70] To do this He came in the flesh, in our state. He was made sin for us by God so that we might be made the righteousness of God in Him and be restored to that state in which Adam was originally. Because He did this in my place I do God's will when I regard this as a certain truth. For Kohlbruegge, in the incarnation Christ did not come in the nature of Adam before the fall, but rather "in flesh," the state of man separated from God.[71] This was life apart from God, that is under the law and judgment of God. "Now Jesus was the person of the sinner, had become sin for us. The whole curse of the law, the eternal condemnation rested on Him."[72] (Kohlbruegge of course did not teach that Christ committed any sin or was personally sinful.) We are justified

65 Huenemann, *op. cit.*, p. 128.

66 *Ibid.*, p. 129.

67 *Ibid.*, p. 130.

68 *Ibid.*, p. 149.

69 *Ibid.*, p. 152.

70 *Ibid.*, p. 153.

71 *Ibid.*, p. 158.

72 *Ibid.*, p. 159.

before God in Christ through faith. Yet our faith, as we ourselves are, is sinful and according to the flesh, so that it is not our faith that justifies but the faith and faithfulness of Jesus Christ. The biblical phrase "faith of Jesus" is not understood by Kohlbrueggians as our faith in Jesus but of Jesus own faith and faithfulness on our behalf.[73]

The third part of Kohlbruegge's catechism is "That God Fulfills His Promises to Me." Here however he does not deal with the commandments, as does the Heidelberg, for the law is not for him the means and measure of our sanctification. Thankfulness is "to take leave of my 'I can, I should, I would,'" and "proclaim His righteousness only, preach His name, and seek refuge at the throne of His grace. . . in order by grace to please God. . . ."[74] We cannot please God with "works that He did not command," to quote Kohlbruegge on Heidelberg Question 2. These works are an effort at self-sanctification. True sanctification is the actualization of justification in the life of the believer. True thankfulness is to accept what God has offered to me and use it with joy. Kohlbruegge cites the dog as the most thankful of God's creatures because he is faithful to his master and approaches him in the most humble way precisely at the time when he has been punished! "He is thankful to God who confesses that it is impossible for him ever to be thankful to God."[75] Christ is the Christian's "new man" just as Adam is his "old man." The man in Christ walks in the Spirit and brings forth the fruit of the Spirit, that is to deny himself and do God's will which is to believe (I John 3:23). Our conversion, when we have put off the old man and put on the new, occurred "in the crucifixion and resurrection of Christ. . . " We become partakers of this when:

> a certain moment occurs in our life in which, by the Spirit of faith, we are transferred into this grace (salvation) and pass from death into life. That is the complete transformation of a person which reconciles him to the righteousness which is valid before God, a transformation which is also called a new birth.

Kohlbruegge says that the mark of that rebirth is "That I fear God, love and honor my neighbor, and not comfort myself with my rebirth but with the eternal faithfulness and mercy of God."[76] For Kohlbruegge sanctification is the work of God in the *Gemeine* — the building up of the body of Christ in the fellowship of the believers, that is the church.

---

73 *Ibid.*, p. 169.

74 *Ibid.*, p. 174.

75 *Ibid.*, p. 178.

76 *Ibid.*, p. 187.

KOHLBRUEGGIANISM AND THE GERMAN-RUSSIANS

So far we have looked at the circumstances and concerns of Kohlbruegge's life that helped formulate his doctrine. And we've taken a summary look at that doctrine without much comment or criticism. Before we do that, there is another question: How did this teaching of Kohlbruegge enter the Reformed Church in the U.S., and more particularly, how did it become the basis on which the Eureka Classis was formed? Remembering that this one classis did not go into the merger but remained faithful to the Reformed faith and to preserving the Reformed Church? Was this teaching in South Russia before these people came here? Or did they get it after they were here? Or both there and here? I remember forty years ago when I first came into Eureka Classis there were many statements made about the early days. So I thought I would ask some of the old-timers. I made a lot of phone calls here, there and just about everywhere. And what did I learn. There are no more old-timers. I myself am one of them now, and those I asked couldn't remember any of the answers anymore!

But I felt I couldn't write this chapter without the answer to that question of the origin of Kohlbrueggianism in Eureka Classis. Then one day I recalled seeing something in the booklet, *Experiences From My Missionary Life In The Dakotas* by the Rev. Peter Bauer, that referred to Kohlbruegge. Pastor Bauer served too many congregations to get to them frequently enough.

> To help overcome this shortcoming, we installed reading services in all the congregations in which the elder read the sermon to the congregation in my absence. I had learned about the writings of Kohlbruegge in Worms, South Russia from Pastor A. Vencianer, who had been a pupil of Kohlbruegge, and I introduced them into all my congregations. Several years later an elder once said to me: "Pastor, did you know that you would no longer be with us today if you had not introduced Kohlbruegge's writings into the congregation?" I said to the man, "This I know right well, that is why I placed them into your hands.[77]

So there we have it. Already in Russia the influence of Kohlbruegge was felt in the Reformed Churches, and it was brought over here.

But I still thought there must be other sources as well, especially as I looked through fifty years of *The Witness* magazine and saw all the articles setting forth the distinctive Kohlbrueggian teaching. Then I heard this story. A theological student from Germany was traveling through Iowa on the train. He became ill and was put

---

77 P. Bauer, *op. cit.*, p. 11.

off the train at Dubuque. He did not recover but died and left a box of books. Pastor Jacob Stark came into possession of these books, books by Kohlbruegge, and consequently became convinced of this teaching and then began teaching it himself.

However afterwards I came across a more authorized version of this story in the book, *Zeugnisse Reformierter Lehre* (Testimonies of Reformed Doctrine) by Pastor Stark. He was pastor at the Presbyterian church at Sherrills Mound near Dubuque. In 1877 a student came to Rev. Stark, Rudolph Grau by name, who was sick and broke. For awhile Rev. Stark extended his hospitality to him. This student had been acquainted with Adolph Zahn, a Kohlbrueggian, at Halle in Germany and had attended the student-parties at his home, which were actually Bible studies. The student had brought with him the writings of Zahn, Wickelhaus (a good friend of Kohlbruegge) and of Kohlbruegge. Stark read these and was stirred deeply by them. So much so that he couldn't let go of them and was by them led into the Scriptures. At this point he had to part with many things he previously held as his only comfort on the way to blessedness, that is, the holy "I" and the self-life of the regenerate. From a pious man he had to become an unclean sinner with no advantage over the godless and sinners but found life only through faith in Christ.

The more he studied the more convinced he became, and he became the leader if this "new teaching," though there was soon much opposition to it in the Presbyterian Church. By his home training and excellent studies at Princeton Seminary, he was well suited for leadership, though, as he says, he had to unlearn many things that he had learned at Princeton before he had read Kohlbruegge. He had spent three years at Princeton and was a fellow-student with Benjamin B. Warfield, the famous Presbyterian theologian and Princeton professor.

Stark was an editor of the *Presbyterianer* (the Presbyterian), but when the editorial office became a theological battleground, the paper was discontinued. He then became a founder of the *Waechter* (the Watchman), a vehicle for sending forth the new teaching. In 1883 he became pastor at Waukon, Iowa, for twelve years. But in the controversies over doctrine he made some strong personal attacks and was deposed from the ministry of the Presbyterian Church. Then in 1896, while living on a farm, he was invited to preach a missionfest in South Dakota. It was his first contact with the German-Russians. Though he had been deposed they showed him great respect and could not get enough of his sermons. For eleven years he preached among the German-Russians and continued the publication of the *Waechter*. These were years of much joy and pleasure in his work. He died of cancer at age sixty.[78]

So according to my understanding it was through Pastor Jacob Stark that

---

78 Jacob Stark, *Zeugnisse Reformierter Lehre* (Central Publishing House, Cleveland, OH, 1909), pp. vii-xvi.

the German Presbyterians and the German-Russians in the Reformed Church in South Dakota were strengthened in Kohlbrueggianism. Now there may have been others also, since the Reformed churches at Garner, Iowa, and Newton, Wisconsin, came under this influence. Newton pastor D.W. Vriesen mentions attenders from Kohlbruegge's church at his home congregation in Suderwyck, and speaks of Pastor Geyser preaching there in his autobiography *Aus meinem Leben*. But at least we have two contacts of Kohlbrueggianism with the German-Russians: Pastor Peter Bauer and Rev. Jacob Stark. (Perhaps when this gets in print and reaches the congregations and other interested readers that more sources will surface. I won't be a bit surprised!)

EXPERIENCES WITH KOHLBRUEGGIANISM

Before concluding this chapter with some of the criticisms that have been made of Kohlbrueggianism and my own evaluations, I would like to include some of my own experiences and impressions on coming in the Eureka Classis in the mid 1950's. At that time Kohlbrueggianism was the dominant, almost universal, message heard in the pulpits of classis. I soon acquired a five-foot shelf of Kohlbrueggian writings, all German, I think. The following evaluations are not intended to be derogatory though some may seem negative. What they attempt to do is bring out how some of the distinctive Kolbrueggian emphases were understood by the people, some people.

One of the first questions I was asked repeatedly at the beginning of my ministry was, "Do Reformed people need to be converted?" I understood from a Reformed covenantal perspective that our children belong to the Lord. They wondered whether these children need to be "converted," as do those outside of the covenant in the world. What I realized later was that the question really meant, "Since our salvation is wholly in Christ and not in us, are we therefore to expect any personal change?" In my first sermons I preached with considerable zeal that the distinct Reformed emphasis was "doing all things to the glory of God." But that seemed to fall on deaf ears - maybe astonished ears. What they understood as the glory of the Reformed Faith was that we do nothing. Christ has done it all — even believe for us - and there is nothing we can or should do. Since we as Christians are totally depraved, there is no difference between us and the world. Sometimes this was taken to mean we could live like the world, and it was reportedly said after some indiscretion or immorality, "that's another one Jesus will have to pay for." Preaching about our sinfulness and even denouncing prevalent sins was well received: "Good sermon." But it did not seem to produce much change. Since our salvation is all in Christ (objectively) and not in us (subjectively), one elder raised the question, "Do I wear my boots in heaven?" meaning, "Will I still have my sinful nature in heaven?"

I'm sure that these responses to his doctrine would have upset Kohlbruegge as much as they did me. And I'm not for a moment suggesting that our older pastors promoted or approved of these aberrations. Most church members showed a sincere interest in the preaching of the Word of God, and as in all denominations and churches there are those whose lifestyle contradicts their profession. Of those pastors that I have known who might be designated as Kohlbrueggians, they were all devout and godly, devoted to the proclamation and practice of the Word of God. Of one of the older ministers it was said, "He doesn't believe in "Christian experience," yet I could only respond that I had never met anyone who demonstrated a greater experience of faith and knowledge of the Lord. In another instance an older minister said to me, "Norman, Norman, it's always the "I," "I," "I." I was a little bit offended by this at first, but afterwards benefited from it. Many hours of my ministry were spent in discussion of these questions concerning the place of the law in our lives as Christians, and whether we really live by grace if we are trying to keep the commandments, since Christ has fulfilled all righteousness for us. Truthfully and thankfully I can say that over the years even where we differed we have respected and loved each other in the Lord, and have shared a common faith, the Reformed faith — that our salvation is in the Lord.

CRITICISM AND EVALUATION

In this closing portion we will look at some of the criticisms that have been brought against Kohlbrueggianism and my own brief evaluation. Kohlbrueggianism has always been sharply attacked. Perhaps that is because it was itself an attack on both traditional Reformed orthodoxy and piety. As we have seen, Kohlbruegge himself reacted against these, and his writings are unrelenting in his criticisms of them. Likewise Jacob Stark went on the attack and brought the censure of the church on himself. Stark's tone is seen in the concluding segment of his *The Church and Her Doctrine,* a segment not included in the booklet but found in *The Witness* and entitled "Kohlbrueggianism."[79] He writes:

> And whoever finds in Kohlbruegge a false concept of the Redeemer, may be wholly sure that he himself believes on an antichrist. . . . Whoever finds antinomianism (opposed to the Law) in Kohlbruegge, ought not to doubt, that he himself is wholly a servant of the law and lies under its curse. This error is not to be attributed to Kohlbruegge, but is always on the side of his opponents. And if these masters be saved - saved at all - then they must learn something about all these contested points of doctrine and learn precisely that what they have contradicted and

---

79 J. Stark, *The Church and Her Doctrine (Kohlbrueggianism)* (*THE WITNESS* Vol. XIX, No. 1, Jan. 1939) p. 6.

maligned in him. In all cases it is only the truth of salvation that has been contested. Nothing else and nothing more. . . . Our Churches' final destiny will be dependent on what we will do with it. Do we yet wait for other teachers of righteousness?

These points of doctrine are set forth in the same piece. Stark rather angrily complains that it is the orthodox Reformed theologians who have opposed Kohlbruegge. Why?

Cause and plausible basis for it was given by the fact, that Kohlbruegge in some instances really goes farther in the reformation doctrine, grasps it more deeply, yes, executes it with less deference than even the Reformers. Thus though apparently led to it by the Reformers, especially Luther, yet he was the first since the time of the Apostles, who grasped and presented the doctrine of **the image of God** in its entire extent and exact truth. Thus he obtained a clearness about **the human nature of the Son of God** and His position **under the law** which no one else had. Accordingly he received light and clearness of the whole **doctrine of the Holy Spirit, of regeneration, justification and sanc-tification.**[80]

The first criticism of Kohlbruegge came from F. W. Krummacher, the pastor of the Reformed Church at Elberfeld. After Kohlbruegge had preached his famous sermon on Romans 7:14 as the guest preacher: "The celebrated guest has *only one side* on his instrument — his constant theme is 'man is flesh and sold under sin, free grace does it alone and does it completely'."[81] Thus the charge of "one-sidedness" was brought against Kohlbruegge and has been repeated ever since.

Perhaps the criticism that stung him the most and hurt him most deeply was in the letter written by his former friend Isaac Da Costa in response to the same sermon: "There is in your teaching a true and blessed teaching of justification by faith without the works of the law. Yet it is not free altogether from the dangers of antinomianism . . . in respect to the Law. . . this doctrine and disposition are not grounded on the infallible word of God." Da Costa then goes on to criticize Kohlbruegge by saying that there is not a greater difference between east and west than between Kohlbruegge's teaching and that of the Heidelberg Catechism. In opposition to Kohlbruegge's doctrine Da Costa says, "This confession that we are still far from what we ought to be is seen in respect to the fact that sanctification follows after conversion and justification, not that we make ourselves holy in our

---

80 *Ibid.*, pp. 6, 7.

81 Huenemann, *op. cit.*, p. 81.

own power, partly or completely. But our sanctification is the forming of the image of Christ in us by the Holy Spirit."[82]

Abraham Kuyper did not criticize Kohlbruegge in this matter because he knew of his concern for the Christian life. But he was critical of Kohlbruegge's son-in-law, Prof. Eduard Boehl, and of the Neo-Kohlbrueggians.[83] In particular he criticized Boehl's doctrine of the image of God that

> Man is created 'in' not 'after' God's image, that is, the image is not found in man's **nature** or **being**, but outside of him in God. Man was merely set in the radiance of that image. Hence, remaining in its light, he would live in that image. But stepping out of it, he would fall and retain but his own nature, which before and after the fall is the same.[84]

Kuyper refutes this position by appeal to Genesis 5:1 where Scripture says that Adam "begat a son in his own likeness, and after his image." Kuyper argues,

> Hence to beget a child in our image and after our likeness means to give existence to a being bearing our image and resemblance, although as a person distinct from us. From which it must follow what when Scripture says, regarding Adam, that God created him in His image and after His likeness. . . it cannot mean that the divine image shone upon him so that he stood and walked in its light; but that God so created him that his whole being, person, and state reflected the divine image, **since he carried it in himself.**[85]

Thus the criticism of Kohlbruegge's contemporaries. But the criticism and controversy goes on. In the United States Rev. H.A. Meier professor at the Mission-House of the RCUS in Plymouth, Wisconsin, attacked Kohlbrueggianism in the seminary publication in 1905 and 1906. The *Waechter* charged Meier with heresy, and a complaint was brought against him from the Eureka congregation but nothing came of it.[86] In more modern times, while there is some appreciation expressed for Kohlbruegge, as by Barth and Berkhouwer, the same criticisms continue. Even Barth

---

82 Bristley, *op. cit.*, p. 41.

83 Neo-Kohlbrueggians were the theological descendants of Kohlbruegge who in succeeding generations took some of his principles to extremes.

84 A. Kuyper, *The Work of the Holy Spirit* (Wm. Eerdmans Publishing Co., Grand Rapids, MI, 1956), p. 218.

85 *Ibid.*, p. 133.

86 J. I. Good, *History of the Reformed Church in the U. S. in the Nineteenth Century*, (New York, the Board of Publications of the Reformed Church in America, 1911) p. 605.

says that he let justification swallow up sanctification, grace swallow up nature and mortification obliterate vivication.[87] Professor Louis Berkhof summarizes most of these criticisms in his preface to Boehl's *The Reformed Doctrine of Justification*; salvation is merely by imputation, the image of God is a sphere in which man lives, neither the fall nor regeneration change the inner nature of man, sanctification is by imputation leaving the regenerate man just as wicked as the unregenerate.[88] To all these criticisms by the renowned professors, Jacob Stark would say,

> Whoever is involved in such errors, will not understand Kohlbruegge, and constantly takes offense. A Reformed professor and a doctor of theology wrote: "Kohlbruegge was a man of God, full of faith and the Holy Spirit; but his exaggerations of the doctrine of justification, his false conception of the person of Christ, and his antinomianism are not to be approved." A man full of faith and of the Holy Spirit and yet a heretic![89]

For my own evaluation of Dr. Kohlbruegge and his disciples and their teaching, I would say that for all the denials of the place of subjective experience in the life of the believer, the Kohlbrueggian doctrine is rooted in the subjective spiritual experience of H.F. Kohlbruegge. He does speak of Scripture and experience. In God's providence his thinking was forged through his own rejections and reactions to them. This is not to psychologize his theology. It is a theology of the Word. But an understanding of the Word that focuses on one idea that had its inception through his own spiritual experiences. He has made it a theological idea and has read both the Bible and the catechism in the light of that idea. The plain words of the Heidelberg Catechism cannot be understood in a Kohlbrueggian sense. His theological idea has to be read into it. The handling of the catechism by the Kohlbrueggians is close to modern literary interpretation which makes a document say what the reader wants rather than what the author intends.

I would like to suggest the following answer to the questions raised by Kohlbruegge. Dr. Geerhardus Vos writes in *The Pauline Eschatolgy:*

> In the Apostle's construction of Christian truth, two distinct strands show themselves. The first we may call the **forensic** one. It revolves around the abnormal status of man in the objective sphere of guilt, and deals with all that is done outside of man, in order to its reversal, so that instead of **unrighteous** he may become

---

87 Huenemann. *op. cit.* p. 210.

88 E. Boehl, *The Reformed Doctrine of Justification*, (Grand Rapids, Wm B. Eerdmans Publishing Co., 1946) Preface by L. Berkhof, p. 10.

89 J. Stark, *"The Witness"*, *op. cit.*, p. 6.

in legal standing **righteous** before God. The other. . . may be called the **transforming** one. It has to do with everything that pertains to the subjective inward condition of him to whom the grace of God is imparted. The former effects justification, the latter regeneration and sanctification. . . . Each (of these two strands) after a fashion may lay claim to relative completeness. Hence. . . some writers from a sense of personal preference have chosen the one line, and tracing it out, have felt that they were offering the student a full-orbed compass of the Apostle's religious thought. All the time they were forgetting, or perhaps with some intentional partiality ignoring, that alongside of it, there runs the other twin strand making up the other semi-cycle of the teaching. . . a loose juxtaposition of two tracks of thinking without at least an attempt at logical correlation is inconceivable. . . the two strands shall not be entirely equal in rank within the system of doctrine, for that would yield a dualism hard to put up with. . . . The solution can hardly be other than that the forensic principle is supreme and keeps in subordination to itself the transforming principle. Justification and sanctification are not the same, and an endless amount of harm has been done by the short-sighted attempt to identify them. But neither are these two independent one of the other; one sets the goal and the other follows.[90]

Vos finds the answer in the resurrection, "the most radical and all-inclusive transforming event." Yet we read that Christ "was delivered for our offenses and raised again for our **justification**" (Romans 4:25). By this foundational principle, the acquisition of righteousness through the resurrection of Christ, we have the basis on which the believer is declared righteous (justified); and by the same event, the resurrection of Christ, the Spirit is gained for our transformation! Kohlbruegge was not all wrong; neither was he all right!

CONCLUSION

"God moves in a mysterious way," the hymn writer tells us. And the Lord Himself reminds us, "Your ways are not My ways" (Isaiah 55:8). Who could have written such a scenario of the story of the saving of the Reformed Church in the U.S.: The German-Russians and Kohlbruegge? Only the Architect who said, **"I will build My Church."**

---

90 G. Vos, The Pauline Eschatology, (Grand Rapids, Wm. B. Eerdmans Publishing Co., 1953), pp. 148-151.

WESTMINSTER THEOLOGICAL SEMINARY
Philadelphia, Pennsylvania

DR. CORNELIUS VAN TIL
Professor of Apologetics

REVEREND PROFESSOR JOHN MURRAY
Professor of Theology
DR. EDWARD J. YOUNG
Professor of Old Testament
(On the *Queen Mary* on Professor Murray's retirement to Scotland)

C H A P T E R   S I X

The Influence of Westminster Theological Seminary on the Reformed Church in the United States

Rev. Howard Hart

There can be little doubt that Westminster Theological Seminary has had a powerful and fundamental impact on our beloved Church, the Reformed Church in the United States (RCUS). Since the late 1920's this orthodox institution has renovated the scenery of Reformed teaching in this country as well as some of the Asian domains.

Let us look at the history of this blessed place of Calvinistic instruction, and then see some of the impact it made on the RCUS.

HISTORY

Westminster Theological Seminary (WTS) was founded in 1929 in Philadelphia, Pennsylvania. The grand purpose of the seminary was to train and equip men to preach the Reformed Faith. The focus of the teaching was the Lordship and grace of Jesus Christ. When I attended the Seminary (1958-1961), I was impressed not only with the great learning of my professors, but their profound piety and dedication to Jesus Christ. Their determination to be faithful to the infallible Word was experienced in every class session. I was in awe not only with the content in the lecture halls but also with the godly demeanor and dedication to Jesus Christ exhibited by the teachers. I was presented with Christ and His glory.

The seminary was founded by faculty members who had been teaching at Princeton Theological Seminary. Since 1812 Princeton was "the" seminary to attend. The high standards of scholarship and the quality of the professorship were the best offered on our continent, if not in the world. The seminary loved the Word of God and was dedicated to an orthodox Presbyterian faith. Princeton was "the" defender and propagator of a rich Calvinistic theology. By the 1920's, however, Princeton was slipping into the camp of those who did not hold a high view of Scripture. The need of the day, for the Modernists, was a more popular and humanly acceptable gospel and ministry (not unlike the present day emphasis of church growth, new life churches, and "practical" Christianity). Several professors at Princeton were determined to continue the exposition of biblical truth which Princeton had been noted for in the past. The leader of this group of dedicated Christian teachers was J. Gresham Machen. He was determined to see the "old" Princeton survive in the midst of the blatant rejection of supernaturalism that had infected Presbyterianism and Princeton itself. Westminster Seminary was founded in the midst of the controversy caused by liberal higher criticism's attacks on the true faith. In the past Princeton's outstanding theologians and leaders had brought distinction to the faculty. Among them were Archibald Alexander, Charles Hodge, J. A. Alexander, B. B. Warfield, William Henry Green, Gerhardus Vos, Robert Dick Wilson, and J. Gresham Machen. It has been said that in the period just preceeding its reorganization, Princeton stood at the very height of influence against Modernism and Indifferentism, which had long been at work in the Presbyterian Church in the United States of America. Princeton stood in loyalty to the Scriptures against the New England and the New School theology of the day. "Old" Princeton met the serious challenge of the day and was an encouragement and assistance for the struggling forces of historic Christianity throughout the world. But opposition within the seminary and opposition without succeeded in overthrowing the "old" Princeton. The reorganization in 1929 meant that the old Princeton had come to an end.

With the passing of the old school it became imperative to begin a new seminary. Westminster Theological Seminary opened its doors in Philadelphia on September 25, 1929, as the real successor of the old Princeton. Robert Dick Wilson, J. Gresham Machen, Oswald T. Allis, and Cornelius Van Til, all of whom had been teaching at Princeton before the controversy of reorganization, along with R. B. Kuiper, Ned B.Stonehouse, Paul Woolley, and Allan A. MacRae, formed the new institution, either as faculty or students, or both. The next year one of the finest theologians in Scotland and in the United States joined the above eminent teaching staff. His name was John Murray. He had received theological training at Princeton and had taught there.

The real continuity between old Princeton and Westminster Seminary was clearly stated by Dr. Machen at the opening of Westminster. He said,

> Though Princeton Seminary is dead, the noble tradition of Princeton Seminary is alive. Westminster Seminary will endeavor by God's grace to continue that tradition unimpaired; it will endeavor, not on a foundation of equivocation and compromise, but on an honest foundation of devotion to God's Word, to

maintain the same principles that old Princeton maintained. We believe first, that the Christian religion, as it is set forth in the Confession of Faith of the Presbyterian Church is true; we believe, second, that the Christian religion welcomes, and that it is capable of, scholarly defence; and we believe, third, that the Christian religion should be proclaimed without fear or favor, and in clear opposition to whatever opposes it, whether within or without the Church, as the only way of salvation for lost mankind. On that platform, brethren,we stand. Pray that we may be enabled by God's Spirit to stand firm. Pray that the students who go forth from Westminster Seminary may know Christ as their own Savior and may proclaim to others the gospel of His love.[1]

The new seminary was founded because of the decline of many churches in the United States as well as in North America as a whole. Professor John Murray pointed out that Westminster Seminary was founded at a critical time in North American church history. He said,

The seminary came into being at a time when the very things for which it was established were being repudiated by a large section of Reformed churches in North America and in Europe. . . . When the enemy came in like a flood, God in His abundant mercy and sovereign providence raised up a standard against him.[2]

Faculty and students were drawn from many different Reformed and even liberal churches of the day. All were intent on the study of the Word of God and its application for the present evil world. Biblical Christianity was defended at the seminary. The teaching was Reformed and not fundamentalistic or baptistic. Westminster did not and does not reduce the gospel to a few "fundamentals." What is sought is to prepare ministers who proclaim the "whole counsel of God" (Acts 20:27).

Several years ago, after some years of discussion, Westminster was reorganized into two Seminaries, one at the old Philadelphia, Pennsylvania, campus, and a new campus at Escondido, California.

Let me quote extensively from the 1995-1996 catalogue of Westminster Theological Seminary in California to give you a flavor of the past and present purpose, conviction, characteristics and doctrinal position of Westminster.

Westminster Theological Seminary in California is a Christian

---

1 *Christianity Today*, Sept. 1930, p. 4.

2 *The Presbyterian Guardian*, July 10, 1944, pages 197-198.

institution of higher education offering instruction in biblical, theological, and ministerial disciplines with a view toward the intellectual and personal preparation of office bearers and other members of the church. The seminary is transdenominational and is committed to confessional Reformed theology. The purpose of the seminary is thus to bring glory to God as an academic institution that serves the Lord Jesus Christ both in the church and in the society at large by nurturing church leaders and members through graduate theological education and other instruction in the Word of God.

The present relationship of the RCUS and WTS is strained. There is an attitude among many of the brothers in the RCUS that WTS is not upholding the "old" Westminster's apologetics and the high view of Scripture that the Church demands for herself. The Synod has sent representatives to talk to Westminster in Philadelphia. Let me quote a committee report adopted by our 249th Synod held in 1995 that deals with the "Doctrine of Scripture at Westminster Seminary (Philadelphia),"

The Special Committee to Study the Doctrine of Scripture at Westminster Seminary (Philadelphia) hereby amends its original report as follows. First, in place of the paragraph titled "Conclusions and Recommendations," we submit the following:

Your committee concludes that there is a cause for concern about various forms of expression used by some professors at Westminster Seminary (Philadelphia), that, at the very least, obfuscate the historic, orthodox understanding of Scripture as defined by the Reformed Creeds. One, for example, describes the inspired writers as "editing" and "reshaping" the text. While we recognize that Moses and Jeremiah carefully chose words and phrases that would cast their accounts in a certain light, the proliferation of such phrases in this professor's writing seems to suggest at times that the Biblical authors were more interested in creating history than reporting it. . . . Another professor espouses a theory of multi-perspectivalism, according to which he comes very close to asserting that man's subjective and subtle perspectives provide the normative key to interpret Scripture. . . .
In the course of time, this may end up destroying their understanding of the unity of the biblical message, which historically meant that the given sense of difficult texts can be known only as they are searched out in other passages that are more clear.

The committee then recommends that the members of Synod keep a "weather eye open" as to the theology of the Word at Westminster (Philadelphia).[3]

THE INFLUENCE OF WESTMINSTER THEOLOGICAL SEMINARY ON THE MINISTERS AND MINISTRY OF THE REFORMED CHURCH IN THE UNITED STATES

Your servant sent out a questionnaire to the present Westminster graduates in the RCUS to poll their opinions on how WTS influenced their lives and their ministry in the RCUS. We presently have thirteen WTS graduates in the RCUS, nine responded to the questionnaire. Questionnaires were also sent to several Elders in the RCUS who have been under the ministry of several WTS men and four of the five responded. From their and my observations I would like to present twelve basic influences this "grand old seminary" had on the ministers and ministry of the RCUS.

1. The WTS men brought and bring to our beloved part of the vineyard of Christ a militant commitment to the authority, infallibility and inerrancy of the Scriptures. The influence of WTS broke the back of the beginning of the inroads of Neo-Orthodoxy in the fifties and sixties in the RCUS. Today, the Church is "bullish" on Scripture. Other Reformed denominations have recognized our faithful stand on Scripture as the only rule of faith and practice.

2. WTS graduates brought with them a reformational theology into a Church that was in most of its theology and practice Reformed. At the same time there were indications that the RCUS was dying. New vigor was injected into the tiny RCUS. The present President of the Executive Committee of Synod, the Rev. Vernon Pollema says, "I believe that WTS broadened the Reformed Church in the United States' view of the Reformed Church and Reformed faith, moving it away from parochialism. WTS also stimulated the RCUS to get on with the task of missions, which is the life-blood of the church. Were it not for a renewed effort in home missions, what would the RCUS look like today?"

The Rev. Paul Treick, a son of the RCUS, gives us similar sentiments, "Without question, God providentially used Westminster to give hope back to the RCUS at a time when we had no theological seminary of our own. Here was a seminary that stood out in terms of scholarship, but equally important, an institution that virtually stood alone to train men to expound and 'contend for the faith once delivered unto the saints.' We are more consistently Reformed in our theology as a result of Westminster. Westminster did not have a denominational ax to grind. It was simply determined to instruct men in the truth of the Scripture so they could

---

3 *1995 Abstract, Reformed Church in the United States*, p. 75.

preach it without compromise against the onslaughts of every false gospel. This gave the RCUS a renewed incentive, not simply to hold our own or relive the painful battles of the past, but through new mission works to bring the Gospel to the lost. In this, Westminster got us out of our shell so we realized that there were yet 7,000 that had not bowed the knee to Baal."

3. WTS gave to its students an appreciation for Biblical scholarship. This is an extremely important point. We live in a day of intellectual "pop and fluff." Anti-intellectualism is rampant in our society and church world. There are some that exhibit the feeling that our denomination is "too careful" about her candidates for the ministry. It might even be said that seminary training is not necessary and possible even harmful to Christians. This mentality will bring the church back to the dark ages. An untutored or blank mind will only bring disaster. The knowledge of a few little fundamental facts about a given idea is very dangerous. We are to preach the "whole counsel of God," and this means depth of understanding and knowledge of the Gospel. WTS men bring with them a sense that the congregation is not stupid but deserve the "meat" of the Word of God. Being a good theologian is a prerequisite for being a good pastor.

4. The courts of the church set up study committees to think through problems and present theological propositions and answers to the contemporary church that is continually being tested from without and sometimes within by errors. When one looks at some of the Special Study Committees' members we see a great influence of Westminster graduates on the present beliefs of the RCUS. Study committees like: Association for the Advancement of Christian Scholarship, Deaconesses, Ecclesiastical Divorce and Remarriage, Infant Communion, Ordination Vow, Reformed Church in the United States Ecclesiology, Right to Die, Theonomy, and Voting in Congregational Meetings, we see a Biblical approach by WTS men being faithful to the Word of God. The studies show the WTS depth and theological acumen that is appreciated not only by the RCUS but also by other Reformed bodies. These "studies" will, for the most part, survive the test of time and be an influence to the church at large.

5. WTS men are trained to preach the Bible. They are not storytellers or "topical" preachers. They tell the congregation the meaning of the text with which they are dealing. They take a grammatical and historical approach in the presentation of the Word of God and have a healthy understanding of the Biblical Theological approach to Scripture. The Rev. Steven Schlei says, "I have never regretted my decision to attend WTS. It gave me the tools to confidently exegete the Bible. In my opinion, it was the best theological seminary in the U.S. (and probably the world) when I attended, and it probably still is the number one seminary in the U.S. today."

6. Without WTS there would have been in the 1950s until the 1970s a dearth of adequately prepared men for the ministry. The Mission House, then in the Evangelical and Reformed Church, had already lost it's foothold on the Reformed faith. WTS filled in the gap. At the present time we have men from other Reformed seminaries. These seminaries have also been influenced by WTS and for the most part reproduce the scholarship and attitude of WTS. Many of the more recent seminaries have WTS men on their faculties.

Elder Clifford Mettler of our congregation in Menno, South Dakota states that WTS "was a place we could have men go to be taught the Calvinistic faith." WTS has produced many fine Calvinistic pastors.

Rev. Robert Grossmann states. "The Eureka Chassis had by 1955 engaged a healthy conservative reaction against theological liberalism. Conservative reactions however, become sterile and unhealthy if they continue only in reaction. To avoid these evils, reaction must be followed by biblical reformation. This reformation must ask and must be able to answer the question, 'How can we be even more biblical and more Reformed than we have been in the past?' The future must be built upon solid biblical ground, not upon human reaction. WTS trained for us a generation of ministers able to work for such a biblical Reformation. . . . The modern RCUS is very much a product of the stubborn adherence of our fathers to biblical authority and truth, and the competent ministry in that truth of the next generation, mostly trained at WTS."

7. WTS men testify that they were influenced by a godly faculty. These pastors in turn influenced their congregation to live a life that was conformable to the example of Jesus Christ. The Rev. Robert Grossmann, a son of the church and third generation minister in the RCUS says. "Can one not have been personally inspired and influenced by the Reformed dynamism of Van Til, the firm doctrinal standards of Murray, the passionate and gentle love for the Word of Young, the vast historical knowledge of Wooley, and the godly example of Christian manhood each exemplified? One of the first two or three privileges and treasures of my life was to study under these great but humble men of God."

8. "Dr. Cornelius Van Til's presuppositional apologetic, which begins and ends with the Triune God, is certainly foremost in my mind and has most influenced my ministry" (The Rev. Paul Treick, a son of the RCUS). The Rev. Steven Schlei testifies that, "This giant of the faith (C. Van Til) gave me an absolute confidence in the truth of the Christian religion. He taught me how to defend the faith against all challengers. He steered me away from rationalistic hyper-Calvinism and taught me to understand Scriptures from a paradoxical perspective."

When we examine men in orthodoxy and purity of intent, for licensure, or for ordination, we have a separate section on Apologetics. If a man does not know and believe in a presuppositional apologetic, that is gathered from the Word of God, the man is rejected. Apologetics is the defense of the faith against the modern mentality that causes a large brood of tensions for the Christian, since the credibility of the Christian faith is always under attack.

Apologetics takes the defensive and offensive posture to build up the Christian in his faith. The RCUS is becoming one of the last bastions in this country for the biblical apologetic. In keeping with presuppositional apologetics, we are a self-consciously Calvinistic denomination. We make no excuses for our position on the historic Christian faith.

9. Influence on a son of the church is best illustrated by the words of the Rev. Lloyd Gross, now retired from the active ministry. Here are excerpts from his testimony.

> The influence of WTS on my theology is immeasurable. I shifted in my own theology from a latent antinomianism to the view of the law of God as articulated in the Heidelberg Catechism, the Belgic Confession, and the Westminster Confession. Before entering WTS I held an incipient orthodox Lutheran view of the law which is that it mainly shows us our sinfulness. WTS held up clearly for me the Reformed view of the law that it indeed shows us our sinfulness, drives us to Christ, and that we earnestly strive now to keep all the commandments of God to show our thankfulness to God for our redemption. The emphasis on the Third Part of the Heidelberg Catechism became more apparent to me at Westminster. Also, at Westminster I shifted from a Neo-Kohlbrueggian theological emphasis to a more Calvinistic emphasis. . . . I brought the Kohlbrueggian perspective to WTS. . . . When I studied at Westminster the first year I did not receive the teaching of Kohlbruegge. Instead the professors kept giving me Calvin, Kuyper, Bavinck, Warfield and Hodge. Except for Calvin these men were new to me, but I had studied Kohlbruegge in my pre-seminary days and read his works in German. Some of the older elders and ministers in the RCUS recommended Kohlbruegge to me . . . . I was much disturbed upon entering Westminster in 1955 that those professors never quoted him or referred to Kohlbruegge. One day, toward the end of my first semester, I encountered Professor Young, for whom I had developed great respect. I asked him his view of Kohlbruegge. His reply stunned me. He said, "Who?" I went to WTS thinking I would study Kohlbruegge only to find that one of my very respected and learned professors had not heard of him. This drove me to serious

reflection, study and prayer. It was the theology of Murray and Van Til in my second year at WTS that convinced me of the Calvinistic Reformed Faith as articulated in the Three Forms of Unity and the Westminster Confession.

Strangely, I was influenced to go to Westminster through my pastor, the late Rev. Walter Grossmann. Rev. Grossmann in God's providence is perhaps the single reason I attended Westminster. Even though he was a strong admirer of WTS, he was influenced by Kohlbrueggian theology. However, so strong was Rev. W. Grossmann's influence on my life, that when I indicated I might attend Mission House Seminary instead of Westminster he threatened to cut off all communication and friendship with me. To quote him, he said, 'Unser Freundschaft ist über,' meaning, our friendship is over if I attended Mission House instead of Westminster.

In my judgment that was a turning point in the old Eureka Classis. A very dear friend of mine had already entered Mission House. Had I, along with him as an RCUS student, also attended that institution it is not all improbable that the pendulum would have swung to Neo-Orthodoxy in the RCUS.... After I, as the first native son of the Eureka Classis attended WTS, a number of WTS graduates were received into the RCUS and the Neo-Kohlbrueggian theology and the Neo-Orthodoxy of the Mission House gave way to the theology of Calvin and the Scottish and Dutch reformers.

The Rev. Norman Jones, a WTS graduate and former editor of the *Reformed Herald*, says, "Apart from Westminster men coming into the RCUS, our denomination would probably have gone Barthian, liberal or fundamentalistic, or perhaps just melted into the UCC (United Church of Christ).

10. The Rev. Norman Hoeflinger. Again to quote the Rev. Lloyd Gross. "The steady influence of Rev. Norman Hoeflinger, the first WTS graduate to enter the RCUS is incalculable. I can not overstate his influence upon me when I entered the ministry in 1958 three years after his arrival. He brought with him the clear Westminster theology...." Other ministers of the RCUS have reported similar sentiments. The author of this chapter has had contact with Norman for over twenty-eight years. He brings with him all that is right with the RCUS and Westminster Seminary. He was president of the Eureka Chassis for many years. He served on numerous committees with me.

11. Many of the men that attended WTS were from different personal and

ecclesiastical backgrounds. There were men from Orthodox Presbyterian backgrounds, Christian Reformed backgrounds, Baptist backgrounds, etc. coming into the RCUS. Most of them were from WTS from the 1950s through the 1970s. Some were school chums and had the same training in the Reformed Faith. They melded very well together. There were five sons of the church with WTS training with eight others who have assorted backgrounds. They became a very close knit group. Their fellowship was jovial and warm hearted. There were times when they thought they had all the answers, but in general they were careful expounders of the Bible. There is still a deep respect among the WTS graduates for each other.

The Rev. Robert Sander states, "To a larger or lesser degree all the men of the Synod have an influence on the thinking of each other both in stated meetings and in our relationships on less formal occasions. Surely, our trend in thinking is governed by our theological depository. This comes from the tremendous influence Westminster has upon us in the things of God. How can we, knowingly or unknowingly, do otherwise than influence our brothers in the faith. So, we are driven back to our days at Westminster." It must be said that up until this day the Westminster men that are left from the 1950s to the 1970s have solid friendships.

"Even though WTS has slipped away somewhat from its moorings, it is still known, nationwide, as a seminary staunchly and vocally committed to the defense of the inerrant, infallible, written Word of God," says the Rev. Robert Sander.

12. Professor John Murray. During my years at Westminster (1958-1961) this man was the greatest influence on my life. He taught me how to love systematic theology, biblical interpretation and knowing what the texts of the Bible said by a thorough examination of the words and construction of the verse. Professor Murray was the foremost lecturer of Systematic Theology in the world. All his lectures began with prayer. They were short but powerful supplication to the Almighty God. The lectures were earnest and moving declarations of the Word of God. He had been lecturing for thirty years on some of the content of his presentations, yet Murray's style was lively and alive. To him the truth was a wonderful and living thing.

I remember asking him a question in class, a rare occurrence in his classroom. He did not give me an answer. A few days later I met him in one of the narrow hallways of Machen Hall. He said, linking my arm to his, "Mr. Hart, the question you asked the other day...," then he gave a full answer to my query. He had thought the question through. No instant theology with Professor Murray. He taught me that scholarship is to bring wisdom. His profound insight and teaching has had a tremendous impact on the Reformed Church in the United States WTS graduates. We learned to be exact in our study of the Bible. Professor Murray wrote,

> But what I am going to stress is the necessity for diligent and
> persevering searching of the Scripture; study whereby we shall turn

and turn again the pages of Scripture; the study of prolonged thought and meditation by which our hearts and minds may become soaked with the truth of the Bible and by which the deep springs of thought, feeling and action may be stirred and directed; the study by which the Word of God will grip us, bind us, hold us, pull us, drive us, raise us up from the dunghill, bring us down from our high conceits and make us its bondservants in all of thought, life and conduct. The Word of God is a great deep; the commandment is exceeding broad; and so we cannot by merely occasional, hurried and perfunctory use of it understand its meaning and power.[4]

The theology of John Murray was in every respect thoroughly Reformed. The model of his work was the *Institutes* of John Calvin. Calvin was a theologian of the Holy Scriptures as well as a commentator of the Bible. Calvin noted that the service of his life was for the covenant people of God. The same may be said of Professor Murray. Our dear professor taught us Reformed orthodoxy out of the Scriptures, and in so doing he taught us how to be Reformed theologians who love and live the Word. That is his legacy to the RCUS through his students.

In closing this chapter, allow me to look to the future of the RCUS and the influence of Westminster Theological Seminary.

In recent years our ministers have not been coming to us with Westminster backgrounds. They are good men and sound in the Faith. I hope that this book and this chapter will help them understand the "Westminster mind."

The "old" Westminster is gone. Her influence, however, is still with us. It will not be very long and "old" graduates will be gone as well. Let us pray that we will thank God for Westminster Theological Seminary and her students who made an impact on the contemporary church scene.

Postscript: Here is a list of WTS graduates that are still serving the RCUS. Messrs. Scott Clark, Lloyd Gross, Robert Grossmann, Howard Hart, Norman Hoeflinger, Norman Jones, Vernon Pollema, Robert Sander, Steven Schlei, Paul Treick, Herman Van Stedum, Jim West, and Steven Work.

---

4 *The Presbyterian Guardian*, February 25, 1945.

1991—245TH SESSION OF SYNOD—GARNER, IOWA

CHAPTER SEVEN

Our Heidelberg Heritage

Rev. Paul H. Treick

Our beloved Heidelberg!— this is an expression one seldom hears about a confession or a creed of the church. After all, a confession is composed of doctrines which are supposed by many to be dry and unemotional theological statements. Yet, love for the Heidelberg Catechism has characterized the 250-year history of the Reformed Church in the United States and continues. It is not a love for a book or a document as such, but a love for the faith it expresses so well.

Along with us, Christians of many languages from all over the world have uttered these words as they have known the "comfort" so beautifully and soundly expressed by this document first published in 1563. What is it that makes the Heidelberg Catechism so unique?

The continuing history of the Reformed Church in the United States is due in large part to the use of the "Heidelberger." The defining word here is "use." What benefit is a creed for us if it is not used? What good is a creed carefully preserved on our "beloved historical document" shelf, if it is not also in our hearts and heads? How can a creed benefit the church if it is not taught to believers and to their children? It is alleged that indoctrination of our covenant children is somehow suspect or simply wrong. Critics say it leads to "dead orthodoxy." We would counter by saying that not knowing what to believe leads to "unorthodoxy." The anti-creedal trend in the twentieth century has been to render mere lip-service to the historical, confessional statements of the church, but not make them living documents in the life of the church. If you want to see a dying church, look at one which no longer teaches or adheres to its own creeds. If you want to see a dead church, look at one which can no longer define what it claims to believe. If its belief is unknown, then what reason is there for its existence? The exodus from the historic Reformed faith in recent years has not been the fault of the creeds, but a failure to make them the center of instruction and discipline.

In some quarters, attempts are made to rewrite theology so frequently that a book like the Heidelberg Catechism seems like little more than a relic of the past. The results are clearly seen today and they are disastrous. The pathetic trend of today is doctrinal avoidance where theological awareness is exchanged for feelings. Doctrinal ignorance is often lauded. Feelings, opinions, and experiences have become the basis for truth. People fear that doctrines (usually considered to be too old-fashioned and divisive) will drive people away from the church. In reality, the opposite is true — people leave when they no longer know or can state what they believe. When people are no longer able to distinguish between truth and error, they easily fall prey to liberalism or neo-evangelicalism.

Doctrines are simply teachings and everyone follows some teaching. Everyone believes something — whether true or false. Today's anti-creedal environment says, "No book but the Bible; no creed but Christ." As cleaver as this might sound, this *is* the creed of many who prefer to disguise their actual beliefs either because of ignorance or because their doctrines are too bizarre to be presented up front.

THE CATECHETICAL METHOD

The Heidelberg Catechism, along with the Belgic Confession of Faith and the Canons of Dort are the official creeds of the Reformed Church in the United States. These all compliment each other and were united as a package of creeds by the Synod Dort in 1618. Of these, the Heidelberg is unique since it is a catechism. It is designed as a teaching tool to be memorized and to become a part of the daily confession of the believer. The latter two creeds are excellent statements of the Reformed faith, but their form and purpose are more suitable as administrative statements than pedagogical tools.

The word "catechesis," derived from the Greek, describes the teaching and instruction given to "catechumens" in preparation for confirmation. The word "catechism" is from the Greek word *Katēcheō* which means to "sound from above" and came generally to mean "to give instruction concerning the content of faith" (see Luk. 1:4; Acts 18:25; Rom. 2:18; 1 Cor. 14:19 for the use of this word). The method of this instruction involved a teacher asking questions and the student responding with carefully worded answers provided by the teacher. We see in Galatians 6:6 (where this word is used twice) the contrast between the catechumen ("him that is taught in the word") and the catechizer ("him that teacheth in all good things").

The word "catechism" is often associated with Roman Catholicism, perhaps because of the papal sanctions and blessings associated with it. The Protestant Church, however, was the first to write a catechism. Luther's larger and shorter catechisms appeared in 1529. The Heidelberg and the Westminister Larger and Shorter Catechisms are the most important of the Protestant contributions. Peter Canisius (1534-1566), a Roman Catholic Jesuit priest, was the first to issue a catechism within the Roman Church.[1] All catechisms are not of one sort — there are good and bad catechisms depending on the doctrinal content of each.

The use of catechisms became quickly associated with the rite of "confirmation" — not as the Roman Catholics practiced it, but covenantally, where the baptized child would be taught the promises of the Gospel in order to confess them by examination and confirm them as his own. The covenant, the catechism, and confirmation are thereby inseparably intertwined. Calvin, in speaking of confirmation favored . . .

> a catechizing, in which children or those near adolescence would give an account of their faith before the church. But the best method of catechizing would be to have a manual drafted for this exercise, containing and summarizing in simple manner most of the articles of our religion, on which the whole believers' church ought to agree without controversy. A child of ten would present himself to the church to declare his confession of faith, would be examined in each article, and answer to each; if he were ignorant of anything or insufficiently understood it, he would be taught. Thus, while the church looks on as a witness, he would profess the one true and sincere faith, in which the believing folk with one mind worship the one God.
>
> If this discipline were in effect today, it would certainly arouse some slothful parents, who carelessly neglect the instruction of their children as a matter of no concern to them; for then they could not overlook it without public disgrace. There would be greater agreement in faith among Christian people, and not so many would go untaught and ignorant; some would not be so rashly carried away with new and strange doctrines; in short, all would have some methodical instruction, so to speak, in Christian doctrine.[2]

In accord with this, in the Second Helvetic Confession (Swiss) by Heinrich Bullinger (1566), we read,

> The Lord enjoined his ancient people to exercise the greatest care

---

1 David Schaff, *Our Fathers Faith And Ours — A Comparison Between Protestantism and Romanism*, (New York, G. P. Putnam's Sons, 1928) p. 20.

2 John Calvin, *Institutes of the Christian Religion*, IV. xix.13.

that young people, even from infancy, be properly instructed. Now since it is well known from the writings of the evangelists and apostles that God has no less concern for the youth of his new people, when he openly testifies and says: "Let the children come to me; for to such belongs the kingdom of heaven" (Mark 10:14), the pastors of the churches act most wisely when they early and carefully catechize the youth, laying the first ground of faith, and faithfully teaching the rudiments of our religion . . . . Here let the Church show her faith and diligence in bringing the children to be catechized, desirous and glad to have her children well instructed. (Chapter XXV)

Let us never underestimate the importance of catechetical instruction for the believer and for the church as a whole. To the extent that this practice has been neglected we have seen the theology of the church shift and drift. Certainly there are other methods of instruction, but the catechetical approach is difficult to rival in terms of its overall structure and progressive building up of the faith. If just one generation is not instructed in the basic truths of the Gospel the damage done to the next generation is very difficult to recover from.

It is common to attempt to begin instruction with moralistic lessons and a lot of emphasis on how to love God and our neighbor — a noble thought, but a terrible mistake. The basis of the Christian life that glorifies God is a knowledge of sin followed by repentance and faith in Christ. Obedience to God's law, growing out of thanksgiving, can only come when there is a salvation to be thankful for. The catechism is well-suited to give to children as well as adults the step by step guidance in these blessed truths.

Parents, take heed that you may say to your children, as Paul to Timothy, that "from a child thou hast known the holy scriptures" (2 Tim. 3:15).

THE UNIQUE CHARACTER OF THE HEIDELBERG CATECHISM

Our purpose in this chapter is to uncover the course of development which laid the foundation for the Heidelberg. The book known as the Heidelberg Catechism did not appear out of a vacuum, but was the fruit of God's providence. Many events and numerous godly men contributed to the final product. To give a complete history of the Heidelberg Catechism would require volumes, since to put ones finger on the pulse of the German Reformation is to feel the heartbeat of the Heidelberg Catechism.

At the time of the Reformation catechisms abounded throughout Europe. Protestants were eager to teach their followers and defend their faith to both ecclesiastical and civil authorities. Many catechisms were written before and many after the Heidelberg.[3] The distinctiveness of the Heidelberg does not lie merely in the question and answer format, but it lies in the very personal, pastoral nature of the questions and answers. This is exemplified in the very first question, "What is **your** only comfort in life and in death?" The answer provides the response of a confessing Christian, "That **I**, with body and soul, in life and in death am not **my own**, but belong to **my faithful Savior** Jesus Christ . . . ." The Heidelberg not only outlines the essential doctrines of the Christian faith, but it reveals the course of the Christian's life from sin to salvation to thankfulness. It employs the basic outline of the book of Romans and it follows the definition of the word "redemption" — to be set free from the bondage of sin by purchase through the blood of Jesus to glorify God. It incorporates the fundamental teaching that our salvation includes both our body and our soul (*ie.* a Calvinistic world and life view). This approach is in distinction to the false dichotomy of the scholastics who saw man's salvation in terms of the soul, but not of the body. In that sense the Heidelberg Catechism is both doctrinal and practical. Among catechisms the Heidelberg is a unique treasure from which we have drawn great wealth for many generations. It was the stated creed of the RCUS from its organization in the United States, having been already accepted by the German and Dutch immigrants who came to this country.

The format of the Heidelberg was intended to be pastoral — the pastor asking the questions and the student responding with the answers. Early catechisms, including Calvin's first catechism, were arranged in paragraph format, without questions and answers.[4] Later, it was seen that the question and answer method (the catechetical method) was more effective.[5] Some began using this catechetical method the wrong way — where the student asked the question and the pastor gave the answer. Leo Juda, of Zurich, did this in his first catechism. He reversed this in the second catechism, so the minister asked the questions and the pupil gave the answers. This is still the present method. A number of editions of the Heidelberg were augmented with detailed explanations of each question, numerous Bible texts,

---

3 The first Protestant Catechism (which inclined to the Reformed faith), according to August Lang (Lutheran historian) was a *Dialogue-book* by Rev. John Bader, of Landau, 1526. In 1527 a catechism appeared in St. Gall and was used until the Heidelberg replaced it in 1615. *Luther's Larger and Shorter Catechism* was published in 1529.

4 See John Calvin, *Instruction in Faith* (1537), Paul T. Fuhrmann, Trans. & Ed., (Louisville, Westminster/John Knox Press, 1992).

5 Some, such as J. I. Good refer to this as the "Socratic" method. While this method resembles the Socratic method, it differed greatly from the premise of Socrates (an unbeliever) which held that all men had an inherent or innate knowledge which the instructor was to draw out of the student by a series of questions. In contrast to this, the catechetical method assumes just the reverse — that man's knowledge is totally corrupted. A proper catechism, therefore, provides not only the question but also the correct answer.

prayers, and even hymns written to express each Lord's Day of the catechism.[6] It was also widely used in homes so fathers could instruct their children.

In this 250th year celebration, happily catechism classes and the memorization of the Heidelberg Catechism still continue among the covenant children of the Reformed Church in the United States. This is still much the same as in the days of the Reformation in the sixteenth century. This practice is continued not out of blind adherance to tradition, but because it has proven to be the most effective method of instilling these precious truths in the minds of our children. It gives them not only a ready grasp of deep truths and definitions for their own benefit, but aids in explaining the Gospel to others.

Some have opined that this catechatical method is spurious because children are giving answers to questions that someone else has prepared. It isn't their own answer. We're putting words in their mouth. That is exactly the purpose of catechizing. Were we to allow each child to formulate his own answers to the questions, they would each be formulating a new creed according to their childish understanding. In teaching any other subject, the same method is employed. Water is not just wet, but we tell students that it consists of specific amounts of hydrogen and oxygen. In catechizing, it is expected not just that children are able to parrot the answers, but to demonstrate an understanding of them. It is always our hope and prayer that the Holy Spirit will use this instruction to create a true and living faith in their hearts. A thorough examination is required for confirmation — to determine that the answers recited are also understood and have become the basis for a knowledgeable confession of true faith in Jesus Christ.

The Heidelberg Catechism is not just a children's book. It is a book for all who are the children of God. One of the most effective tools of evangelism today is still the Heidelberg. Because of its strong biblical basis, it possesses an ageless quality. It must be used, not as a substitute for studying the Bible, but in conjunction with the Holy Scriptures. A thorough knowledge of the Heidelberg should initiate a more intensive study of other creeds, namely, The Belgic Confession of Faith, the Canons of Dort, and other Reformed creeds as well.

In the words of Zacharius Ursinus in the introduction to his Commentary on the Heidelberg Catechism, catechetical instruction is necessary for the following reasons:

1. Because it is the command of God (Deut. 11:19)

---

6 Examples of these are: *Catechismus, oder Kurtzer Unterricht Christlicher Lehr*, Schaffhausen, (Gedruckt, bei Johann Ulrich Ziegler, 1789); Christoph Stähelin, *Catechetischer Haus-Schatz, oder Erklärung des Heidelbergischen Catechismi*, (Zurich, bei F. Hanke, 1724); F. P. Kindler, *Der Heidelberger Catechismus*, (Erlangen, 1846).

2. Because of the divine glory which demands that god be not only rightly known and worshipped by those of adult age, but also by children, according as it is said, "Out of the mouths of babes and sucklings hast thou ordained strength" (Ps. 8:2).

3. On account of the comfort and salvation; for without a true knowledge of God and his Son Jesus Christ, no one that has attained to years of discretion and understanding can be saved, or have any sure comfort that he is accepted in the sight of God (John 13:3; Heb. 11:6).

4. For the preservation of society and the church. If we are correctly instructed in our childhood out of the sacred Scriptures concerning God and his will, and do not then commence the practice of piety, it is with great difficulty, if ever, we are drawn away from these errors which are, as it were, born in us, or which we have imbibed from our youth, and that we are led to abandon the vices in which we have been brought up, and to which we have been accustomed.

5. There is a necessity that all persons should be made acquainted with the rule and standard according to which we are to judge and decide, in relation to the various opinions and dogmas of men, that we may not be led into error, and be seduced thereby, according to the commandment which is given in relation to this subject, "Beware of false prophets" (Matt. 7:15).

6. Those who have properly studied and learned the Catechism, are generally better prepared to understand and appreciate the sermons which they hear from time to time. . . .

7. The importance of catechization may be urged in view of its peculiar adaptedness to those learners who are of weak and uncultivated minds, who require instruction in a short, plain, and perspicuous manner . . . .

8. It is also necessary, for the purpose of distinguishing and separating youths, and such as are unlearned, from schismatics and profane heathen, which can most effectually be done by a judicious course of catechetical instruction.

Lastly. A knowledge of the catechism is especially important for those who are to act as teachers, because they ought to have a more intimate acquaintance with the doctrine of the church than others, as well on account of their calling, that they may one day be able to instruct others....[7]

AUTHORIZATION AND AUTHORS

The unique character of the Heidelberg Catechism is the product of the time in which it was written and the exceptional preparation God gave to those responsible for its composition. The heritage of the Heidelberg for the RCUS goes back much farther than our years here in the United States. While the authors of the Heidelberg are significant, the impetus it needed to be widely distributed was due in large measure to the one who authorized and defended it. In the sixteenth century, the writing of a confession such as the Heidelberg Catechism could easily cost you your life.

When we survey the history of the Heidelberg Catechism, the names of Elector Frederick III, Zacharias Ursinus, and Casper Olevianus are most conspicuous. These were all gifted workmen of God who were used in a very special way at a crucial time in the history of the church. The sixteenth Century was not only a time of tremendous change in the church, but also in the lives of those used in the Reformation. In observing the lives of these men, we will also be exposed to some influential events and individuals who paved the way for the Heidelberg. In looking at this history, behold the hand of God and give Him all the glory.

We should remember that this period of history was at the latter half of the Renaissance which was the rebirth of cultural interest — especially an interest in studying the classic writings of the past. Those engaged in this study were known as "humanists" (not to be equated at all with the secular humanism of today). This revival began in Italy in the twelfth century and gradually moved northward. It's affect north of the Alps in the sixteenth century was characterized more by theological study — especially the writings of the Christian classics from the New Testament period and following. These men were known as "Christian humanists" (such as John Colet, Johannes Reuchlin, Thomas More, Jacques Lefèvre, and Erasmus). Many of these young humanists turned Protestant, such as, Ulrich Zwingli, Philip Melanchthon, John Calvin, Theodore Beza, and Casper Olevianus. The interest shifted to the task of reforming the church according to apostolic principles. It may be true that "Erasmus laid the egg that Luther hatched."

ELECTOR OTTO HENRY OF THE PALATINATE

Frederick's predecessor, Otto Henry (d. 1559), was a Low-Lutheran and a Christian humanist. At this time three groups dominated the Protestant scene — High-Lutheran (closer to the Roman Catholics), Low-Lutheran (more liberal and

---

7 Zacharias Ursinus, *Commentary on the Heidelberg Catechism*, (Grand Rapids, Wm. B. Eerdmans Publishing Co., 1956) pp. 14-16.

humanistic), and Reformed. Northern Germany was generally High-Lutheran and the south, since it was reformed more by the Calvinists, was Low-Lutheran . Otto was committed to improving the condition of the University of Heidelberg, which since its change from Catholicism to Protestantism had deteriorated. His desire was to hire the best professors he could find to bring it out of the scholasticism of the Middle Ages. Being more committed to humanism than mere confessionalism, he hired some Reformed professors, most prominent were Peter Boquin (French) and Thomas Erastus (Swiss). No small controversy with Lutherans ensued, but they remained at Otto's insistence and offered a strong foothold for the Reformed at the university.[8] Thus the door was open for Frederick to appoint Ursinus and Olevianus during his later tenure as Elector.

Otto Henry also was quite broad-minded about allowing the Reformed a place in the realm. It should be remembered that in 1555 the Peace of Augsburg[9] was signed which gave each prince the authority to determine the official religion of his domain according to his own religion (*Cuius regio, eius religio*). Those citizens who refused were allowed to sell their land and depart. In addition, cities could permit different faiths, if they were already established. This peace applied only to Roman Catholics and those Protestants who subscribed to the Augsburg Confession (1530).[10] Significantly, Calvinists and Anabaptists were excluded from this freedom. However, Otto, being quite broad-minded and somewhat sympathetic to the Reformed, gave permission for Reformed refugees to settle in Frankenthal despite warnings from Phillip Melanchthon that this would create friction.[11]

Perhaps one of the most significant acts of Otto Henry was to reform the worship in the Palatinate according to the Low-Lutheran position. His Church Order of 1556 departed from the High-Lutheran practice of exorcism. He threw out the altars except for the main altar for Lord's Supper, and he ordered that pictures should be removed from the churches.

---

8 James I. Good, *The Heidelberg Catechism In Its Newest Light*, (Philadelphia, Publication and Sunday School Board of the Reformed Church in the United States, 1914), pp. 124-132.

9 This ruling was tremendously significant in that it permanently shattered both the political unity of Germany and the medieval unity of Christendom. It remained the law of the land until the end of the Thirty Years War and the Peace of Westphalia in 1648. It was not until the end of the Thirty Years War that the Reformed Church was given official status in Germany.

10 The 1530 edition of the Augsburg Confession (a Lutheran document) allowed for the physical presence of Christ in the Lord's Supper. A 1531 edition had this particular reference removed. The Protestant princes signed this "Altered Augsburg Confession". Frederick III signed this Alterd Augsburg Confession which was generally accepted by the Low-Lutherans. If the Reformed church was to have any freedom to worship they were forced to agree with the Augsburg Confession. The Altered Confession was broad enough to allow the Reformed to sign it until the time when the Heidelberg was officially recognized in Germany in 1566.

11 James I. Good, *loc. cit.*

A final preparation for Frederick's reign was Otto Henry's intervention in the heated disputes between two very vocal and zealous men — Tileman Hesshusius (High-Lutheran) and William Klebitz (Reformed). Here, as controversies erupted around such issues as images, hymn books, the form of Lord's Supper, and a degree given to a Reformed student from the University of Heidelberg (which was Lutheran at the time), it was Otto Henry who offered the greatest concessions and sympathy to the Reformed.

So, the stage was set for Frederick III to assume the Electorship at the death of Otto Henry in 1559. God had providentially been laying the foundation before Frederick's time so that out of this High-Lutheran state, one of the greatest confessions of the Reformed faith could be written.

ELECTOR FREDERICK III (THE PIOUS) OF THE PALATINATE

Elector Frederick III (1515-1576) of the Palatinate in Germany might be said to be the "father" of the Heidelberg Catechism since he authorized and defended the writing of the Heidelberg. His reference to the Heidelberg Catechism as "my catechism" reflects not only his love for the doctrines of the Heidelberg, but the responsibility he felt for its creation and defense.

As were many of the Reformers, Frederick was born into a Roman Catholic home, the eldest son of Duke John II of the Palatinate. In 1537 he married Mary a daughter of Margrave Casimir of Brandenburg. She was an outspoken High-Lutheran, even warning Frederick about Zwinglian (ie. Reformed) influences in Heidelberg. As a condition of marriage, she got him to read the Bible. Through her influence he was converted from Roman Catholicism to Lutheran, but a Low-Lutheran, and much more inclined to the Reformed position than the High-Lutheran. He was a very quiet and peaceful man, and did not invite controversy. While he was often attacked viciously, he did not respond in kind. The castle at Heidelberg was characterized by a godly atmosphere. It is said that he and his wife prayed and sang a psalm (psalm-singing was forbidden among the High-Lutherans) at the beginning and close of every meal. Every day he prayed for his people and was generous with his wealth.[12]

In 1559, two weeks after Otto Henry died, Frederick was appointed as the Elector of the Palatinate. His predecessor had created some sense of peace and stability, but there was definitely a undercurrent of controversy between the three major factions — Roman Catholic, Lutheran, and Reformed. The Hesshusius and Klebitz debates and attacks heated up. Most of the controversy centered around the Lord's Supper, not only in the manner in which it was served, but especially whether

---

12 Thea B. Van Halsema, *Three Men Came To Heidelberg and Glorious Heretic*, (Grand Rapids, Baker Book House, 1963), p. 69.

the physical or spiritual presence of Christ was present. Frederick accepted the Low-Lutheran position which said that the body of Christ was not "distributed," but "exhibited" at the Lord's Supper.

While Frederick did not initially declare that he was Reformed, it became increasingly apparent that he came down on the side of the Reformed whenever controversies had to be settled. This was in part due to his peaceful nature, but perhaps more so, to his deepening conviction that all doctrine must be derived from the Bible alone.

Frederick felt that since the Catholics had gained greater unity with the developments at the Council of Trent (meeting in three stages from 1545-1563), all Protestants should present a united front against Catholicism. It is clear that Frederick never espoused the High-Lutheran position. Phillip Melanchthon (also Low-Lutheran) played an important role in supporting Frederick. It was Melanchthon who advised Frederick to settle the dispute as to the formula used in the Lord's Supper by using the biblical formula of 1 Cor. 10:16 instead of the formula used in the Augsburg Confession (ie. Christ's body and blood are "communicated" to believers, but it avoided saying that the elements "are" the body and blood of Christ. He added an important clause which said that this "communication" did not occur without thought, as occurs when mice gnaw at bread).[13]

But Frederick was still a Low-Lutheran and had his son Christopher instructed in Luther's Catechism. Within his own heart Frederick was not satisfied with the conclusions on the matter of the Lord's Supper and set out on an intensive study of the Bible to find the truth. Day and night he labored, searched, and prayed that God might reveal the truth to him. During this search his motto was also formulated, "Lord, according to Thy will."[14]

This search of the Scriptures is significant, for Frederick used nothing but the Bible to seek the truth. This is precisely the Reformed principle to determine the truth even though Frederick may not have employed it because he was self-consciously Reformed at that point in time. The Bible had become the rule of faith with a different emphasis than Luther had held. Frederick forwarded the Reformed principle of theology which said, "only what is commanded in the Bible," as opposed to the Lutheran principle of , "only what the Bible does not forbid." The Augsburg Confession contained no biblical references to the Bible as the only rule of faith. Contrast this to the Heidelberg Catechism and its strong biblical basis. This is a first sign that Frederick was openly becoming Reformed in his theology.

Gradually, we see Frederick shift away from Lutheranism toward Reformed

---

13 James I. Good, *op. cit.,* p. 144.

14 *Ibid., op. cit.,* p. 146.

theology. He also became tired with the authoritarian nature of Hesshusius (already dismissed from his position at the University of Heidelberg) which he was now demonstrating in his church. He appointed a consistory to rule in the church, headed by a strong Reformed man named Zuleger.[15] In 1560 Casper Olevianus was appointed as a professor of theology at the University of Heidelberg. Fear began to set in that Frederick was becoming a Calvinist. His wife, Mary, was so upset at Frederick's leanings that she called upon his son-in-law, Duke John Frederick of Saxony (a High-Lutheran), to have prayers in the churches to the end that Frederick might be kept in the Lutheran faith. Mary remained Lutheran for some time, but later changed and also became zealously Reformed. It was certainly true that the High-Lutherans were now a minority and that the large number of Low-Lutherans made the later change to Calvinism in the Palatinate easier.

By 1561 the majority of the faculty at Heidelberg University was Reformed. One stiking example is the the the fact that Heidelberg University supported the teachings of Jerom Zanchius (1516-1590) who was driven from Strassburg by the Lutherans for his teaching of the doctrine of predestination.[16] For a Lutheran university to support the position of a Reformed theologian evidences the Reformed position of the University at this time. Zanchius later became a professor of Reformed theology at the University of Heidelberg. Following a conference at Naumburg, which attempted to unite the Protestants, Frederick made his break with the authority of the early Lutheran faith (which he called "popish"), and with Melanchthon (who with Luther authored the Augsburg Confession of 1530) Frederick was inclined now to distance himself from Melanchthon, concluding that if Melanchthon could be so wrong on the first Ausburg, then why not also on the later editions. While they were a slight improvement over the original Augsburg confession, Frederick deemed these to be in error also.[17] Melanchthon's 1540 Altered Augsburg Confession, which Frederick eventually signed, stated in Article X that "with the bread and wine the body and blood of Christ are truly shown forth"

---

15 *Ibid.*, p. 147.

16 See Jerom Zanchius, *The Absolute Doctrine of Predestination*, Translated by Augustus M. Toplady, (Grand Rapids, Baker Book House, 1977).

17 *Ibid.*, p. 159. See footnote 8 also. Melanchthon was the primary author of the Augsburg Confession of 1530. More significantly, he authored the Altered Augsburg Confession of 1540 (*Confessio Augustana Variata*). In this confession there was enough latitude concerning the physical presence of Christ to satisfy the Low-Lutherans, and the Reformed who wished to find some area of agreement with their Lutheran counterparts. The High-Lutherans repudiated this Altered Ausburg Confession. Elector Frederick III signed this confession, but refused the earlier versions. John Calvin also subscribed to Melanchthon's Altered Confession. While Melanchthon was not totally embraced by the Reformed, he and his followers had also lost respect and influence in the Lutheran Church was gradually becoming solidified in High-Lutheran doctrine.

instead of "are truly present."[18]

It was in 1561 that Frederick took an openly Reformed position in various areas. Again, he was driven to the Bible for more study. Reformation took place in the worship and the churches. Statues were covered with black cloth, the veneration of the wafer in the Lord's Supper was halted, pictures in churches were covered with whitewash, the use of the organ ceased, Latin hymns were replaced by Luther's psalms and other hymns, stone baptismal fonts were removed, altars were thrown out and replaced with communion tables, the golden chalice for Lord's Supper was replaced with wood or pewter, bread was used in Lord's Supper instead of the wafer, lay baptism was halted, and communion to the sick was lessened so that it did not appear to be a saving work. Zacharias Ursinus was appointed to the faculty at Heidelberg and Olevianus became the head of the Palatinate church. More and more Reformed writings were coming out of the Palatinate which put fear in the hearts of the High-Lutherans that the Palatinate had fallen to the Reformed. They were right.

In 1562 Thomas Erastus,[19] a Reformed professor at Heidelberg and a physician, demonstrated his extensive knowledge of the Reformed doctrine of the Lord's Supper with the publication of a remarkable booklet on the body of Christ in the Lord's Supper. The doctrine of the ubiquity of Christ was denied and here we see the sacraments are called "signs and seals." Frederick ordered the publication of this work. A second order by Frederick in this year was that a catechism should be written. His desire was that this new catechism should be, above all, biblical. The suggestion for this catechism first came from Olevianus and the majority of the writing of it would be by Ursinus. A commission representing the court, the university, and the churches was set up. It was this commission that gave the primary authorship to Ursinus and Olevianus. In the introduction to the first three editions of the catechism, Frederick III states that it originated, "with the counsel and assistance of our whole theological faculty, also all superintendents and principal church councilors."[20] That would include such faculty members as Bouquin, Tremellius, Ursinus, Olevianus, Diller, Erastus, and Frederick himself.

---

18 John T. McNeill, *The History and Character of Calvinism* (NY: Oxford University Press, 1962) p. 197.

19 Thomas Erastus, a Zwinglian and although helpful in this area of the Lord's Supper, later became an opponent to Olevianus. He opposed Olevianus' establishment of a presbyterian government and church discipline. Erastus held that the state has the right to intervene and overrule in church affairs. He denied that the church had the power to excommunicate — only the state had that power. He served both on the Heidelberg faculty and as Elector Frederick's personal physician. He eventually was forced to leave Heidelberg. His teaching (much like Richard Hooker's in England) became known as Erastianism.

20 Emil Buehrer, The Reformation, (Green Bay, Reliance Publishing Company, 1945) p. 92.

God used Frederick's reign at just this time in history to produce for us a beautiful and biblical expression of the Reformed faith which remains for us today. As we will see later, the catechism of Frederick came under severe attack, yet God caused it to be preserved against almost unbelievable odds.

THE AUTHORS

Zacharias Ursinus (Baer) at age 26 and Casper Olevianus (Van der Olevig) at age 28 were the primary authors of the Heidelberg Catechism. Yet Frederick participated in the structure and everything had to be subject to his assent, including the literal expressions. The Synod of the Palatinate would ask for a change in Question 78 before the first edition was published in 1563[21] and in a later edition Frederick had Question 80 added.[22] Each author formulated his own draft without consulting each other about the main features. The effect was that the first drafts were far apart in form even though both the Genevan Catechism of Calvin and the Emden Catechism of à Lasco were used as a guide. Olevianus' composition existed of a simple development of the Covenant of Grace, and Ursinus' division was misery, redemption, and thankfulness. Olevianus deemed the structure of Ursinus' work as best for this catechism.[23]

These two men were well adapted to perform this monumental work since they were bosom friends and of like faith. Both were brilliant scholars. They belonged to the second generation of Reformers, when the vibrations from the initial blast of the Reformation were less pronounced. Theirs was a period when less of the outward and more of the inward, formative work needed to be done. While the writing of the Heidelberg Catechism will probably remain as their claim to fame, yet we should remember that this was but one work in their lives. They faithfully served the cause of the faith and did a great deal to further the understanding, formulation, and defense of the Reformed faith.

ZACHARIAS URSINUS (1534-1583)

Zacharias Baer, whose last name was Latinized (in Latin "bear" is "ursus") to become Ursinus, was a native of Breslau, the capital of Silesia. His father was a deacon at the Magdalen Church. He was a gifted scholar whose embrace of mathematics and philosophy served him well to express the faith with keenness and clarity. He possessed a quiet personality and avoided public discourse. In 1550, at

---

21 *Ibid.*, p. 168.

22 Philip Schaff, *The Creeds of Christendom*, Vol. III, (New York, Harper & Brothers, 1882), p. 336. This 80th Question was designed by Frederick to be a counter to the Council of Trent which adjourned Dec. 4, 1563. This question caused a temporary prohibition of the catechism in the German Empire.

23 W. Heyns, *Handboek voor de Catechetiek*, (Grand Rapids, Eerdmans-Sevensma Co.) p. 53.

the age of 16 he enrolled at the university at Wittenberg where Philip Melanchthon (1497-1560) was not only his professor, but became his lifelong friend. After seven years of study he traveled widely. In Geneva he met John Calvin (1509-1564); in Zurich he met Johann Bullinger (1504-1575) and Peter Martyr (who became a very close friend). His acquaintances were impressed by Ursinus and he in turn was influenced by them. After a short tenure of teaching in Breslau, he was called in 1562 by Frederick III to become Professor of Philosophy (and in the same year made Doctor and Professor of Theology) at the University of Heidelberg.

Zacharias Ursinus

As a professor he gave himself totally to his work and was closely attached to and loved by his pupils. He did not enjoy being disturbed by lengthy visits in his study and so he attached as sign above his door which read, "Amice, quisquis huc venis: aut agito paucis, aut abi, aut me laborantem juva" ("Friend, whoever you are who enters here: either make your matter short, or go, or assist me in my work").[24]

With the change of power back to Lutheranism, following Elector Frederick's death in 1576, Ursinus was forced to leave Heidelberg since he could not receive Luther's catechism or Lutheran doctrine. He was called, by the second son of Frederick, John Casimer, to the newly established Reformed Theological School in Neustadt. The school flourished during his stay there. In failing health, the Lord called Zacharias Ursinus to Himself at the age of 49 years. Here he knows fully the "only comfort in life and in death" which he proclaimed so vigorously in this life.

PHILLIP MELANCHTHON

When requested to write a catechism which would express the Reformed faith, we should remember that Ursinus did not begin this work in a vacuum. He was influenced by his past training and the writings of others. As noted earlier, Ursinus was a close friend and, in some respects, a follower of Phillip Melanchthon (1497-1560) who was a Low-Lutheran. It would be in error to think that Ursinus was himself a Melanchthonian. Unlike Melanchthon, Ursinus believed in predestination, he believed that Christ's physical body was at the right hand of God (see Heidelberg Catechism Questions 46, 76 and 80), and he rejected the teaching that

---

24 Henry Harbaugh, *The Fathers of the German Reformed Church in Europe and America*, Vol. I, (Lancaster, Sprenger & Westhaeffer, 1857), pp. 240-241.

Christ was physically present in the elements of the Lord's Supper. Melanchthon would not have assented to these teachings.[25]

It might be noted also that Melanchthon was well-respected among the Reformed theologians. In 1543 John Calvin dedicated to Melanchthon a publication in which he set forth the errors of Dr. Albert Pighuis, an opponent of the doctrine of grace. Calvin also edited Melanchthon's *Loci Communes* which was translated into French.[26] Calvin did not have such a relationship with Luther, although he did write to him on occasion. Calvin used Melanchthon to get through to the less than congenial Luther, for Calvin said, "For so far as I could understand by report, and by letters from different persons, the scarcely pacified temper of the man might, on very slight occasion, break out into a sore."[27] So, it is not surprising that we find a very cordial relationship between Ursinus and Melanchthon. While divided by theological issues, the Reformers often had to consider the greater evil and enemy in Rome.

While often siding with the Reformed when disputes arose, the influence of Melanchthon on Ursinus was more personal than theological. Melanchthon was a peaceful man and aided the Reformed cause at times, because he wanted to distance himself from Catholicism and from the caustic attacks by the High-Lutherans against the Reformed. We should be aware that there were also sharp differences between the High-Lutherans and the Low-Lutherans, especially in the area of the ubiquitous presence of Christ's body. In examining the evidence, it is clear that Melanchthon was closer to the High-Lutheran doctrines than to the Reformed.[28] Perhaps we can also conclude that Ursinus, like Melanchthon, had the desire to see a more united front against the papal powers who wanted both Lutheran and

---

25 The Marburg Colloquy betwen Luther and Zwingli having failed, Martin Bucer invited Luther to meet in Wittenberg in 1536 to seek some union. The resulting document, the Wittenberg Concord, is illustrative of Melanchthon's position on the Lord's Supper. In drafting this Concord, Melanchthon wrote, that "with the bread and wine the body and blood of Christ are truly and substantially present, offered, and received." Paul C. Empie and James I. McCord, Marburg Revisited (Minneapolis: Augsburg Publishing House, 1966) p. 59.

26 Bonnet, Jules, *Letters of John Calvin*, Vol. I, (Edinburgh: Thomas Constable and Co., 1855) p. 349. Jules Bonnet cites the following statement from a letter of Calvin to Melanchthon, "Would that the union between all Christ's Churches upon earth were such, that the angels in heaven might join their song of praise!" Melanchthon's *Loci Communes*, first published in 1521, was a systematic treatment of Luther's theology. In this work Melanchthon treated the doctrines of free will, the Law-Gospel dichotomy, and justification by grace through faith. He strongly repudiated scholasticism.

27 *Ibid.*, p. 412.

28 J. D. Douglas, ed., *The New International Dictionary of the Christian Church*, (Grand Rapids: Zondervan Publishing House, 1974) Carl S. Meyer states in an article on Melanchthon, "Recent scholarship has asserted Melanchthon's integrity as a Lutheran theologian against those who fault him for deviations." p. 647.

Reformed churches destroyed. In this there was sometimes cooperation, and even some attempts to mollify the various parties. Yet, on the basic issues of Calvinism, Ursinus stood with Calvin and Melanchthon did not.[29]

AMBROSIUS MOIBANUS

Another noteworthy influence on Ursinus was his childhood training in the church under his pastor Ambrosius Moibanus. Moibanus was a Protestant whose theology was developed before the specific details of the Lutheran or Reformed position were clearly formulated or the heated debate had begun. Later in his life, Moibanus, a student of Calvin's *Institutes,* wrote a letter to John Calvin in which he states that Calvin's writings met with his approval.[30]

Moibanus, as did many in the early Reformation, wrote a catechism for the instruction of the youth in the truths of the Bible. His first catechism (1533) was in Latin, his second (1535) in German, and a third (1537) in Latin. The format of the catechisms also changed. The first was in a ten topic arrangement common at that time — Piety, the Law, the Gospel, Christ, the Sacraments, Baptism, the Lord's Supper, Love and Good Works, Calling, and Prayer.[31] The second and third editions each had an appendix with catechetical questions and answers. Not only the catechetical form, but the practical and personal approach of Moibanus' catechism is reflected in the Heidelberg Catechism. Ursinus learned Moibanus' catechism and it left a lasting impression on him. The truths and style that Ursinus learned as a youth stayed with him. These he incorporated into the Heidelberg Catechism some fifteen years later. Moibanus' beginning emphasis on Christian piety and man's relationship to God is reflected in the Heidelberg beginning with the "comfort" — with the emphasis on man's personal redemption and reconciliation more than merely outlining the decrees of God. We see Moibanus' influence in Ursinus' treatment of God as a "heavenly Father" (Question 26); of faith as a "hearty trust" (Question 21); in his treatment of the requirements of God's law as being "love" (Question 4); and in the teaching on the sacraments as promises and assurances. Moibanus' catechism laid the foundation for Ursinus to direct his catechetical instruction in terms of man's sin, redemption, and thankfulnesss. We might note how closely this discipling method is to our Lord's command, "Deny yourself, take up the cross, and follow me." Ursinus' boyhood instruction was remembered and built upon. The Heidelberg Catechism demonstrates a more mature Reformed theology than Moibanus, yet his style is in evidence.

---

29 See James I. Good, *op. cit.*, p. 45 where he concludes that Ursinus gave up Melanchthonianism for the Reformed faith after he want to Zurich.

30 James I. Good, *op.cit.*, p. 245.

31 *Ibid.*, p. 87.

From this, let the church of today also take note of the blessed influence which children receive when they are catechized early and soundly (*cf.* 2 Tim. 1:5 and 3:14,15). If what is learned as a youth is actually committed to memory, it will provide a deep spiritual reservoir for every endeavor of Christian life.

OTHER INFLUENTIAL CATECHISMS

Ursinus was well-acquainted with various other catechisms which were available to him.[32] Some of these catechisms proved to be sources for the Heidelberg. Olevianus, on the other hand, was quite familiar with Calvin's catechism in France and Calvin's teachings from his stay in Geneva where he studied under Calvin. However, he did not have as an extensive a catechetical background as Ursinus had.

> James I. Good lists the following sources (in addition to Moibanus mentioned above):
> 1. The Strassburg catechisms by Capito, 1527; Bucer, 1534, and Zell, 1535 and 1537.
> 2. The Zurich catechisms of Leo Juda, 1534, 1535, and 1538, and of Bullinger, 1559.
> 3. Calvin's catechism, 1537 and 1541. Sometimes also Calvin's Institutes.
> 4. The à Lasco catechisms, à Lasco's 1551; Micronius' 1552; the London compend 1552; and the Emden, 1554.[33]

In addition to these catechisms, we should be aware that Ursinus had himself written two catechisms — a larger and a shorter catechism[34] — before he was given the task to write the Heidelberg. His larger catechism was drawn largely from the Catechism and Institutes of John Calvin. Of the 323 questions in this Larger Catechism, 173 refer back to Calvin's catechism, 58 are references from à Lasco's catechisms, 28 are derived from Bullinger, and 31 from Melanchthon's "Considerations of Ordinances".[35] In Ursinus' larger catechism the central theme was the covenant of grace — a theology which was in the process of being formulated and more carefully defined.

---

32 *Ibid.*, p. 41. There were scores of catechisms, filling several thousand pages, published before 1563 and unto the end of the sixteenth century in Germany and Switzerland.

33 *Ibid.*, p. 42. In addition to the four groups listed, there was also the Brenz catechism of the Palatinate which Otto Henry had incorporated into the Church Order. It has some phrases similar to the Heidelberg, but nearly the entire catechism deals with the sacraments. It would be considered to be Low-Lutheran.

34 The larger catechism (called *Catechesis Maior*) was Ursinus' *Summa theolgiae* with 323 questions and focusing largely on the covenant. It was written in late 1561 or 1562. His shorter catechism (called *Catechesis Minor*) was written shortly after in the year 1562.

35 *Ibid.*, p. 45.

It has been said that Olevianus also used his catechism as a basis for the Heidelberg, but that is not likely. His longer catechism, *Fester Grundt, das ist, die Artickel des alten, waren ungezweiffelten Christlichen Glaubnis*, was published after the Heidelberg. He spoke of writing this larger catechism in a letter to Bullinger, but it was first published in Heidelberg by Michel Schirat in 1567.[36] He had written some materials on the matter of the covenant of grace before 1563, but not a catechism as such.

Ursinus' shorter catechism (108 questions) was quite unlike the larger. It was not centered as much on the development of covenant theology, but the outline of it is significant in determining where the outline of our Heidelberg began. The format of this smaller catechism had a familiar three-fold division — 1. Sin; 2. Redemption; and 3. Thankfulness. Clearly, our Heidelberg Catechism was an expansion of this unique division. Where did Ursinus arrive at this three-fold format? Most likely he got it from a book of instruction republished at Heidelberg in 1558, entitled, "A Brief and Orderly Statement of the True Doctrine of Our Holy Christian Faith for House-fathers" (based on a work by Gallus of Ratisbon).[37] This book appeared between Ursinus' writing of his larger and shorter catechisms and followed the outline of: 1. The law, including sin and penitence; 2. The gospel or faith; and 3. Good works. This book was Lutheran on the sacraments, which were included in the second part of the outline.[38]

On the doctrine of election, Ursinus in both the larger and smaller catechisms, is very clearly a Calvinist and not sympathetic to Melanchthon. More is said on the doctrine of election and double predestination than even Calvin wrote in his catechism. When the Heidelberg Catechism was written there are markedly less direct references to election, leading to the erroneous conclusion that it was conciliatory toward the doctrines of Melanchthon. This change of emphasis may be because of the nature of the Heidelberg itself. It's purpose is not to simply define a doctrine, but to call the elect of God to repentance and faith. The sovereign grace of God is foundational throughout (see especially Questions 26, 52 and 54). In Ursinus' explanation of Question 54 in his commentary there is a lengthy explanation of both the nature of the Church and also of the eternal predestination of God. Here he says, "The common place of the eternal predestination of God, or of election and reprobation naturally grows out of the doctrine of the church: and is for

---

36 Lyle Dean Bierma, *The Covenant Theology of Casper Olevian*, Doctoral Dissertation for Duke University (Ann Arbor, University Microfilms International, 1980), p. 7.

37 *Ibid.*, p. 47.

38 *Ibid.*

this reason correctly connected with it."[39]

Is the Heidelberg avoiding the doctrines of the covenant and election? Certainly not. While the Heidelberg and Ursinus' shorter catechism do not expound covenant theology as such, it is important to note that the whole structure of the Heidelberg is covenantal in its purpose and application.[40] It is specifically intended to be the tool to instruct our covenant children. It is covenant theology in practice. The doctrine of the covenant and of election are only briefly mentioned by name, yet the basis for the "comfort" spoken of in the Heidelberg are the comforts that Christians find in these doctrines. The doctrine of election or predestination was viciously attacked by many who opposed the Reformed Church. This is still true today. Ursinus rightly saw the doctrine of God's sovereign, electing grace as a comfort, not a mystery or a threat. The Christian's comfort rests in the unshakable stability of his salvation. The doctrine of election provides this for the believer. In addition, the concept of God is not merely that of a sovereign, but of a loving Father. Question 28 rightly teaches the confidence that the believer has in God the Father for the future — that "no creature shall separate us from His love, since all creatures are so in His hand, that without His will they cannot so much as move." The elect are the children of God by adoption. God,who is our Father through Christ, unfailingly cares for His children. What greater comfort can a child of God have than this?

Quite a number of questions in the Heidelberg Catechism inquire of the learner, "What comfort or benefit is this to you?" (see Questions 1, 2, 28, 36, 43, 45, 49, 51, 52, 57, and 58). A striking example of this approach appears in Question 52 which asks, "What comfort is it to you that Christ shall come to judge the living and the dead?" In most treatments of the second coming of Christ and the judgment the concept of it being a comfort is lacking. Yet, comfort is exactly what the true believer experiences when he contemplates the return of our Lord. Such comfort can only belong to those who are assured that, by true faith in Jesus Christ, the promise of the covenant is theirs forever. The stress on the passive obedience of Christ on the cross which atoned for all our sins, and the active obedience of Christ which merited for us all our righteousness, is foundational to the whole

---

39 Zacharias Ursinus, *The Commentary of Dr. Zacharias Ursinus on the Heidelberg Catechism*, translated by the Rev. G. W. Willard, (Grand Rapids, Wm. B. Eerdmans Publishing Co., 1956), p. 293. Fully eleven pages are given to thoroughly setting forth the matter of predestination and election.

40 *Ibid.*, p. 97. Here we read Ursinus' definition of the Covenant as "a mutual promise and agreement between God and men, in which God gives assurance to men that he will be merciful to them, remit their sins, grant unto them a new righteousness, the Holy Spirit, and eternal life by and for the sake of his son, our Mediator. And, on the other side, men bind themselves to God in this covenant that they will exercise repentance and faith, or that they will receive with a true faith this great benefit which God offers, and render such obedience as will be acceptable unto him. This mutual engagement between God and man is confirmed by those outward signs which we call sacraments. . . ."

structure of the catechism and of our comfort. The stress on comfort and benefit has led some of the more scholastic critics to accuse the Heidelberg of being merely pragmatic and self-centered. While this approach is practical, it is not mere pragmatism, and it is certainly not centered on man as evidenced from the very first question and answer. Furthermore, the Heidelberg exhibits the central unity of the covenant by placing the Law of Love (Question 4) in its first part and the ten commandments in the third. This is the genius of Reformed covenant theology.

JOHN À LASCO

A study of the history of the Heidelberg Catechism would be incomplete without recalling the oft forgotten contributions of John à Lasco. The dominant theme in the Heidelberg Catechism regarding comfort finds its basis in the à Lasco catechism (1546) where a number of questions ask, "What comfort is it . . . ?"

This catechism was written by a remarkable man of God, John à Lasco, the founder and organizer of the Reformed Church in East Friesland, the Netherlands, the lower Rhine, and in England.[41] He was born in Poland of a family of nobility. His study at Zurich under Zwingli's influence directed him to a more Reformed view of worship and the celebration of the Lord's Supper. He held unswervingly to the position that faith and life must be subordinate only to the Word and will of God — in contrast to the prevailing view that popes and councils determined all truth for faith and life.

The fiery à Lasco undertook the duties of his office as pastor of the Reformed Church at Emden, and as superintendent of ecclesiastical affairs in East Friesland. Where Luther desired a gradual change in worship, à Lasco aimed for a thorough and decided reformation so as to avoid gradual and successive changes. Regarding change he stated,

> For such changes serve to render religion at first uncertain, and then contemptible, in the judgment of the uncultivated. If, therefore, a change of cultus is to be introduced, I desire it to be done in such a way, that no additional changes will be necessary in (the) future; that is, that all papal abominations, as soon as their sinfulness shall be made evident, be abolished, without exception; and in the introduction of new customs, an effort be made to conform as much as possible to the original purity and simplicity of the Apostolic Church, in order thus to supersede the necessity of any subsequent improvement."[42]

---

41 Henry Harbaugh, *op. cit.*, pp. 190-218.

42 *Ibid.*, p. 198.

Sensing the need for a confession of faith for the Frisian Reformed Church, à Lasco wrote a catechism (1554) based on Calvin's. This catechism which was known as the Emden Catechism, was used in all the foreign Reformed churches for a time and provided an important source for Ursinus in the preparation of the Heidelberg Catechism. Several questions of à Lasco's catechisms (he wrote several) have the theme of comfort which belongs to the believer.

It is interesting to see this theme of comfort and that of the covenant combined in Ursinus' Larger Catechism. It reads as follows:

> "What firm comfort do you have in life and death?" That I am formed of God according to his image. And after I had lost this image willingly in Adam, God, out of His infinite and free mercy, received me into the covenant of his grace, in order that He, on account of the obedience and death of His Son, sent unto us in the flesh, may give to me, a believer, justice and eternal life; and this covenant He had sealed in my heart through His spirit, re-forming me in accordance with the image of God and calling me 'Abba Father' through His Word and visible sign of the covenant.[43]

In comparison, Ursinus' second, shorter Catechism, reads as follows:

> What is your comfort by which in life and death your hearts sustains itself? That God, for Christ's sake, has truly forgiven my sins and given me eternal life, that in it I may glorify him forever."[44]

In these forerunners of the Heidelberg we see the change of emphasis on the matter of the covenant, and the comfort theme is expanded to the beautiful expression of our only comfort found in the first question and answer of the Heidelberg Catechism. There is comfort in belonging to the covenant and people of God and of knowing by faith the meaning of "I will be your God, and ye shall be my people." The Heidelberg Catechism is designed to focus on and impress this covenantal truth upon the hearts of the pupils in a very convincing way.

Thus, Ursinus preferred to view and teach the Christian faith in terms of the comfort we receive from being a member of God's covenant family. Within that covenant community God has his elect people. While the teaching of the sovereign electing grace of God was certainly a truth precious to Ursinus (see Heidelberg Catechism Question 54), yet he may have felt that this doctrine might appear too harsh for young children (or those not familiar with the Reformed faith) to under-

---

43 James I. Good, *op. cit.*, p. 65.

44 *Ibid.*

stand. So concludes James I. Good. I think this is to miss the depth of thinking that went into the Heidelberg. Ursinus' view of the Christian faith is rightly defined more in terms of the covenant of grace than in terms of election. The elect are the faithful "remnant" of the covenant people (Romans 11:5-7). Covenant administration does not proceed from election, but the assurance of one's election must develop out of a strong covenant consciousness. Within God's covenant He has His elect, and in the final analysis only the elect will ever know the eternal blessings of the covenant. The covenant-breaker will have heard of the blessings, but will only experience the curses.

Casper Olevianus

The comfort that Christians have is based on both of these truths — the security of election by God unto salvation in Christ, and the communion with God that we have as His covenant people. These two important doctrines are carefully and beautifully interwoven into the fabric of the Heidelberg to give us the promise, the ground and the fruits of our salvation.

CASPER OLEVIANUS (1536-1587)

The oft forgotten coauthor of the Heidelberg Catechism is Casper Olevianus. He did not contribute as many words to the catechism as Ursinus — but let us not underestimate the tremendous contributions he made in the formulation of covenant theology and Reformed ecclesiology. He stands shoulder to shoulder with the Reformers of his day.

Casper Olevianus (van Olewig) was a native of Olewig, a village near Treves (Trier) in France. His father was a baker who also held the office of mayor and senator. He was educated in Paris, Orleans, and Bourges. Here he became acquainted with and accepted Reformed theology. Later he studied theology in Geneva, Zurich, and Lausanne where he was influenced by such eminent leaders as Farel, Calvin, Peter Martyr, Beza, and Bullinger. He was appointed by Frederick III to become the eloquent courtpreacher in St. Peter's Church in the Palatinate. Recognizing his commitment to Reformed theology and extraordinary abilities, he was appointed to share in the writing of the Heidelberg Catechism.

It was through a terrible tragedy that Frederick III first became acquainted with Olevianus. When Olevianus was a student of law at Bourges, he became close friends with Herman Louis, the son of Pfalzgraf Hermann Ludwig (later Frederick known as Frederick III of the Palatinate). One day, while strolling along the Eure

River, both young men were invited to join another group of students in a boat trip across the river. This group of students was rather drunk. Olevianus declined to go with them, but Herman Louis went. In the course of the crossing the boat was overturned and all the occupants drowned. Olevianus dove into the water to save his friend, but was not successful. In doing this Olevianus himself very nearly drowned. Here Olevianus also promised God that should he be saved from death he would give himself to the service of the Gospel in his homeland.[45] Olevianus was rescued and he kept his promise by giving himself to the study of the works of John Calvin.

After graduating with a law degree in 1557 he went back to Treves for a short time. In 1558 he actually went to Geneva to study theology under John Calvin himself, and later on to Zurich to become a student of Peter Martyr, Bullinger and Beza. On his way back to Geneva, he met William Farel, the "persuader," who along with Calvin, convinced him that he must return to his homeland to teach the doctrines of the Reformed faith. He was now well-armed with Reformed theology, especially the teaching of the Covenant and Presbyterial Church government learned at Geneva. These would become important later in his ministry.

This young man, now twenty-three years old, returned to Treves filled with exuberance and fire to teach the Reformed theology. He was hired to lecture in Latin on Melanchthon's Dialectics at an academy known as The Bursa. It should be remembered that Treves was the city of the "Coat" (a coat supposedly worn by Jesus Christ which the Roman church taught the people to venerate). The size of the audience was so small he decided to preach (on his twenty-third birthday) in German on the subject of the doctrine of justification by faith. In his sermon he attacked the Roman mass, the worship of saints, religious processions, and other evils of the church. This was on August 10, 1559. Word of this spread rapidly to the enemies of the Reformed faith. The authorities favorable to the Roman Catholic Church ordered him never again to use the lecture hall to preach. At this time they did not forbid him to preach elsewhere in the city of Treves, which had a growing Reformed movement. His church grew to 500-600 adults. In a letter to the ministers of Strassburg (written from prison) Olevianus states that about half of the citizens embraced the Gospel.[46] The Elector, Johan von der Layen, returned from a meeting at the Reichstag in Augsburg, and was informed by the Roman Catholic sympathizers that this Calvinistic movement was getting out of hand. By August 25, the Elector's investigators issued a decree forbidding Olevianus from preaching entirely.

The Treves city council, in attempting to weaken the grip of power held by the Elector declined to obey. On September 6, with 170 of his knights, Elector Johann returned and agreed to some political freedoms. He still could not gain

---

45 Bierma, *op. cit.*, p. 3.

46 James I. Good, *op. cit.* p. 235.

sufficient support on the city council to stop Olevianus from preaching. His answer was force. He left the city and placed it under siege from late September to October 11. The city council capitulated to the Elector's demands and Olevianus and his colleagues were placed under arrest with capital charges of high treason.[47]

Through the intervention of Frederick III of the Palatinate (along with six other Protestant electors), Olevianus and eleven of his colleagues were released from prison on December 11, 1559 (after paying a fine of 3,000 gulden) and required to leave the city. After their release other Protestants were soon forced to flee the city. Olevianus' mother lived there for another twenty years until the next Elector of Treves drove out all Protestants. She fled to Herborn. The Jesuits were then given the task of reconverting all the Protestants. A holiday, "The Whitmonday Procession," was founded by the Jesuits in 1560, to celebrate the exile of the Protestants who followed the teachings of Olevianus. No Protestant was allowed to live in Treves for 200 years, until in 1784 an edict of religious toleration was issued. In 1817 the first Protestant church service was held.[48] The city of Treves, for better or worse did realize that a prophet had been in their midst! His name was Casper Olevianus.

Olevianus' journey now took him from prison to Heidelberg. Frederick III invited him to return to Heidelberg with him, where in 1560 he became an instructor in preaching at the College of Wisdom (which had just been converted to a seminary). In 1561 Olevianus was promoted to Professor of Theology at the University of Heidelberg where he was also given a degree of Doctor of Theology. Soon after this he married a girl, Philippina, whom he had met in Strassburg.

Olevianus felt he was better suited to preach than to lecture, so he accepted the position as pastor of St. Peter's Church and later the Church of the Holy Spirit.[49] His influence here was truly reformational (and revolutionary!), as he not only preached Calvinistic theology, but organized the church of the Palatinate along the lines of Presbyterianism which Calvin had established in Geneva. Especially, the practice of church discipline was instituted (as opposed to the idea that the civil authorities alone could institute and execute discipline).[50] Perhaps Olevianus' most noteworthy contribution to the theology of the Reformation is in the area of covenant theology. He is deemed by many to be the founder of covenant theology

---

47 Lyle Dean Bierma, *op. cit.* p. 5. *cf.* also James I. Good, *op. cit.*, pp 204 *ff.* for a detailed account of this ministry of Olevianus in Treves.

48 James I. Good, *op. cit.*, p. 241.

49 It was Olevianus' desire to have his friend Peter Martyr fill his seat, but when he turned down this request, it was Zacharias Ursinus who filled the vacancy left by Olevianus. Olevianus and Ursinus became close friends and co-workers as a result.

50 Lyle Dean Bierma, *op. cit.*, p. 6.

(not the first to expound it, but to define and systematize it).[51]

When appointed to work with Ursinus on the production of a catechism, Olevianus brought with him not only a sound Calvinistic theology, but a zeal which grew out of the fires of affliction, in order to produce a catechism filled with sound doctrine and the heartfelt comfort of knowing that "whatever evil He sends upon me in this troubled life, He will turn to my good; for he is able to do it, being Almighty God, and willing also, being a faithful Father." (Heidelberg Catechism Question 26)

Following the writing of the Heidelberg Catechism, Olevianus labored faithfully as a pastor and was especially responsible for the formation of a Reformed ecclesiology in the Palatinate.[52] After the death of Elector Frederick III (in 1576), the Lutheran doctrines and customs were immediately reinstated by Frederick's son, Ludwig. Since Olevianus was the primary leader in the Reformed church in Heidelberg, he was singled out as an enemy. He was suspended from office of pastor and professor, forbidden to correspond with any of the scholars, prohibited from holding any private assemblies in his house, and he was even placed under arrest. Another adherent of Reformed doctrine, Count Ludwig, of Sayn-Wittgenstein-Berleberg, was also deposed. He immediately called Olevianus to instruct his sons and also to preach in Herborn (Rhine-Westphalian area). Here Olevianus labored vigorously and tirelessly during the last ten years of his life, especially preparing the way for the introduction of the presbyterial order of church government in the provinces of Nassau, Wittgenstein, Solms, and Wied. This form of government was adopted in this region in 1581.[53]

In 1587, at the age of 50, Casper Olevianus entered into his eternal comfort, leaving behind his wife, two sons and a daughter. In his last testament he gives

---

51 The earliest treatise on the subject of the covenant was that of Henry Bullinger, *A Brief Exposition of the One and Eternal Testament or Covenant of God* which was written in 1534. This predates Olevianus' writings on this subject by nearly 30 years. Yet, Olevianus was a student of Bullinger for some time before writing on the subject himself. John Murry says that "Bullinger mapped out the lines along which the thinking of covenant theologians proceeded." (J. Murray, *Encyclopedia of Christianity* Vol. III [Marshallton, DE: The National Foundation for Christian Education, 1972] p. 204.) For a translation of Bullinger's Treatise, see Charles S. McCoy and J. Wayne Baker, *Fountainhead of Federalism: Heinrich Bullinger and the Covenantal Tradition* (Louisville, KY: Westminster/John Knox Press, 1991) pp. 99-139.

52 The teaching of the key of Christian discipline in Question 85 of the Heidelberg Catechism was a courageous move in the Palatinate. It was a direct challenge to the prevailing position that the state alone had this power. Were it not for the fact that Frederick III, a part of the civil establishment, commissioned the writing of the catechism, the Heidelberg would have met with immediate opposition if not banishment by the state. Olevianus, who learned much concerning Christian discipline from Calvin, must be credited for stressing this matter both in the catechism and in the Palatinate.

53 Henry Harbaugh, *op. cit.*, pp. 257 - 258.

evidence of his firm faith in the Almighty, saying,

> Herewith I also commend my body and soul to my beloved God, Father, Son, and Holy Ghost, through the eternal High Priest, relying upon His gracious covenant and promise, that he will, to all eternity, be my God, and the God of my seed, and that he will never deal with me in anger, as he has sworn to me in His oath (Isa. 54:9).[54]

Another example of Olevianus' fatherly concern for his covenant children comes in a letter three days before his death, written to his son Paul, who was too ill to be at his side,

> My dear son Paul, with the patriarch Jacob I say: I wait for thy salvation, O Lord! for I have arrived at that point where I exclaim, with the apostle: I have a desire to depart, and to be with Christ, to whom also I commend and commit thee; as I did in holy baptism, so also I do now, when I am about to depart to the Lord. In like manner do I also commend your dear mother, your brother, and your sister to Him, and the word of His grace. True, I would gladly have seen you once more; yet I could not urge you to come, as it is very cold, and your leg is not yet recovered. Yesterday I arranged all my affairs, as it is meet for a pious father to do; and our noble prince, John has ratified, by a document, his liberality toward you, without laying any restraint upon your liberty. Hourly do I expect to make my pilgrimage to the Lord. Do not undertake hastily to come to me. We will see each other again, according to God's gracious covenant, in eternal life. I commit to you your pious mother, even as I know your love to her. Care for your young brother Ludwig, as for my beloved one; and, with that wisdom which is constitutional with you, treat him gently. Mind not high things, but condescend to men of low estate; and so direct your studies that many may be benefited by them. The blessing of God be with your going out and coming in. Amen. And let your spirit repose upon the free and gracious sacrifice of the Son, expecting the heavenly inheritance only through and in the will of the Son of God. Amen. Your father, Casper Olevianus, of Treves, minister of the Word of God. Lord Jesus, receive my spirit."[55]

Such an epistle of at the end of a life's journey demonstrates the depth of faith and

---

54 *Ibid.*, p. 259.

55 *Ibid.*, p. 260.

conviction which characterized the life's work of Olevianus.

Apart from the trial by fire in prison and the providential connection with Elector Frederick III, there are several elements that are significant in the theology and contributions of Olevianus — his contributions in the area of church polity and discipline, his formation of a more consistent and mature covenant theology than heretofore. We are deeply indebted to God for this faithful laborer in our Reformed heritage.

PETER RAMUS (1515 -1572)

Pierre de la Ramée, a french philospher, better known by his latin name, Peter Ramus, had an effect on the thinking of Casper Olevianus. At the time of the Reformation, the predominant philosphy was still based on the pagan dualism (scholasticism) of Aristotle. The Roman Catholics had merely modified the heathen philosophy of Aristotle. Aristotle not only held that all of life is divided into the realms of form and matter (the spiritual and the physical). He also employed a form of logic to arrive at truth. Ramus led a movement which was critical of the Aristotelian method. In 1561 he was converted to Protestantism which involved Ramus' application of his principles to the area of theology, especially in the area of "federal" or "covenant" theology.

Today, we would not agree with all the conclusions of Ramus' philosophy, but one significant conclusion that Ramus and Olevianus came to was that you cannot reform theology without also reforming the whole philosophy of life and approach to truth. On this we would certainly agree. Since the Reformation brought the church back to the Bible as the sole source of all authority for faith and life, it was necessary that the Bible' not logical syllogisms, be seen as the source of truth. Ramus replaced the deductive logic of scholasticism with the inductive method of reasoning. He was still left with a constant and unacceptable method of dichotomizing (dividing everything into two parts). Ramism was a semi-Platonic system of thought which is unacceptable to the Reformed church today. The error was to use Aristotelian logic to refute Aristotle. Using that method which turned logic into rhetoric, one does not reach a Christian philosophy such as Cornelius Van Til has done in this century, but, at best, one can only become Platonic which is also non-Christian. More needed to be done in this area of study, but Ramus did make an important contribution in breaking with the scholasticism of the church of Rome.

Ramus had four presuppositions:

The first is a twofold confidence in the ability of man to know, and in the "knowledge" of that which is known. The second is an assumption that the form of presentation is to be determined by the desire for communication rather than the nature of the subject matter. The third is that the cause of a thing is more evident than a statement to its effect. And the fourth, a general and universal is more evident than a particular and single.[56]

Ramism had a great influence on Puritan federal (covenant) theology and also came to Heidelberg in 1569 after visits to Strassburg, Basel, and Zurich. At Heidelberg he made a public profession of Protestantism in the French Reformed Church at Heidelberg. Elector Frederick III was impressed with Ramus and was inclined to have him as a professor there. He appointed him to fill a vacated chair in the ethics department. Among the professors who accepted him was Olevianus. The university senate, predominately Aristotelian, however, refused to have Ramus join the faculty and immediately appointed another man, ignoring Frederick's appointment. Their reason: Heidelberg University was Aristotelian and Ramus was Platonic. Frederick did appoint him to teach a course in the classics and later in Aristotelian philosophy, but much opposition against him was raised by both students and faculty. Zacharias Ursinus prevailed upon Frederick III to suspend any further lectures by Ramus.

Ramus returned to Paris. In August of 1572 he fell victim to the St. Bartholomew's Massacre in which Roman Catholics deceived the Reformed with the promise of protection, when in fact, they ambushed and slaughtered over 2,000 Reformed Christians. Assassins entered his fifth floor room at the college. They pillaged his room, then despite his plea for mercy shot him in the head, dragged his body about the room , and then threw it out the window. Students then dragged him about the streets to the River Seine where a surgeon cut off his head and had his body thrown into the river. They retrieved the body, and literally hacked it to pieces. Such was the hatred for this reformer.[57]

The significance of Ramus is that Ursinus and Olevianus were on opposite sides of the Ramus controversy. Olevianus stressed the practical which was more consistent with Ramism; Ursinus stressed the analytic which was more consistent with scholasticism. Together these temperaments and outlooks resulted in the production of the Heidelberg.[58] We do not read that this difference in philosophical approach ever caused a real breach between Ursinus and Olevianus. There is a difference of opinion regarding how much of Ramus' philosophy affected the work of Olevianus. It is doubtful that Olevianus ever fully embraced Ramism for it is not

---

56 W. Robert Godfrey, Jesse L. Boyd III, ed., *Through Christ's Word*, "Federal Theology" by W. Wilson Benton Jr. (Phillipsburg, NJ, Presbyterian and Reformed Publishing Company) 1985, p. 196.

57 James I. Good, *op. cit.*, pp. 112 - 113.

58 James Good notes that there was one dispute regarding Question 35, but "God's grace prevented it." (*op. cit.*, p. 115).

evident in his work.[59] What is significant is that Olevianus recognized the error of Aristotelianism and saw the need for a more consistent biblical philosophy.

OLEVIANUS AND COVENANT THEOLOGY

Any overview of the life of Olevianus without seeing his contribution to covenant theology would be incomplete. While Ursinus stressed covenant theology in his first, Larger Catechism, the covenant receded into the background in his later writings. In the case of Olevianus, his interest and formulation of a consistent covenant theology grew more prominent after the completion of the Heidelberg Catechism. We cannot say that Olevianus was the first to use covenantal theology, but it is clear that he was instrumental in its development. While in Zurich he became acquainted with the early covenant theology of Zwingli and Bullinger.[60]

For Olevianus, "the covenant of grace is the kingdom of Christ, or better: through the covenant of grace that the kingdom of Christ is brought about. In the covenant it takes shape."[61] He says that the articles of the Apostles' Creed are really a summary of the covenant of grace — the Father is the first party; the Son is the Mediator of the covenant, the Holy Spirit is the Applicator of the covenant, and the Church is the second party of the covenant. In his *Fester Grund*, a catechism he wrote after the writing of the Heidelberg Catechism, he beautifully states the basis for the covenant of grace in saying, "One's salvation consists in union and communion with God."[62]

Olevianus saw the covenant of God as the covenant of works with Adam before the Fall and the covenant of grace after the fall which God secured in the crucifixion of Christ.[63] Olevianus stood between the early covenant theologians and the later 16th and 17th Century covenant theologians. The school which Olevianus founded in Herborn saw the professors there expound and expand upon the covenant theology of Olevianus.

Zacharias Ursinus, who also studied the covenant extensively, was the first

---

59 Lyle Dean Beirma, *op. cit.*, pp. 230-238, has a lengthy discussion on Ramus. His conclusion is that Olevianus never adopted the philosophy or theology of Ramus. Olevianus entered the debate between Ramus' empirical theology and Beza's rationalism in order to neutralize Beza's predestinarianism with the covenant idea of Calvin. This placed Olevianus in opposition to Ursinus who "remained a defender of the Aristotelian-Reformed orthodoxy."

60 Lyle Dean Bierma, *op. cit.*, p. 215, and Dr. H. Faulenbach, Dr. D. Meyer, Dr. R. Mohr, ed., *Casper Olevian (1536 bis 1587)*, (Köln, Rheinland-Verlag-GmbH, 1989), pp. 85 - 86.

61 Dr. H. Faulenbach, Dr. D. Meyer, Dr. R. Mohr, ed., *op.cit.*, p. 87. (translation mine)

62 Lyle Dean Bierma, *op. cit.*, p. 211 and p. 93. In two of Olevianus' greatest works, the *Expositio* and *De Substantia*, the covenant is the major theme, as it was in the majority of Olevianus' writings.

63 *Ibid.*, p. 86.

Reformed theologian to speak of a covenant of nature (or "works" as it was referred to later) in addition to the covenant of grace. This covenant of nature was initiated by God with man at creation and remains with man. This is that part of God's image in us which results in the perception of the divine will and gives the ability to determine right from wrong. This was a step toward a fuller formulation of the covenant and understanding of the nature of man. Calvin also speaks of the "sensus divinitatus" as the sense of the deity in man even after the fall (see Rom. 1:21). Ursinus saw the Christian not only as a member of the covenant but as a member of Christ Himself — a union with Christ in all things (see Heidelberg Catechism Question 43)

Olevianus was the first theologian to speak of a covenant with the devil (which man entered into at the Fall), a covenant which believers have with other creatures, and a pretemporal redemptive arrangement between the Father and the Son (which we sometimes today call the covenant of redemption).[64] He also spoke of the covenant of grace in terms of a mutual covenant instead of a unilateral covenant. By this he did not deny the fact that God unilaterally imposed the covenant on man, but that the essence of the covenant requires faithfulness and obedience on the part of man. This covenantal consistency is clearly seen in the unique position of the law of God in the Third Part of the catechism under "Thankfulness." The covenant of grace does not abrogate moral requirements on the part of the believer, but the believer, who now has a different relationship to God, has a different relationship to the law — a joyful, thankful service rendered to a heavenly Father whose covenant not only requires us to be faithful, but by the fulfillment of redemption, has rendered us willing servants. Man, after the Fall, sees his sin and misery in the fact that he cannot fulfill the Law of Love — the basic requirement of God (Question 4 of the Heidelberg Catechism).

Olevianus spoke of a "general administration of the covenant promise to all within the visible church — elect and non-elect alike — and a special administration of the substance of this promise to the elect alone. The . . .outward administration of the covenant promise". . . was given to all of Israel (ie. circumcision), but . . . "the administration of the substance of the covenant promise only to the elect" (ie. spiritual circumcision). Therefore, "while the reprobate in the visible church partake of the visible signs of the covenant, they do not partake of its substance."[65]

Both Ursinus and Olevianus were quick to point out that any obedience is due to the work of God's Holy Spirit working in us (Phil. 2:12,13). The mutual aspect of the covenant is seen in the administration of the Word and sacraments (see Heidelberg Catechism Question 82). Reconciliation between the King and subject

---

64 Lyle Dean Bierma, *op. cit.*, p. 227.

65 Bierma, *op. cit.*, pp. 126-126.

involves a mutual commitment. This commitment is by the grace of God through His Holy Spirit. It appears that when Olevianus interprets, "I will be your God, and you shall be my people," he is taking the latter part of this covenant promise to be **both** a statement of promise by God **and** a required commitment on the part of his people. Here we see the sovereignty of God and the responsibility of man brought into harmony. This was indicative of a move away from the supralapsarianism of that day toward sublapsarianism.

Olevianus and Ursinus together have given us a rich heritage in the precious doctrines of covenant theology, of which the Heidelberg Catechism is more the product than the instruction manual. Due to the work of these men the roots of covenant theology were established on the continent of Europe and later developed further by Scottish and British theologians (such as Robert Howie, 1565 - 1654; Robert Rollock, 1555-1598; William Ames, 1576 - 1633, and others).

THE FINISHED PRODUCT — THE HEIDELBERG CATECHISM

From the quiet, contemplative theology of Ursinus and the eloquent, practical theology of Olevianus a new catechism was produced which literally shook the world. It brought comfort to some and made others very uncomfortable. Other creeds were harsher and more negative toward their enemies. The Heidelberg, while defining the essentials of the Reformed faith, did not set out to simply condemn the errors of others, but to deal with the personal sin of man, the way of salvation, and the purpose of God's redemption — His glory. This is the genius and uniqueness of the Heidelberg. It did not set forth the all the details of the covenant, but it put the covenant responsibilities into practice. It did not set forth in detail the doctrines of God's sovereignty as the Canons of Dort did later, but it assumed these as the foundation of man's salvation.

In many ways the Heidelberg Catechism grew out of theological contro-versy, as creeds generally do. And it was a creator of controversy by those who hated the Reformed faith. For those who saw in it a summary of biblical truths, it was a confession of comfort. For pastors in their churches and fathers in their homes it was an implement of tremendous value to instill the promises of the covenant in the hearts of students and children. It was a statement of faith useful for the church, but no less so for the homes. We might think that everyone would have embraced it with great affection, but storm clouds rapidly overshadowed it in its infancy.

The ink on the pages of the Heidelberg Catechism was barely dry when it became the center of controversy. Much of the abhorrence for the Heidelberg centered around its teaching on the sacraments. Those who opposed it saw this as the point of attack and missed seeing how the sacraments as set forth in the catechism were the natural outworking of the covenantal basis of the catechism. In the Heidelberg Catechism the sacraments were set forth as the covenantal signs and seals which God has appointed for his covenant people. By directing their attack against the sacraments, opponents were causing the tail to wag the dog. Yet, the sacraments were the most visible points to attack. Had these assaults not been heroically thwarted by the grace and power of God, the Heidelberg might have been put to ashes — the heritage destroyed by the heretics.

If Frederick took credit for the production of the Heidelberg and was willing to call it "my catechism," so too he would have to defend it with his life. And defend it he did. This was a critical time in the life of the Reformed Church, for in the Heidelberg, doctrines were defined and allowed to see the light of day. Opposition to Frederick and his catechism grew until in the year 1566 Frederick was summoned by Emperor Maximilian to defend the Heidelberg (and the Reformed faith) at the Diet of Augsburg.

Maximilian (inclined toward the High-Lutherans) wanted unity in the empire, but the Calvinists here, as in France and in the Netherlands, were stirring up controversy. They were branded as rebels. As the diet convened Maximilian appeared to take the side of the Catholics. Few sided with Frederick and the Reformed. Lutherans were not willing to unite with the Reformed for the cause of Protestantism in general. The Elector of Saxony, a Low-Lutheran, had the foresight to see that if the Lutherans and Reformed were not united, Catholicism would rise to power. The Protestants at the diet did not agree to isolate Frederick, so it would be up to the Catholics (with the help of High-Lutherans) to bring charges against him. This they did as they charged Frederick with casting out images, altars, and introducing Reformed liturgy.

Maximilian issued a decree against Frederick that if he would not cast out all the Reformed changes that were made in the regions of Neuhaus and Sinzheim, he would be deposed. With that deposition would go the Heidelberg Catechism! Frederick had less than two days to prepare his defense which would take place on May 14, 1566. Frederick protested against the procedures and against the fact that he was condemned before he had an opportunity to defend himself. In other Diets we have seen theologians such as Luther defend the faith. Here, a layman, a civil ruler, would be taking up the cause of Christ and the Reformed faith. His son, John Casimir, stood at his side carrying a Bible.

Taking a page from Luther's defense at the Diet of Worms, Frederick finally appealed to the conscience which must be bound by the Word of God. In his defense he said,

> So far as matters of a religious nature are involved, I confess freely
> that in those things which concern the conscience, I acknowledge
> as Master, only Him, who is Lord of lords and King of kings. For

the question here is not in regard to a cap of flesh, but it pertains to the soul and its salvation, for which I am indebted alone to my Lord and Savior Jesus Christ, and which, as His gift, I will sacredly preserve. Therefore I cannot grant your Imperial Majesty the right of standing in the place of my God and Savior.[66]

Frederick then began to defend the faith as set forth in the Heidelberg Catechism,

But that my catechism, word for word, is drawn, not from human, but from divine sources, the references that stand in the margin will show. For this reason also certain theologians have in vain wearied themselves in attacking it, since it has been shown them by the open Scriptures how baseless is their opposition. What I have elsewhere publicly declared to your Majesty in a full assembly of princes; namely, that if any one of whatever age, station or class he may be, even the humblest, can teach me something better from the Holy Scriptures, I will thank him from the bottom of my heart and be readily obedient to the divine truth.[67]

Frederick closed his defense with courage and commitment borne out by the words,

Should, contrary to my expectations, my defense and the Christian and reasonable conditions which I have proposed, not be regarded of any account, I shall comfort myself in this that my Lord and Savior Jesus Christ has promised to me and to all who believe that whatsoever we lose on earth for His name's sake, we shall receive an hundred fold in the life to come.[68]

Silence fell on the assembly until his sole friend, Elector Augustus of Saxony, slapped him on the shoulder and exclaimed, "Fritz, you are more pious than all of us." He was right.[69] Maximilian adjourned the assembly which was to meet again in six days to consider the decree he had made. At this meeting the Protestants held together, fearing that what might happen to Frederick might also be brought against them. Frederick did not agree with them on the matter of the ubiquity of Christ, but they were willing to overlook this for the sake of unity. They declared that Frederick was an adherent of the Augsburg Confession despite the one doctrine

66 James I. Good, *op. cit.*, p. 193.

67 *Ibid.*

68 *Ibid.*

69 Frederick III is often referred to as "Frederick the Pious" since that remark.

on Lord's Supper that he objected to and therefore they would side with Frederick. On May 24, the diet was called together again by those who would not agree with Frederick's exception. Now Frederick was called on to allow nothing else than what was taught in the Augsburg Confession to be preached. They deemed the teachings of Frederick to be more dangerous than Calvin's. These teachings should cease, the teachers driven out and their books destroyed. Frederick refused to do this. On the matter of the Lord's Supper, Frederick took his Bible, laid it on the table, and urged anyone present to teach him something better out of the Bible. No one dared.

Frederick left the council that day. Maximilian's decree was overturned, but he was still determined to rid his realm of Calvinism. There was celebration in Heidelberg as Frederick returned and had retained his reign. The next day at a church service he grasped Olevianus' hand and publicly admonished the whole congregation to demonstrate the same faithfulness that he had shown.

A final diet convened in September of that year exonerated Frederick. Not only was Frederick cleared of charges, but the Heidelberg Catechism was allowed to be used in Germany. Had Frederick failed, his catechism might well have been destroyed. It was a victory for Frederick, but more importantly a victory for the Reformed faith.

Frederick would likely be a forgotten man were it not for the Heidelberg Catechism which continues today as the fruit of Frederick, Ursinus, and Olevianus. Without question, the courage and abilities which God gave these men was responsible, more than any others, for the establishment of the Reformed Church in Germany. In God's providence these men were able to learn and develop the doctrines of the Reformed faith from institutions and men of many countries, primarily Switzerland, France, and the Netherlands. Their catechism was returned

The original title page of the 1563 German edition of the Heidelberg Catechism. It was published by Johann Mayer in the city of Heidelberg, from which the catechism also draws its name today. Sometimes it is referred to as the Palatinate Catechism.

The full title on the cover page reads: "Catechism or Christian Instruction the way it is practiced in Churches and Schools in the Electorate of the Palatinate."

to these lands and many others in gratitude.

Heidelberg Effect

The Heidelberg Catechism, like few other books at that time, became an international catechism. It was first published in the German language and since 1563 it has been read by many thousands of people in scores of languages throughout the world. Our own efforts to provide the Heidelberg Catechism for Zaire may be the most recent — with translations in Swahili, Tschiluba, Kiluba, and Lingala. In the 17th Century the Dutch published a Greek version of the Heidelberg bound with the Canons of Dort and the Belgic Confession of Faith.

The Dutch were instrumental in bringing the Heidelberg Catechism to their trading partners. The Dutch East India and West India Companies had the Heidelberg translated into the languages of the countries they traded with the hope of converting these people.[70] Their own coat-of-arms was placed on the title page of the catechism. When they established colonies, they often sent missionaries with the ships. In contrast, the East India Company of Great Britain was forbidden from introducing Christianity to their colonies for fear of exciting the hostility of the natives.[71]

Some additions and deletions appeared in the course of history. The first edition of the Heidelberg did not have Question 80, the second had most of what we now have, and the third edition added the phrase which said that the Mass was an "accursed idolatry." The Swiss added to the 27th question a sentence which said that, "God is not the author of sin."[72] In Hungary, Empress Maria Theresa forbade the use of the Heidelberg. Her son, however, allowed the use of an altered edition which removed all references to the Roman Catholic Church.[73]

King Frederick William I of Prussia stated in his 1717 regulations, "that in all the evangelical churches and schools of my dominion there shall be used and taught no other catechism than the Heidelberg Catechism, to which I myself hold allegiance."[74] Henry Bullinger, the successor of Zwingli at Zurich, said, "I am confident that no better catechism has made its appearance. God's name be praised

---

70 This mission enterprise was a requirement of their charter from the Dutch government.

71 *Ibid.*, p. 11.

72 *Ibid.*, p. 17.

73 *Ibid.*, p. 17. Question 30 was largely omitted; Question 80 had the last sentence removed. In 1891 the complete version was again published and used in Hungary.

74 Otto Thelemann, *An Aid to the Heidelberg Catechism*, (Grand Rapids, Douma Publications, 1959) p. xx.

for it. May He grant it abundant success."[75] We can all join in the sentiments of Henry Alting, Professor at Heidelberg and Groningen (d. 1644) that, "the Heidelberg Catechism is at the same time milk for babes and strong meat for adults."[76]

Various shorter versions of the catechism also appeared — the first in German by Count John Casimir (son of Frederick III)[77] in 1585, then a short version was produced by the Synod of Dort entitled, "A Compendium of the Christian Religion." Various other short versions were produced through the years. Some, as early as 1597, were set to poetry in various languages. And as mentioned earlier, some editions included the teachings of each Lord's Days set to music. Many versions of the Heidelberg Catechism are spotted with the blood of martyrs — Reformed Christians who were shamefully martyred for the cause of the faith, of which the Heidelberg Catechism was a vital part.[78]

There is probably no other Reformed Church existent today in which the Heidelberg Catechism plays such a central role in the instruction of the covenant youth as in our beloved Reformed Church in the United States. After 250 years here in the United States, and for years before that, we continue to utilize it in very much the same way as the families and churches of our forefathers. May this never change for the sake of our youth and the glory of our Lord from whom we draw this everlasting comfort for body and soul.

A Unique Creed

We should understand the unique character of the Heidelberg Catechism as a "creed-catechism." There were great Reformed creeds and many good catechisms to teach the faith. The creeds were statements of doctrine and the catechisms were used only for catechizing. But it was not until the Heidelberg that a catechism became a creed and a creed became a catechism. Frederick was very cautious in endorsing the Heidelberg, since only the Augsburg Confession was legal in Germany. The Heidelberg was carefully written to instruct the youth, but it was also written to be the creed of the Reformed Church in Germany. Children recited it in the schools, and ministers would preach catechetical sermons from it.

---

75 *Ibid.*

76 *Ibid.*, p. xxi. We might be surprised to find B. B. Warfield among the critics of the Heidelberg. He charged in the Princeton Review, 1908 p. 565, that the Heidelberg is hedonistic and contains a spiritual utilitarianism because it asks such questions as, "What is my comfort, benefit, profit, etc." This, he said would attract a child to religion by selfish ideas of enjoyment. (J. I. Good, *op. cit.*, p. 296.)

77 John was responsible for bringing the Reformed faith back to the Palatinate after a brief lapse into Lutheranism after the death of his father, Frederick III.

78 *Ibid.*, pp. 19, 20. James I. Good rightly notes that at the center of the Heidelberg history written in blood is the "blood of Christ".

In the turmoil of the history of the Reformed Church in the United States in the 1930's, the stubborn refusal to give up the Reformed faith and the Heidelberg Catechism attests to the powerful influence that the Heidelberg has had upon us as a denomination. The proposed merger of the RCUS with the Evangelical Church of North America placed the Heidelberg on the same par as Luther's Catechism — a compromise that would surely have enraged our forefathers from Heidelberg!. Those committed to a Reformed position would have been allowed to choose the Heidelberg, others could have followed Luther's, and for the undecided, both! What a bargain! — the faith for a bowl of pottage. The Reformed get to keep the Heidelberg and still end up with the benefits of this huge denomination. Those committed to the Reformed faith knew that this compromise was unholy, and also that the use of the Heidelberg would soon end. And end it did in the resulting united churches. It is difficult to say whether the people held on to the Heidelberg, or whether the Heidelberg held on to them. Either way, through a firm commitment to the biblical faith as set forth in the Heidelberg, God was pleased to preserve both the Heidelberg as a confession and, more importantly, His church. This steadfastness which God wrought is part of our Heidelberg heritage. There will certainly be challenges in days to come. Be prepared.

In recent days the RCUS has again officially adopted the Belgic Confession of Faith and the Canons of Dort. These were the creeds of the RCUS at its beginnings in the United States. It is fitting that on this anniversary of the 250th Synod we should be able to lay claim to all three again. It was feared by some that having three creeds would undermine the importance and the use of the Heidelberg. If it falls into obscurity, it is not the fault of other creeds, but of those who are willing to neglect them all. The Synod of Dort was really the first to bind these three creeds together as necessary and complimentary confessions of the Reformed Churches.[79] The teachings of the Heidelberg are beautifully supplemented and "fleshed out" by these other expressions of biblical teachings. The Heidelberg Catechism will always be the unique teaching tool of these three. The Heidelberg is very much at home with what is sometimes referred to as the Three Forms of Unity.

This is the remarkable nature of the Heidelberg. It is loved dearly by those who love the faith. It is hated intensely by those who deny the faith. Yet the Heidelberg, and the true faith it expresses, still stand and cannot be ignored. It's teachings are fundamental. Due to its firm biblical foundation, it has proven itself to be not only an enduring creed, but a rich blessing for many generations. It is not

---

79 Otto Thelemann *op.cit.*, p. xx, quotes from the Synod of Dort (1618), "That the doctrine contained in the Palatinate Catechism is in accordance with the Word of God, and that it contains nothing which on the ground of dissonance with the Word of God needs to be altered or amended, and that it is also an exceedingly correct hand-book of sound Christian doctrine, adapted with special skill not only to the capacity of youths, but also of adults."

simply a children's instruction book.

It's enduring quality is seen in the picture of children at their parents knee struggling to memorize the first question, to the catechumen coming to catechism class with a Heidelberg stuffed in the back pocket of his jeans, to the funeral service where it is often quoted to provide a special sort of comfort and warmth for the families of those who have carried these words of comfort in their hearts throughout their lives.

Ursinus perhaps best describes the design of the catechism in his closing words of the introduction to his *Commentary on the Heidelberg Catechism*:

> The design of the doctrine of the catechism is our comfort and salvation. Our salvation consists in the enjoyment of the highest good. Our comfort comprises the assurance and confident expectation of the full and perfect enjoyment of this highest good, in the life to come, with a beginning and foretaste of it already in this life. This highest good is that which makes all those truly blessed who are in the enjoyment of it, whilst those who have it not are miserable and wretched. What this only comfort is, to which it is the design of this catechism to lead us, will be explained in the first question . . . . [80]

> **What is your only comfort in life and in death?**

> That I, with body and soul, both in life and in death, am not my own, but belong to my faithful Savior Jesus Christ, who with his precious blood has fully satisfied for all my sins, and redeemed me from all the power of the devil; and so preserves me that without the will of my Father in heaven not a hair can fall from my head; indeed, that all things must work together for my salvation. Wherefore, by His Holy Spirit, he also assures me of eternal life, and makes me heartily willing and ready from now on to live unto him.

THE HERITAGE

Countless people through the years have carried on the Heidelberg tradition. That is well, but will we and our children continue to carry on the Heidelberg's truths? Will we continue to commit it to our heads and our hearts? Will we faithfully teach our covenant children to walk in the doctrines it so clearly expounds? Would we be willing, as many before us, to put our life on the line to cling

---

80 Zacharias Ursinus, *op. cit.*, p. 16.

to the Christian faith as set forth in the Heidelberg? The use of the Heidelberg is very much a part of our past, but will we take that heritage with us into the future?

To recount the rich heritage of our forefathers is an exercise in futility and no more than "name-dropping" unless we still walk in those shoes and are committed to instill these truths in the hearts and minds of the generations to come. Just to preserve and honor a heritage as a thing of the past is to make an idolatrous icon of it. To persevere the faith expressed in our Heidelberg heritage will be a blessing to us and to our covenant children. The Heidelberg is not just a book to memorize, but to use so that the Scriptures might be opened to us in a most beautiful and comforting way.

The Heidelberg Heritage is not something we should speak of merely in the past tense. We are the ones who, with others of like precious faith, must carry this heritage into the future. We appear to pale in comparison to some of the men instrumental in producing the Heidelberg, yet we should not view ourselves as under them. As Dr. Cornelius Van Til used to teach, each generation must stand on the shoulders of those preceding to further the cause of Christ and His Kingdom.

As a Reformed Church, celebrating our 250th Synod by the grace of God, the Heidelberg is a vital part of our heritage. It can only be our fervent and continued prayer that the Heidelberg Catechism will always be "our beloved Heidelberg" — an expression of our only comfort — for generations to come.

Praise God for our Heidelberg heritage!

Bibliography

Bierma, Lyle Dean, *The Covenant Theology of Casper Olevian*. Ann Arbor: UMI Dissertation Services, 1995.

Buehrer, Emil, *The Reformation*. Green Bay: Reliance Publishing Company, 1945.

Calvin, John, *Institutes of the Christian Religion*. McNeill, John T., Ed., Transl. and Indexed by Ford Lewis Battles. The Library of Christian Classics Vol. XX. Philadelphia: Westminster Press, 1960.

Catechismus, Oder Kurtzer Unterricht Christlicher Lehr. Schaffhausen: Johan Ulrich Ziegler, 1789.

Empie, Paul C. and McCord, James I., *Marburg Revisited*. Minneapolis: Augsburg Publishing House, 1966.

Faulenback, Dr. H., Meyer, Dr. D., Mohr, Dr. R., editors, *Casper Olevian (1536 bis 1587)*. Köln: Rheinland-Verlag-GmbH, 1989.

Fuhrmann, Paul T., Transl. and Ed., *Instruction in Faith (1537) by John Calvin*. Louisville: Westminster/John Knox Press, 1992.

Godfrey, Robert and Boyd, Jesse L. III, editors, *Through Christ's Word*. Phillipsburg: Presbyterian and Reformed Publishing Company, 1985.

Good, James I., *The Heidelberg Catechism in its Newest Light*. Philadelphia: Publication and Sunday School Board of the Reformed Church in the United States, 1914.

Harbaugh, Rev. Henry, *The Fathers of the German Reformed Church in Europe and America*, Vol. I. Lancaster: Sprenger and Westhaeffer, 1857.

Heyns, W., *Handboek voor de Catechetiek*. Grand Rapids: Eerdmans-Sevensma Co. Date unknown.

Kindler, F. P., *Der Heidelberger Catechismus*. Erlangen: 1846.

Schaff, David S. DD., *Our Fathers Faith and Ours*. New York: G. P. Putnam's Sons, 1928.

Schaff, Philip, *The Creeds of Christendom*, Vol. III. New York: Harper & Brothers, 1882.

Spitz, Lewis W., Ed., *The Protestant Reformation*. Englewood Cliffs: Prentice-hall, Inc., 1966.

Stähelin, Christoph, *Catechetischer Haus-Schatz, Oder Erklärung des Heidelbergischen Catechismi*. Zurich: F. Hanke, 1724.

The Encyclopedia of Christianity, Vol. III. Marshallton, DE: The National Foundation for Christian Education, 1972.

The Heidelberg Catechism. Publications Committee, RCUS. Freeman, SD: Pine Hill Press,

1986.

Thelemann, Otto, *An Aid to the Heidelberg Catechism*. Transl. by Rev. M. Peters, Grand Rapids: Douma Publications, 1959.

Ursinus, Zacharias, *The Commentary of Dr. Zacharias Ursinus on the Heidelberg Catechism* . Transl. by Rev. G. W. Willard, Grand Rapids: Wm. B. Eerdmans Publishing Co, 1956.

Van Halsema, Thea, *Three Men Came to Heidelberg*. Grand Rapids: Baker Book House, 1963.

Zanchius, Jerom, *The Absolute Doctrine of Predestination*. Transl. by Augustus Toplady. Grand Rapids: Baker Book House, 1977.

CHAPTER   EIGHT

Whither the RCUS?

Rev. Jim West

The future of any Church depends upon the animating power of the Spirit of Christ, who inflames our hearts for the Gospel and keeps us faithful to the Word of God. The Reformed Church in the United States must not discount the role of the Holy Spirit, nor assume that the official acknowledgment of the historic creeds is an automatic guarantor of her future orthodoxy. It is not inconsequential that the Reformed Church in Heidelberg that Olevianus shepherded was called The Church of the Holy Ghost. Indeed, the church is God's holy temple only by the indwelling of the Holy Spirit (1 Corinthians 3:17).

History tells us that there is often a great chasm between a church's official creed and its working creed, that is, what it actually does believe and practice. Creeds are not interesting fossils or museum pieces that magically connect us to the church militant or triumphant. They contain doctrines that must be believed and believed heartily. The recent adoption of the Three Forms of Unity do not make us more orthodox unless there is a corresponding trust in the doctrines contained in those Creeds. When the Lord prosecuted the Church at Laodicea, He did not do so because the Church had impoverished itself creedally. On the contrary, the church was "rich" with theology. The Church even declared, "I am rich, have become wealthy, and have need of nothing" (Revelation 3:17). Many commentaries understand this to refer to spiritual wealth instead of mammon. If so, the Church at Laodicea expressed pride in her creedal heritage. Yet, the Lord prosecuted the Laodiceans, saying, you "did not know that you are wretched, miserable, poor, blind, and naked" Revelation 3:18). Is it possible for a church to bask in the sunshine of its creeds in a prideful way, boasting before the Lord instead of boasting in the Lord? Yes — the lukewarm Church of Laodicea did precisely that! To such churches the Lord said, "As many as I love, I rebuke and chasten. Therefore be zealous and repent" (Revelation 3:19). Yes, the church is commanded to repent! Repentance is a continual activity for the Church. As Spurgeon once said, "The proof that I repented yesterday is that I am still repenting today."

The RCUS must not only be doctrinally sound in her official creed, but doctrinally sound in her working creed. The hearts of her members and leaders must be sound too.

CHRISTIAN DISCIPLESHIP OF YOUTH

One of the ways that she can be doctrinally sound is to instruct her youth in the great doctrines of God's sovereign grace. Catechetical training (a synonym for Christian discipleship) is one of the hallmarks of the RCUS. As one reviews the past, it is clear that this is one of the great strengths of the RCUS. Faithful instruction of the covenant youth in the doctrines of Scripture as summarized by the Heidelberg Catechism, in church history, Bible history, memorization of Scripture, and the singing of Psalms, hymns, and Scripture songs, — all these must be inculcated into the spiritual bloodstream of our youth.

The purpose of Christian discipleship is to prepare the youth for covenant confirmation. Sadly, confirmation and the very confirmation process are not well thought of. Perhaps this is due to the word "confirmation," as it is often thought of as a distinctly Lutheran and Roman Catholic hybrid. Others have criticized confirmation because of a paedo-communion bias, where even undiscerning babies have been forced to partake of the Lord's Supper. The confirmation process is caricatured as anti-covenantal, as a form of creedal discrimination against our covenant youth. Still others have bought into the "quickie decision" method of child evangelism so that confirmation classes are viewed as both taxing and tedious — some even claiming it places a pharisaic yoke around the neck of Christ's tender disciples. For them, confirmation is "jumping through the hoops," — a robotic exercise that deadens rather than edifies.

This caricature is without foundation. The confirmation process of instruction is a rich blessing for the covenant youth. It is Christian discipleship *par excellence*, and has little counterpart in any church or denomination of which we are aware. Required memorization of the Heidelberg Catechism is for all intended purposes like memorizing large chunks or small slices of Scripture. This is not because the catechism is the Word of God, but because it contains rich veins of 24-karat ore. The Great Commission commands the church to "disciple" all nations. The Apostle Paul sometimes spent three years in one town discipling believers. This stellar commitment to the catechization of the youth should be a sparkling advertisement for the RCUS, in a day of obscurantism and easy believism. Whatever the future of the RCUS, she must not toss this valuable cargo overboard in the interests of a blind ecumenism that may be inspired by merger for the sake of merger. The future of the RCUS is her youth and if her youth are not instructed, there is no future. To diminish the importance of catechetical training in the interests of enhancing acceptability in modern society is to destroy the future of the church.

CREATIONISM

Still another important doctrine that will determine the future of the RCUS is her commitment to creationism, and specifically six-day creation. We live in a day when creation is considered relatively unimportant, especially in relationship with the Gospel. This is a false dichotomy at best. Wherever the apostles went, they preached God as the Creator of the universe and Christ as the Redeemer of His people. Creation is not only important in itself, but it is important for evangelism too. When the early church evangelized, she preached a "creational evangelism." For example, in a day when homosexuality is glorified, it behooves the church to proclaim to the world that the perversity of homosexuality consists in its being anti-Christ and anti-creation. The sodomite rejects the "natural use" of his body that he received when he was created. The same application can be made to feminism, because Paul tells Timothy that the woman is not to "usurp" authority over the man (1 Timothy 2:1). The difference between men and women is not height or strength, but kind and order. God created men men, and women women. And He also created the man "first." Their roles are determined by creation. Some have asserted that while creation is important, six-day creation is not that important. The important emphasis, it is declared, is that God created everything and that man did not evolve out of the primordial ooze. This thinking is simplistic. In the first place, our view of six day creation directly affects our view of the Lord's Day or Christian Sabbath, for if God did not literally rest on a literal sixth day, the sanctity of the Lord's Day would be violated (Exodus 20:7). What is more, if God did not create in six literal days, if the first six days are saga or a poetic device by Moses, we run into a dangerous hermeneutical problem. Can we really be sure of anything in Genesis if the first six days are not literally true? And if the first six days are a mere poetical device, designed to teach the reader that God is Creator and created everything in an orderly manner, we would be able to apply the same hermeneutic to Genesis 3 and begin to question the historicity of the fall of man into sin.

The Gospel is not the only thing offensive to modern men. Creation is also an offense. Far from being an evangelistic handicap, six-day creation underlines the antithesis between the worldling's views and the Gospel. Six-day creation is an advantage because it reveals that God created everything in a chronological, thus orderly manner. This leaves no place for the false god "Big Bang" who is fathered by another false god--chance. It also eliminates every mongrel interpretation that vainly tries to retain creation, but at the expense of ditching a literal interpretation of Genesis. Unbelievers who believe in the eternity of matter, the origin of man from sub-human life, and in chaos, can only be reached by a Gospel that glorifies God as the harmonious Creator.

APOLOGETICS

A third leading edge of the RCUS that must be preserved to guarantee a strong church for the future is a fervent, if not fierce jealousy for the apologetics of Dr. Cornelius Van Til. "Presuppositionalism," as it is called, is merely the belief that every man has certain radical axioms of thought that are in the center of his being. He uses these thoughts both wittingly and unwittingly. The unbeliever's grid or worldview is based upon the premise of his own autonomy, that he is able to interpret objectively all the facts. This is nothing more than "there is a way which seemeth right unto a man,"but without the acknowledgment that "the end thereof are the ways of death." Dr. Van Til pointed out that both unbelievers and believers have rudimentary presuppositions that they use to interpret reality. The Christian assumes that God is self-contained and that His word is all-sufficient. No authority is any higher than the Bible's, not human reasoning, empiricism, utilitarianism, etc. Against the Biblical apologetical worldview stand a host of other apologetical views that are weakened by autonomous viruses which in turn threaten to slay the whole body of Christian truth. In the 4th century Athanasius' jealousy for the Deity of Christ gained him the aphorism, "Athanasius Against the World." Accordingly, the RCUS must be ever determined to argue, "Van Til Contra Mundum," or "Van Til Against the World." Translated into churchly language, this means "The RCUS Against the World."

The reason that the future of the church is dependent upon a consistent, Van Tilian apologetic is due to the insidious nature of sin, that seeks to relegate the authority of the Bible to a place of equal authority with human thought systems. For example, Satan's ploy in the Garden was to convince Adam and Eve to think in terms of neutrality, and thereby abandon their God-centered interpretation of the Tree of the Knowledge of Good and Evil. The Serpent coaxed Eve to refile God's interpretation into the file of neutrality. By inspiring them to test God's interpretation in a supposedly neutral laboratory, they denied the Word of God and exalted themselves as determiners of all things ("good and evil"). Simply put, the Christian faith is totalitarian. It is totalitarian not because "might makes right," but because God commands us to acknowledge the meaning He has put into things. What is a fact? By definition a fact is what is God-created. The Tree of the Knowledge of Good and Evil was God's interpretation of the Tree. Nothing in the entire universe is neutral. God has given meaning to each fact so that the fact and the interpretation of the fact are really one. Psalm 148 and other Scriptures testify that all the facts proclaim the praise of God!

CHRISTIAN EDUCATION

Presuppositional apologetics are the basis of Christian education too, which is indeed the only valid kind of education that there is. This does not mean that Christians cannot serve in government schools as unofficial missionaries. But it does mean that education comes into its own when all the facts are acknowledged as God-created facts. Every academic discipline must come under the scepter of Jesus Christ. As one has said, "Every bush is a burning bush." It is a complete contradiction, even tempting God, for us to disciple our children in the doctrines of the Heidelberg Catechism, and to nullify such instruction by dispatching them to the local Moloch (a false god) school. Although all Christians have blind spots which take time and especially patience to overcome, the mandate for Christian education is a responsibility that cannot wait.

Christian education is so important because the universe belongs to Christ. This means that all facts are Christ-centered facts. Colossians 1:15-17 teaches that Christ is both the Mediator of creation and the Mediator of redemption. The apostle Paul tells us four things about Christ: (1) He is the Creator of all things; (2)He is the Sustainer of all things; (3) He is before all things, and (4) He governs all things. The implication is that everything and everyone has a relationship with Christ. The reason is that Christ is both the "firstborn" of redemption and the "firstborn" of creation. "Firstborn" is an Old Testament word and signifies both the preeminence and the sovereignty of the firstborn son, who received the inheritance. Since the universe is Christ's, the work of the artist must reflect the glory of the Creator. History is hindsight of God's decrees of redemption and providence. Civil Government is ordained by God, and magistrates, as Ursinus instructs us, must "require from their subjects obedience, and external propriety according to both tables of the Decalogue." Calvinism is a complete worldview. Therefore, Christian education is not a choice; it is a commandment.

WORSHIP

Another paramount area is public worship. Biblical worship is by nature God-centered, not man-centered. This is why it revolves around the Word of God and our response to that Word in prayer. The Heidelberg Catechism endorses the "lively preaching of the Word." In a day of the consumer church, where the church is seeking to meet the needs of the public by adjusting its message accordingly, the "lively preaching of the Word" has become a casualty. The entertainment craze has so flooded the church that the Acts of the Apostles is sometimes read as if it were really The Acting of the Apostles! God does not call the Church to act, but to preach Christ crucified and resurrected, as Luke himself implies (Acts 1:1). The Acts of the Apostles is really the Acts of the Word of God.

The RCUS must not abandon the regulative principle of worship in order to gratify man's senses with entertainment or by visual representations of the Second Person of the Godhead. Faith is more important than sense. There is an old Arabian proverb: "He who speaks best must turn men's ears into eyes." It is through the "ear-gate" that God has especially promised to bless His word. "Faith cometh by hearing and hearing by the Word of God" (Romans 10:17). Pictures of Jesus, more than anything else, deny the need for faith. We are justified by faith and we are sanctified by faith. This adds up to walking by faith, not by sight (2 Corinthians 5:7). Christianity must be heard and then believed — not seen and believed (1 Pet. 1:8). The Lord has given the church only two sensual reminders — the Lord's Supper and Baptism. Pictures of the Second Person of the Godhead are not only deceptions which "varnish the sunlight of God's worship," and are a virtual denial of the walk of faith. Doubting Thomas is not dead — he is reincarnated by those who demand sight plus faith.

ECUMENISM

Still another feature of the RCUS is a dynamic ecumenical spirit. A stringent sectarianism which fails to recognize the presence of the Gospel in other communions not only grieves the Holy Spirit, but also fosters a detestable, even demonic pride. The RCUS must continue to extend the right hand of fellowship to other orthodox Christian bodies that have embraced the doctrines of the Reformation. The RCUS must take the flag of the Reformed faith up the mountain and plant it into the soil. But even more, she has the responsibility to take others by hand and lead them to the summit too. Rugged individualism may be good for free enterprise economics, but it is positively injurious for the unity of Christ's Church.

In recent years the fear of picking up a doctrinal virus from too close an association with other denominations has slackened off. Paul's exhortation to the Philippians is not only personal, but has a denominational application too: "Let nothing be done through selfish ambition or conceit, but in lowliness of mind let each esteem others better than himself" (Philippians 2:3). Yes, let us esteem other orthodox Protestant churches better than ourselves.

Yet, in spite of a strong ecumenical spirit toward other orthodox Protestant churches, the RCUS should not peg its survival upon the orthodoxy of other churches. No union should be forced, lest we engage in what one theologian has nicknamed "amateur providence." Amateur providence occurs when we force an issue, such as Sarah's strategy to help out God when she brought Hagar to Abraham.

It is also good to remember that ecumenicism is a two-way street. Not only must we aggressively seek closer ties with fraternal churches, but we should aggressively pursue individual congregations that are Reformed in doctrine offering them the right hand of fellowship within our own pale. Providentially, we are here for a reason. The impact of theological liberalism made its mark upon our forefathers a century ago. In 1934 the chickens came home to roost. Could it be that we crumbled early and then recouped, so that we might become a churchly home to individual congregations that have separated from ailing denominations which are giving up their Reformed heritage. If so, the remaining years of the twentieth century and all of the twenty-first century will be banner years for the RCUS.

MISSIONS AND EVANGELISM

A final consideration relates to missions and evangelism. We can speak about ecumenism all we want, but there is no substitute for an aggressive missions strategy. The old phrase, "evangelize or fossilize," continues to be true. It is true for several reasons, not the least being that the promise of the presence of Christ in His Church depends upon the faithfulness of each church to disseminate the Gospel. Jesus' command, "Go ye therefore, discipling all nations, baptizing them into the name of the Father, the Son, and the Holy Spirit" is the basis of Christ's promise, "And lo, I am with you always, even unto the end of the world." The meaning is not merely that Christ will be with the Church when the Church goes, but that Christ **will not be** with the church at all if the Church does not carry out the Great Commission! What is more, in the past mind-set of the RCUS, missions has been a responsibility that is best carried out by the Synod. In recent years, especially since the church divided into individual classes, that reliance has in part been transferred to the classis. However, the individual churches need to view themselves as mission centers too! In fact, the key to missions is the local church, for only the local church can achieve the sort of hands on policy that is required. The best way to conduct warfare is to place the general staff on the battlefield with the troops, instead of conducting the war from thousands of miles away. A church that tries to evangelize itself out of existence will be blessed mightily.

While it is true that the RCUS must be receptive to wherever she hears the Macedonian call ("Come over and help us"), particular emphasis should be placed upon the cities. One of our primary goals should be to launch a missions campaign in the cities. Satan's booty in the heavily peopled areas must be plundered. New York, Philadelphia, Washington D.C., Los Angeles, Chicago, etc., must be brought under the scepter of Christ. This is perhaps the greatest challenge facing us.

The Bible teaches that we are not here for ourselves. Our purpose is to be the salt of the earth and the light of the world. R.B. Kuiper's analogy about a living church is always appropriate. He compares a dead church to the Dead Sea that is the depository of the waters of the Jordan. It has an inlet, but no outlet. Therefore, it is dead. But a living church is like the Sea of Galilee which receives the waters of the

Jordan and then channels those waters south. It is a sea that is thriving with life. This happens when the church both receives the grace of God and dispenses that grace through the preaching of the Gospel. The RCUS must be like Abraham whom God blessed and then made a blessing to the world. Even better, we should be like the man Jesus described in John 7, when He spoke about the cataract that flows from faith. He said, "He that believes on Me as the Scripture hath said, out of his belly shall flow rivers of living water" (verse 38).

Sin is not only transgression of the law of God, but also "any want of conformity" unto the Law of God. This means that we tend to think highly of ourselves for the things that we do, but forget that the things that we do not do (and that we should be doing) are just as important. James wrote, "Therefore to him that knoweth to do good, and doeth it not, to him it is sin" (James 4:17). We can boast about being faithful, but if we are not faithful witnesses, we are not faithful.

The whole period between the first coming of Christ and His Second Coming is the interim period. Why are we here? Why is there a church in the world in the first place? Why hasn't Christ returned? A paramount function of the church in this age is missions. The elect must be brought into the kingdom. If we feel purposeless, then it is because we are not fulfilling our evangelistic duties. This is true both on a personal and church level.

HOLINESS

Finally, we must not lose sight of something even more important than ecumenicism and missions. The cardinal mark of the church is holiness. We not only confess our belief in the Catholic church, but in "the **holy** catholic Church." The church is not first of all a missionary society. Her primary mark is the holiness of God. The church is the "glorious body of Christ" because Christ died so that He might "sanctify and cleanse it with the washing of water by the word, that He might present it to himself a glorious church, not having spot or wrinkle, or any such thing; but that it should be holy and without blemish" (Ephesians 5:26-27). This means that we must display the marks of the church. Our emphasis should not be putting out brush fires, establishing a Reformed Vatican city where decisions are made from top to bottom, micro-managing the affairs of each congregation, creating a church bureaucracy with professional "ecclesiocrats," or endless adjudications at a classical or synodical level. Rather, we must emphasize holy living to the glory of God for every member of the church.

There is nothing mysterious about a prosperous, thriving Christianity. It is when the church is faithful to the basics that she prospers. A famous football coach once told his players, "Fundamentals, fundamentals, fundamentals." He recognized the importance of faithfulness to the fundamentals. The RCUS must continue to proclaim the rudimentary truths of the Christian Faith. However, we must not stop there. For the same football coach also said, "If you're not fired with enthusiasm, you'll be fired with enthusiasm." Yes, both faithfulness and fire are necessary!

David Martyn-Lloyd Jones once described preaching as "the proclamation of the Word of God by a man who is on fire." our leaders need to be faithful and fiery men who cherish the Reformed doctrines!

We do not look into a crystal ball or to the witch of Endor to learn about the future of the RCUS. The future of the RCUS is as bright as the promises of God! we have an unique product that we must "sell" to the world. How do we do this? Not by emulating Tetzel and the world, but by a faithful and fiery proclamation of the Word of God. When we do this, God will bless us because God always blesses His Word. This continuing reformation by the Word of God can only occur if the RCUS is energized by the same spirited fire that caused our father Calvin to proclaim, "Even a dog barks when its master is attacked, should I not raise my voice when the majesty of God is attacked?" And, "O Lord, as an oblation, I offer thee my heart, sacrificed for Thee!"

> "I am the vine, ye are the branches. He that abideth in me,
> and I in him, the same bringeth forth much fruit:
> for without me ye can do nothing" (John 15:5)

1994—248TH SESSION OF SYNOD—NEWTON, MANITOWOC, WISCONSIN

Front row: Rev. S. Parks, Rev. D. Roe, F. Meidinger, Rev. H. Opp, M. Olivier, B. Johnston (ARP), Rev. H. Hart, W. Schnabel, O. Porras, Rev. M. Koerner, Rev. H. Van Stedum. Second row: C. Greiman, Rev. C. Ploeger, J. Arndt, Rev. S. Schlei, T. Griess, Rev. W. Brice, H. Yoder, Rev. J. Merica, Rev. Kishimba Kasantika (ERCZ), Rev. R. Grossmann, Rev. H. Bowen, Rev. J. West, D. Schlegel, Rev. V. Pollema, H. Smith, D. Mettler. Third row: Rev. R. Potter, Rev. N. Hoeflinger, K. Schimke, A. Stache, E. Ochsner, Rev. J. Sawtelle, E. Greimann, Rev. N. Riffert, J. Heerema, Rev. N. Jones, Rev. J. Taylor (OPC), Rev. H. Metzger (RPCNA), Rev. G. Sawtelle. Fourth row: Rev. D. Vance, Rev. F. Walker, M. Van Ginkel (Hope Haven), Rev. J. Hilbelink (OPC), Rev. P. Treick, T. Orth, R. Schnabel, Rev. D. Dawn, Rev. T. Jorgensen, Rev. P. Grossmann, Rev. D. Clark. Fifth row: Z. Wood, A. Nap (Can. Ref. Chs.), D. McPherson, E. Koppenhofer, D. Zoeteway, C. Zeeb, R. Kusler, R. Honaker, A. Rau, Rev. D. Savage.

INDEX

à Lasco, John, 3, 5, 184, 188, 191, 192
Aberdeen, SD, 85, 108, 112, 114, 121
Alpena, SD, 65, 102, 103, 137
Anderson, CA, 113, 118, 121
Antes, Henry, 19-21
Apologetics, 111, 162, 165, 166, 216, 217
Arminianism, 5, 6, 21, 57
Artas, SD, 65, 75, 84, 102, 105, 106, 121, 127, 137
Ashley, ND, 65, 80, 84, 102, 106, 111, 121, 138
Augsburg Confession, 4, 19, 52, 60, 179, 181, 182, 204, 205, 207

Bacon, Samuel, 111
Bakersfield, CA, iii, 80, 86, 103, 104, 109, 115, 121
Baptism, 25, 36, 37, 43, 91, 114, 183, 187, 218
Barth, Karl, 62, 147, 155
Bauer, Peter, 64, 65, 138, 150, 152
Baur, Ferdinand Christian , 58, 97
Bechtel, John, 20
Beech, Thomas, 111
Belgic Confession of Faith, 5, 14, 22, 118-121, 144, 166, 172, 176, 206, 208
Beza, Theodore, 178, 193, 194
Bismarck, ND, 113, 116, 127, 130, 138
Bodenmann, John, 77, 78
Boehl, Eduard, 155, 156
Boehm, John Philip, 1, 8-13, 17, 19-21, 27, 43, 55, 87, 93, 96, 119
Bonekemper, Johannes, 130-132, 135-139
Boquin, Peter, 179
Bosma, D. E., 49, 80, 85, 102, 105, 108, 110, 123
Brunswick, 16, 30
Bucer, Martin, 87, 186, 188
Buehrer, Emil, 80, 82, 103, 107, 183, 210
Bullinger, Heinrich, 55, 87, 173, 185, 188, 189, 193, 194, 196, 200, 206

Calvin, John, 3-6, 12, 28, 35, 36, 55, 68, 84, 85, 87, 92, 93, 105, 108, 112, 121, 142, 166, 167, 169, 173, 175, 178, 182, 184-189, 193-196, 200, 201, 210, 211, 221
Calvinism, 2, 3, 5, 6, 22, 28, 37, 57, 68, 81, 91, 92, 95, 110-112, 165, 182, 183, 187, 205, 217

Canons of Dort, 5, 12-14, 21-23, 55, 57, 119-121, 172, 176, 202, 206, 208
Carbondale, PA, 117, 118, 121
Carlisle, PA, 30, 56, 89, 90
John Casimir, 203, 207
Catherine the Great, 94, 128, 129
Catholicism, 3, 4, 18, 39, 41, 90, 172, 179-181, 186, 203
Chico, CA, 116, 122
Church Order of Dort, 12, 13
Clark, Scott, 169
Classis Amsterdam, 9, 12, 29, 30, 89
Cocceius, Johannes, 6
Coetus, 1, 3, 5, 8-15, 20, 22-24, 27, 29, 30, 54-56, 89, 93, 96, 98, 119, 123
Colorado Springs, CO, 121
Confirmation, 15, 26, 37, 51, 91, 114, 121, 172, 173, 176, 214
Conn, Harvey, 112
Consistory, 9-11, 13, 25-27, 141, 182
Covenant East Classis, 120, 121
Covenant of Grace, 184, 188, 189, 193, 200, 201
Covenant of Works, 200
Covenant Theology, 6, 189-191, 193, 195, 198, 200, 202, 210
Creationism, 215

Dakota Synod, 77-79, 108
Dawn, David, 107
Deaf Reformed Church, 121
Demers, Steven, 107
Denhoff, ND, 121
Dichotomy, 17, 175, 186, 215
Directory of Worship, 44, 57, 91, 111, 114
Dordt College, 118
Dorner, 38, 39
Dubbs, Joseph H., 2, 10, 11, 15-19, 21, 25, 27, 28, 98, 123
Duckett, Jefferson, 113
Dunkards, 18
Dutch Reformed Church, 5, 41, 44, 55, 96

E & R, 48, 49, 58-61, 63, 65, 66, 72, 78, 84, 88, 102-110, 112, 115
Ecumenism, 21, 91, 95, 103, 214, 218, 219
Elberfeld, Germany, 31, 143, 144, 154
Elector Otto Henry, 178
Emden, Germany, 3, 5, 184, 188, 191, 192
Erastus, Thomas, 179, 183
ERCZ, 116
Eureka Classis, 47-51, 62-68, 70-72, 74-81, 83-86, 92, 96, 100-115, 117, 119, 123, 126, 129, 137, 139, 142, 147, 150, 152, 167
Eureka, SD, 49, 51, 62, 64, 101, 112, 127

Evangelical Synod of North America, 45, 48, 52-54, 59, 63, 69, 72, 88, 91, 98, 99

Falkner Swamp, PA, 19, 55
Forbes, ND, 83, 109
Frederick III, Elector, 4, 11, 55, 87, 90, 106, 125, 131, 178-185, 193, 195, 196, 198, 199, 203-207
French Reformed Church, 4, 199

Garner, IA, iii, 2, 28, 50, 86, 87, 103, 108, 109, 117, 121, 123, 152
German Evangelical Synod, 52
German Reformed Church, 1, 2, 5, 8, 9, 11, 14, 18, 22, 23, 30, 37, 48, 54, 66, 89, 90, 94, 96, 118, 125, 130, 133, 185, 211
German-Russians, 50, 53, 85, 95, 103, 104, 108, 112, 119, 125-127, 135, 139
Gibbons, Roger, 111, 113
GKN, 116, 117
Good, James I., 2, 3, 13, 23, 31, 107, 207
Gotha, 16, 129
Grass Valley, CA, 122
Great Depression, 84, 86, 108
Griess, James, 127, 134
Gross, Lloyd, 106, 110, 166, 167, 169
Grossmann, John, 64, 66, 81, 100, 101
Grossmann, Peter, iii, 86, 107, 111
Grossmann, Robert, iii, iv, 2, 85, 87, 113, 118, 165, 169
Grossmann, Walter, 64-66, 69, 70, 72, 76, 78, 80, 83-85, 101, 102, 104, 105, 108, 110, 167
Guldin, Samuel, 20, 55

Halle, Germany, 16, 38, 58, 151
Hamburg, MN, 104, 117, 121
Harbaugh, Henry, 44, 123, 185, 191, 196, 211
Hart, Howard, iii, 111, 159, 168, 169
Hegel, Georg William Friedrich, 38, 58, 90
Heidelberg, i, 4, 5, 7, 9, 10, 12-16, 20, 23, 26, 27, 34, 36, 37, 43, 51, 52, 55, 57, 58, 60, 70, 71, 73-75, 78, 81, 86, 87, 91, 93, 94, 107, 119-121, 123, 125, 131, 137, 142, 144, 146, 147, 149, 154, 156, 166, 171-176, 178-185, 187-193, 195, 196, 199-211, 213, 214, 217
Heidelberg Catechism, i, 4, 5, 13-15, 20, 23, 26, 27, 34, 36, 37, 43, 51, 52, 55, 57, 58, 60, 70, 71, 73-75, 78, 81, 86, 87, 91, 93, 94, 107, 119-121, 125, 131, 137, 142, 144, 146, 147, 154, 156, 166, 171, 172, 174-176, 178-181, 184, 185, 187, 189-193, 196, 200-211, 214, 217
Heil, ND, 68, 81, 83, 102, 138
Hengstenberg, E. W., 31, 38, 39
Herborn, Germany, 16, 195, 196, 200
Herman, F. L., 30
Herzog, F. W., 65

Herried, 102, 106
High German Reformed Church, 118
High-Lutheran, 178-182, 186
History of the Eureka Classis 1910-1985, 115
Hodge, Charles, 33, 36, 38, 160, 166
Hoeflinger, Norman, iii, iv, 106, 115, 123, 125, 167, 169
Hoeksema, Herman, 109
Hofer, Michael, 137, 138
Hoffman, John, 17
Hosmer, SD, 64, 66, 68, 80, 85, 102, 105, 106, 111, 121, 138
Huguenots, 5

ICRC, 117, 122
Isabel, 68, 83, 102, 109

Jones, Norman, iii, 1, 28, 71, 107, 113, 167, 169, 221
Juda, Leo, 175, 188

Kansas City, MO, 113, 121
Karval, CO113, 117, 121
Klaudt, Robert, 80
Klundt, J., 64
Koerner, 134
Kohlbruegge, Hermann Friedrich, iii, 92, 95, 125, 126, 139-151, 153-157, 166
Kohlbrueggian, 66, 85, 92, 96, 101, 103, 104, 137, 150-152, 156, 166, 167
Korn, William, 49, 80, 84, 103, 106, 110, 123
Krieger, W. J., 50, 65-69, 76, 78-80, 101, 102, 105, 106
Krueger, Kasper, 80, 107
Krummacher, F. W., 31, 39, 90, 143, 154
Kulenkamp, G., 20
Kuss, Carl, 135, 136
Kuyper, Abraham, 144, 155, 166

Labadists, 18
Lancaster, PA, 17, 32, 56, 57, 89, 97, 121, 123, 185, 211
Lancaster Seminary, 97
Le Reveil, 141
Leola, SD, 65, 76, 83, 102, 108, 109, 112, 121, 138
Liberty Bell, ii
Lierhaus, Friedrich, 84, 106
Lincoln Valley, ND, iii, 102, 103
Lincoln, NE, iii, 127, 134
Lischy, 20
Lodi, CA, 101, 116, 122
Lord's Supper, 9, 35, 36, 139, 179-181, 183, 186, 187, 191, 205, 214, 218
Louis XIV, 7

Loveland, CO, 113, 121
Low-Lutheran, 178, 179, 181, 185, 203
Luther, Martin, 3, 125, 139, 140, 142, 147, 154, 178, 181, 182, 186, 191, 203
Lutheran, 3, 5, 15, 16, 19, 20, 29, 37, 38, 52, 53, 58, 60, 91, 94, 95, 98, 114, 126, 131, 132, 135, 136, 139, 140, 142, 144, 166, 175, 178-182, 185-189, 196, 203, 214
Lutheranism, 3, 4, 18, 85, 139, 140, 181, 185, 207

Machen, J. Gresham, 160, 168
Magyar, 104, 105
Manitowoc, WI, 49, 65, 82, 103, 121
Marburg, Germany, 16, 32, 186, 210
Martyr, Peter, 185, 193-195
Maximilian, Emperor, 203, 204
Mayer, Louis, 31, 32, 42, 56, 90, 205
Melanchthon, Philip, 4, 5, 37, 140, 178, 179, 181, 182, 185-187, 189
Menno, SD, 49, 80, 103, 104, 109, 115, 121, 127, 134-138, 165
Mennonite, 19, 95
Mennonites, 18, 126
Mensch, 83, 106, 109
Mercersburg, 12, 29, 31, 32, 34-36, 39-45, 56-58, 63, 86, 91, 97, 98, 114, 119, 123, 133
Merger of 1934, iii, 21, 45, 47-54, 57-60, 62-69, 71, 72, 74, 76-84, 86-88, 91, 92, 96, 98-105, 107, 108, 115, 126, 150, 208, 214, 219
Mid-America Reformed Seminary, 117, 118
Milledoler, Philip, 30, 89
Minot, ND, 113, 121
Mission House, 62, 63, 66, 67, 80, 81, 84, 92, 94, 100, 101, 103, 106, 110, 123, 131, 136, 143, 165, 167
Mitchell, SD, 113, 118, 121
Modesto, CA, iii, 116, 122
Moibanus, Ambrosius, 187, 188
Moravian, 18-21, 55, 96, 103
Muhlenberg, 20
Murray, John, 110, 160, 161, 165, 167-169, 196

NAPARC, 122
Napoleon, OH, 104, 121
Neander, John August William, 31, 34, 38, 39, 58
Nevin, John Williamson, 29, 31-43, 56-58, 90
Nonhof, Melvin, 107, 111
Northern Plains Classis, 121
Northwest Synod, 50, 67, 92, 95, 115
Nuss, Michael, 51, 134, 138

Ochsner, Nikolas, 130, 131
Olevianus, Casper, 87, 178, 182, 184, 193, 195-198

Orthodox Presbyterian Church, 85, 110-114, 122

Palatinate, 3-5, 7-9, 11, 15, 23, 41-43, 55, 87, 88, 92, 93, 129, 131, 178-180, 182-184, 188, 193, 195, 196, 205, 207, 208
Peace Commission, 44, 56, 57
Peace of Augsburg, 4, 179
Peace of Westphalia, 88, 179
Pfeiffer, Erwin, 102, 105
Philadelphia, PA, ii, iii, 8, 10-12, 14, 19, 35, 36, 38, 39, 41, 47, 49, 55, 58, 59, 67, 91, 92, 103, 106, 110, 117, 123, 133, 159-163, 179, 210, 211, 219
Pierre, SD, iii, 85, 113, 121, 198
Pietists, 21, 145
Plan of Union, 59, 69-74, 78, 99
Pollema, Vernon, 117, 163, 169
Potter, Ron, 33
Powell, C.W., 113, 118
Princeton Theological Seminary, 33, 145, 159
Protestant Reformed Church, 83, 106, 109
Prussia, 31, 52, 94, 206
Puritanism, 40-42

Quakers, 18

Ramus, Peter, 198-200
Rapid City, SD, 84, 116, 121
Rauch, Friedrich Augustus, 29, 31, 32, 34, 90
Reformed Church in America, 1, 2, 8, 9, 11, 31, 51, 88, 91, 96, 98, 99, 103, 123, 155
Reformiertes Gemeindeblatt, 49, 69, 106
Reiff, 10, 24
Reliance Publishing Company, 82, 183, 210
Rieger, 10, 12, 93
Rittershaus, 65, 138
Rock Springs, WY, 117, 121
Roman Catholic Church, 60, 84, 194, 206
Ronscorfers, 18
RPCNA, 118

Sacramento, CA, iii, 113, 122
Sander, Robert, 111, 168, 169
Savage, Dorman, 113, 116
Sawtelle, Gene, 117
Schaff, Philip, 11, 28, 29, 31, 32, 34, 37-43, 49, 52-54, 56-58, 90, 91, 97, 107, 173, 184, 211
Scheidt, Edward, 50
Schild, P., 64
Schlatter, Michael, 1, 9-12, 23, 24, 27, 29, 55, 93, 96, 123

Schlei, Steven, 164, 165, 169
Schleiermacher, Friedrich Ernst Daniel, 38, 39, 58
Schmidt, 65
Schneck, B.S., 31, 35, 91, 123
Schwenkfelders, 18
Scotland, SD, 50, 82, 95, 108, 134-136, 138, 160
Second Helvetic Confession, 173
Second World War, 84, 102, 105-109
Shafter, CA, 80, 86, 103, 104, 109, 115, 117, 122
Sill, Henry, 50
Sioux Falls, SD, 116, 121
Skippack, PA, 26, 55, 87
Smith, Lendal, 38, 112
South Central Classis, 116, 121
St. Bartholomew's Massacre, 5, 199
Stark, Jacob, 66, 101, 151-154, 156
Steinecker, H. W., 138
Stevens, Hessel, 111
Stonehouse, Ned, 110, 160
Stuebbe, Calvin, 85, 108, 112
Stuebbe, K. J., 49, 65, 80, 103, 108
Stuebbe, Robert, 103, 104, 108, 109, 115
Sutton, NE, 80, 103, 104, 111, 112, 118, 121, 127, 129, 134, 136, 137, 139
Synod of Dort, 5, 13, 26-28, 93, 207, 208
Synod of the Northwest, 64, 65, 69, 76, 82, 100, 102, 137

The Christian Beacon, 72
The New Born, 18
The Witness, 49, 50, 67, 69, 108, 150, 153
Thiele, 65, 102
Thirty Years War, 7, 88, 179
Tholuck, F.A.G., 38, 39, 58
Three Forms of Unity, 12, 14, 22, 118, 167, 208, 213
Treaty of Ryswick, 7
Treick, Henry, 50, 64, 65
Treick, Paul, iii, 116, 163, 165, 169
Treves, 193-195, 197
Tripp, SD, 50, 65, 66, 80, 127, 134-136

UCC, 61, 94, 102-105, 114, 117, 167
Union Seminary, 41, 91
United Brethren, 18, 53, 99
United Church of Christ, 61, 63, 94, 96, 103, 104, 126, 127, 137, 167
United States Supreme Court, 71
Upham, ND, 80, 102, 103, 121, 138
Ursinus College, 44, 57

Ursinus, Zacharias, 4, 87, 178, 183-185, 190, 195, 199, 200, 209, 211

Van Stedum, Herman, 169
Van Til, Cornelius, 110, 113, 160, 165, 167, 198, 210, 216
Venturia, ND, 102, 106, 111
Vos, Geerhardus, 156, 157, 160
Vriesen, D. W., 91, 92, 103, 152

Waechter, 101, 151, 155
Waldenses, 39
Walker, Frank, iii, 29
War for Independence, 11
War of Spanish Succession, 8
Warren, William, 111, 123
Washington, George, ii, 219
Weimar, Germany, 16
Weiss, George Michael, 9, 10, 55
Wenzlaff, T.C., 127, 130, 137
West, Jim, iii, 169, 213
Western Classis, 121
Western Theological Seminary, 33
Westminster Confession, 6, 34, 166, 167
Whitemarsh, PA, 55, 87
Willows, CA, 116, 122
Witsius, Herman, 6
Wittenberg, William, 50, 65, 103, 185, 186
Wooley, Paul, 47, 165
Work, Steven, 169
World Council of Churches, 97
Westminster Theological Seminary, 159, 162-169

Young, Edward J., 110
Yuba City, CA, 116-118, 122

Zanchius, Jerom, 182, 211
Zeeland, ND, 64, 65, 100, 102, 104
Zenk, Gustav, 50, 106
Zinkand, John, 117, 118
Zinzendorf, Count Nikolas Ludwig von, 18-21, 55, 96
Zogg, Ulrich, 80, 100, 104, 137
Zwingli, Ulrich, 3, 54, 55, 87, 131, 178, 186, 200, 206